STUDYING, INTERPRETING, AND APPLYING THE BIBLE

STUDYING, INTERPRETING, AND APPLYING THE BIBLE

Walter Henrichsen
Gayle Jackson

ZONDERVAN™

GRAND RAPIDS, MICHIGAN 49530

ZONDERVAN™

Studying, Interpreting, and Applying the Bible
Copyright © 1990 by Walter A. Henrichsen and Gayle Jackson

Previously published as *A Layman's Guide to Studying the Bible*, © 1985 by Zondervan, *A Layman's Guide to Interpreting the Bible*, © 1976, 1978 by The Navigators, *A Layman's Guide to Applying the Bible*, © 1985 by Zondervan.

Requests for information should be addressed to:
Zondervan, *Grand Rapids, Michigan 49530*

Library of Congress Cataloging-in-Publication Data

Henrichsen, Walter A.
     Studying, interpreting, and applying the Bible / Walter Henrichsen and Gayle Jackson.
       p. cm.
     Previously published as three separate works.
     Contents: A layman's guide to studying the Bible—A layman's guide to interpreting the Bible—A layman's guide to applying the Bible.
     ISBN 0-310-37781-1
     1. Bible—Study. 2. Bible —Hermaneutics. 3. Bible—Use. 4. Christian life —1960- 5. Word of God (Theology) I. Jackson, Gayle. II. Title.
BS605.2.H47   1990
220.6'1—dc20   89-77397

Printed in the United States of America

07 08 /❖ DC/ 20 19 18

Contents

Studying the Bible

Interpreting the Bible

Applying the Bible

SECTION

How to Study the Bible

1 Bible Study Is for Everyone

The scene before our eyes is the vast expanse of wilderness between Jerusalem and the Jordan River. In preparation for His public ministry, Jesus had fasted 40 days and nights in this barren expanse, alone, hungry, and weary. Satan now confronts Him with three insidious temptations. Three times our Lord wards off his suggestions by quoting from the Book of Deuteronomy.

Recognizing that the Bible is authoritative for the Savior, Satan tries his hand at quoting Scripture too. He selects the psalmist's statement, "For he will command his angels concerning you to guard you in all your ways; they will lift you up in their hands, so that you will not strike your foot against a stone" (Psalm 91:11-12; see Matthew 4:6).

As you compare Satan's words with the text in Psalm 91, it is interesting to note that he does not *misquote* the psalmist. Rather,

9

he misuses the passage by misrepresenting the intent of the writer.

The tactics of our enemy have not changed through the centuries. Since Satan misrepresented the Scriptures to Jesus Christ, the believer today can be assured of the same thing happening to him. But how does the devil do this? From what quarter are we to expect his attacks?

Ways in Which the Bible May Be Misused

Five ways immediately come to mind, and others could be added to this illustrative list.

1. *The Scriptures may be misused when you are ignorant about what the Bible says on a given subject.*

The ordination of avowed, practicing homosexuals into the gospel ministry is an example. Some would have the church believe that the loving, accepting spirit of our Lord Jesus precludes their being barred from ordination. Nowhere did Jesus say they shouldn't be ordained, so the church should ordain them as clergy in good and regular standing. Yet the Old Testament expressly forbids acts of homosexuality (see Leviticus 18:22), and Paul states that homosexual behavior contributes to God's wrath on mankind (see Romans 1:26-27). Ignorance about what the Bible teaches is an open door to the attack of the enemy.

2. *The Scriptures may be misused when you take a verse out of context.*

On the night of His betrayal Jesus said to His disciples, "Until now you have not asked for anything in my name. Ask and you will receive, and your joy will be complete" (John 16:24). Some have taken this to be a carte blanche promise from God. He will grant whatever you ask. That same night, however, a short while after making this statement, Jesus prayed in the Garden of Gethsemane, "Take this cup from me. Yet not what I will, but what you will" (Mark 14:36). Promises in the Bible must be blended with the total context of the scriptural teaching on prayer (see 1 John 5:14-15).

3. *The Scriptures may be misused when you read into a passage and have it say what it doesn't say.*

Toward the end of His ministry, Jesus said, "And these signs will accompany those who believe: In my name they will drive out demons; they will speak in new tongues; they will pick up snakes with their hands; and when they drink deadly poison, it will not hurt them at all" (Mark 16:17-18). Some have taken this descriptive passage to be a command to do all of the things mentioned, reading into it a mandate to do all of these when all Jesus is doing is describing what is going to happen in situations in the early church when certain people had the gift of miracles.

4. *The Scriptures may be misused when you give undue emphasis to less important things.*

Did Judas, the betrayer of our Lord, participate with Jesus and the other disciples in the Last Supper? The evidence is inconclusive, yet some allow themselves to become greatly exercised over an issue such as this, even to the point of contributing toward disunity in the church.

5. *The Scriptures may be misused whenever you use the Bible to try to get God to do what you want, rather than what God wants done.*

Let us use the example of a woman who is in love with a man and wants very much to marry him. Jesus said, "Again, I tell you that if two of you on earth agree about anything you ask for, it will be done for you by my Father in heaven" (Matthew 18:19). Taking this promise to a girlfriend, she asks the woman to join her in claiming this promise in order to "get" the man. This is an obvious misuse of the Scriptures.

The Need for Bible Study Methods

Not every misuse of the Bible can be attributed to an attack from Satan, even in the illustrations just mentioned. It becomes immediately apparent, however, that you must learn to use the Scriptures carefully. Christians must not only become familiar

with the rules of interpretation, but they must apply these rules
to a life-long habit of Bible study. The objective of this section
of the book is to introduce you to Bible study methods. Much
good material is already available on this subject, but the intent
here is to take some methods of Bible study and make them
simple enough for the average layman to incorporate into his
Christian life.

Unlike the subject of interpretation, Bible study methods have a
great deal of flexibility and require some creativity. These methods
are not "rules" of Bible study per se, but are guidelines which, if
followed, will enhance the study of the Scriptures. We will explore
these methods in the following chapters. No matter how masterful
or conscientious a student of the Bible you may be, you must
maintain vigilance in staying fresh and creative. So experiment
with the various methods. Pick and choose from what is offered
and add your own ideas. Make the method yours. Remember,
there is a difference between doing Bible study which can be drab
and perfunctory on the one hand, and studying the Bible which is
exciting and life-changing on the other.

Principles of Bible Study

When I was a fledgling seminarian, a layman sat down with me and
introduced me to five principles of Bible study. He helped me
realize the importance of going to the Scriptures as my primary
source, rather than gleaning spiritual truths from studies other men
have made. By principles, he meant that they ought to be included
in our Bible study, irrespective of the method we might employ.

1. *You must do original investigation.* An incident in the early
church illustrates the importance of the believer getting alone with
an open Bible and depending on the Holy Spirit to be his teacher:
"Now the Bereans were of more noble character than the Thessalonians, for they received the message with great eagerness and
examined the Scriptures every day to see if what Paul said was

true'' (Acts 17:11). The Bereans listened attentively to what Paul and Silas had to say, but elected to check it out with the original source.

It is important that conviction be formed on what the Bible teaches, rather than depending on creeds, commentaries, or even sermons. The latter may cause you to turn to the Word as did the Bereans, but during times of testing it is the authority of the infallible Word personally examined that stands.

Two types of resource materials may be used in Bible study. Biblical encylopedias, dictionaries, and concordances are one type, and should be the constant companion of the student. Commentaries and other expository works are the second type. But these should only be used *after* the principle of original investigation has been applied.

Referring to a good commentary after the study is completed is helpful, particularly if you teach your material to others or lead a Bible study group. It becomes a way of checking your ideas and conclusions with others. If you find yourself in disagreement with the commentator, especially on significant issues, you should then take a fresh look at *your* conclusions.

Original investigation is a necessary and important principle to incorporate into your methodology. There is something fresh and exciting about a truth taught by the Holy Spirit during your personal time in the Word of God.

2. *You must have written reproduction.* Have you ever had the experience of thinking a profound thought, but because you did not write it down you forgot it? If so, you probably discerned that the harder you tried to remember the thought, the more elusive it became. Such a frustrating experience illustrates the importance of incorporating written reproduction into your Bible study methods.

Dawson Trotman, founder of The Navigators, often would say, ''Thoughts disentangle themselves as they pass from the mind through the lips and over the finger tips.'' Writing down your thoughts and drawing them together is one of the key differences between Bible reading and Bible study. A rich reservoir of scriptural knowledge can be stored for future use when written reproduction is employed.

3. *Your study must be consistent and systematic.* Two concepts make up this third principle. Bible study should be consistent. This is implied in the words *every day* in Acts 17:11. The Bereans didn't study the Scriptures one day, then wait a week to do it again. Their approach was *consistent.*

The other concept embedded in this principle is that Bible study must be systematic. A chapter here, a topic there, a passage another time are not the best approaches to studying the Bible. Map out a program of Bible study that will systematically unfold for you a balanced understanding of God's whole Word. Such an approach is suggested in chapter 12.

4. *Your study must be ''pass-on-able.''* This conglomerate may sound strange, but it does communicate an important concept. It is found in Paul's statement to Timothy: ''And the things you have heard me say in the presence of many witnesses entrust to reliable men who will also be qualified to teach others'' (2 Timothy 2:2). It is God's intention that we not only grow and mature in our walk with Him, but also help others to maximize their potential for Jesus Christ.

Each believer is to view himself as a link between two generations. We are to *pass on* to others what we have had the privilege of learning. If we apply this only to the content of our study we encourage people to become dependent on us for ''intake.'' The biblical concept of the priesthood of the believer means that all Christians have both the right and the responsibility of feeding personally on the Word of God. Our Bible study methodology must include the element of pass-on-able-ness to facilitate this great ideal.

5. *You must apply what you study to your life.* So important is this principle that we find it incorporated in the rules of interpretation as well as the methodology about to be studied. A cursory reading of almost any portion of the Bible reveals how important application is from God's perspective. He *expects* His Word to be taken seriously. James tersely said, "Do not merely listen to the Word, and so deceive yourselves. Do what it says" (James 1:22).

Basic Steps of Bible Study

Four essentials form the foundation for all Bible study—observation, interpretation, correlation, application. Because these parts *are* basic to your study of the Word, irrespective of the kind of study in which you engage (such as, analytical, synthetic, or topical), it is necessary to look at each individually and at some length.

Each of the four parts will be presented in such a way as to move from the simple to the more advanced. As you apply these parts to your study of the Scriptures, you will be encouraged to select your own level of difficulty, adding various techniques as you become increasingly proficient.

The format of the following chapters will introduce you to five methods of Bible study, beginning with a basic study and moving toward more advanced steps. Each of them will use the four parts of Bible study—observation, interpretation, correlation, application.

As you begin to do these studies, follow the *Basic* sections only

(to the **STOP** sign). Do *not* go on to the *Advanced* sections till you have mastered the basic approach. The methods do not have to be done in the presented order; you may try your hand on them in any order. The basic studies on the following pages are:

After you are comfortable with any of the *Basic* approaches, you have the choice of going in two directions: (1) Proceed to do the *Advanced* steps of the method you have chosen, or (2) go more in depth in your *Basic* study by turning to the suggestions in Chapters 8–11.

If you are just beginning a program of Bible study, you may want to consider starting with a question-and-answer method to get the "feel" of it. An outstanding series on this method is *Studies in Christian Living,* published by The Navigators. (This set and individual booklets are available from your local Christian bookstore or from Customer Services, NavPress, P.O. Box 6000, Colorado Springs, Colorado 80934.) This series consists of nine booklets, progressing from the simple to the more difficult. Not only do they introduce you to two Bible study methods, they also expose you to all the major teachings of the Bible.

Doing these is not a prerequisite to the material in Chapters 2–6, but if you find the following difficult, you may want to start with the question-and-answer approach.

2 The Verse Analysis Method of Bible Study

The verse analysis method of Bible study is the simplest "on-your-own" study. But don't let its simplicity fool you. It is an extremely profitable and rewarding method of Bible study, and a wonderful place to begin. Many have found the fruits of such a study so rewarding that they find themselves continually returning to it for the feeding of their souls.

Bible study is only one method of scriptural intake. You should also be engaged in a Bible reading program. Ideally, it is from this reading program that you select the verse to be studied. In the margin of your Bible, or on a separate sheet of paper if you prefer, note possible verses to be studied.

When you are ready to begin your study, select from these possibilities the one on which you want to concentrate.

You may also want to consider the possibility of memorizing the verse. This combination of Bible study and Scripture memory is unbeatable in sealing the verse to your own heart.

To draw attention to the four basic parts of Bible study, you will note next to each step a letter indicating the part you are doing.

(O) OBSERVATION
(I) INTERPRETATION
(C) CORRELATION
(A) APPLICATION

As you become more proficient in your use of the *Verse Analysis* method, you may want to refer to the chapters dealing with these parts for additional things to look for.

Basic Verse Analysis

For the purpose of illustration, 1 Thessalonians 5:17 will be used in walking through this procedure: "Pray without ceasing" (KJV).

(O) *Step One*—Select the context of the verse and note the boundaries. If it is difficult to determine this, refer to a modern translation such as the *New International Version*, which notes the paragraph divisions. If the context is a rather long paragraph, you may either want to try breaking it down further or choose another verse to study.

The context of 1 Thessalonians 5:17 is the verses immediately preceding and following: "Rejoice evermore" (verse 16 KJV) and "In everything give thanks, for this is the will of God in Christ Jesus concerning you" (verse 18 KJV).

(O) *Step Two*—Note any observations and/or possible applications. Also look for any problems, stating specifically what the problem is. You will want to add to this section of your study constantly as you proceed through the other steps.

1 THESSALONIANS 5:16-18

(O) • There are three commands—*rejoice, pray, give thanks*.

(O) • These commands all have modifiers—*evermore, without ceasing, in everything*.

(O) • The clause "This is the will of God in Christ Jesus concerning you" seems to apply to all three verses.

(O) • You can interchange the modifiers with one another without changing the meaning of the verses: *"Rejoice evermore, pray evermore, give thanks evermore,"* and so on with the other modifiers.

(A) • Giving thanks (verse 18) is not one of my strong points. I tend to grumble about everything.

(A) • I rejoice (sometimes), but not "always."

(I) • The modifiers all have the idea of being perpetual, that is, there is never a time when they shouldn't be done.

(I) • Can verse 17 be taken literally? Is it possible to pray unceasingly? Or is Paul simply talking about an attitude here?

(I) *Step Three*—Briefly rewrite each of the verses in your own words. Try to express the kernel of thought or main idea the writer is communicating.

1 THESSALONIANS 5:16-18

• Verse 16—Never stop rejoicing
• Verse 17—Never stop praying   God's will for you
• Verse 18—Never stop giving thanks

(C) *Step Four*—Cross reference each of the verses with another similar idea in the Bible. The best commentary on Scripture is Scripture. Look for verses that will help explain, illustrate, or in some way clarify the idea.

1 THESSALONIANS 5:16-18

- Verse 16—Philippians 4:4
- Verse 17—Ephesians 6:18
- Verse 18—Romans 1:21; Ephesians 5:20

(A) *Step Five*—Choose from the possible applications the one God would have you work on, stating the problem, an example of the problem, the solution, and the specific thing God would have you do to apply the solution.

1 THESSALONIANS 5:16-18

- Verse 18—I am convicted by the fact I am unthankful. Just yesterday I realized that I had not thanked my wife for all the hard work she does in cooking, keeping house, taking care of the children, and many other things.
- I purpose before God to begin checking this ingratitude and replacing it with verbal expressions of thanksgiving.
- I will apologize to the Lord and to my wife and ask their forgiveness.
- Each day this week I will ask God's help in this during my morning devotions and seek to implement it during the day.
- I will talk this over with my children and ask them to call to my attention any failures to express gratitude to my wife.

Do not go on to the Advanced section until you have mastered these five basic steps.

Advanced Verse Analysis

After you have done the above study for a period of time, feel comfortable with it, and want to proceed further, you may try the next four steps. Bible study should not become burdensome or complicated. Don't add these steps prematurely to your study. Nor should you feel "less spiritual" if you never add them. Methodology must always be your servant, never your master.

(I) *Step Six*—Select the pivotal idea in the passage. This is the word or phrase around which the thought moves. Ask yourself, *Is the principal thrust of this passage to exhort to some action or to teach a doctrine?* If action, then concentrate on the verbs. The key is likely to be found there. If doctrine, concentrate on the nouns.

1 THESSALONIANS 5:16-18

- Verse 17—The pivotal word is *pray*. It is the *means* of appropriating God's grace enabling you to *rejoice*. *Giving thanks* is the *method* of prayer.

(I) *Step Seven*—In one sentence write the distilled essence or theme of the passage. Tie the verses together into one "big idea."

1 THESSALONIANS 5:16-18

- God's will for the believer is that in prayer he thanks God for all circumstances so as to rejoice perpetually.

(C) *Step Eight*—Chart the passage, seeking to draw the parts into a whole and relating them to one another. The various methods of chart making are outlined in Chapter 10.

1 THESSALONIANS 5:16-18

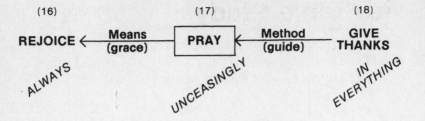

(I) *Step Nine*—Choose a title for the passage

1 THESSALONIANS 5:16-18

- *Title:* "The Will of God in Christ Jesus for Me"

3 The Analytical Method of Bible Study

To analyze something is to study the object in detail, being careful to note even the most minute aspects. This is the objective of analytical Bible study. Here we seek to examine a passage carefully and thoroughly. The purpose is to understand what the writer had in mind when he wrote to his audience.

In many ways the analytical method can be contrasted with the synthetic method of Bible study, which is the topic of Chapter 4. In the synthetic study you will look at the larger picture, as through a telescope. Here in the analytical method you study the parts as through a microscope. Using the illustration of a library, in the synthetic approach you are looking at the composition of the library, while in the analytic approach you are studying the contents of each book.

Analytical Bible study is the "meat and potatoes" of your study of Scripture. As the years progress, you will, in all probability, lean on it as the mainstay of your Bible study program. It is basic for a thorough knowledge of the Word, allowing the student opportunity to interface with why the writer said what he did the way he did. Again, the objective is to reconstruct as clearly as possible the original thinking of the writer.

Question-and-answer Bible studies are a form of the analytical method, as is the verse analysis method presented in Chapter 2. The study on which we are about to embark will launch you into studying a whole passage on your own.

As in verse analysis, a letter indicating the part you are doing is noted next to each of the steps to draw attention to the four basic parts of Bible study.

(O) OBSERVATION
 (I) INTERPRETATION
(C) CORRELATION
(A) APPLICATION

As you become increasingly proficient in your use of the analytical method, you may want to refer to the individual chapters dealing with these parts for additional help.

Basic Analytical Study

For the purpose of illustration, 1 Peter 2 will be the chapter analyzed in walking through the procedure.

(O) *Step One*—Read through the passage carefully. Take a sheet of paper and mark OBSERVATIONS on the top. This will be used throughout the study. Include on this sheet:

1. Observations—Note any and every detail you notice. Bombard the passage with questions such as who? what? where? when? why? and how? Note nouns, verbs, and other key words.

2. Problems—Write out what you don't understand about the passage. Don't say, "I don't understand verse 4." Rather, elaborate on what it is you don't understand. Some of your questions will resolve themselves as you continue your study. Others will be resolved only by referring to an outside source such as your pastor or a commentary. Some of your questions may never be answered.

3. Cross-references—Using the book *Treasury of Scripture Knowledge* or the marginal references in your Bible, cross reference the word, quote, or idea with a similar text elsewhere in the Bible. This will help in your understanding of the passage.

4. Possible applications—You will observe several of these in the course of your study. Note them on this sheet with an (A) in the margin. At the conclusion of your study you will return to these possible applications and select the one on which the Holy Spirit will have you focus.

The following is a sample list of observations taken from 1 Peter 2. They are all listed in this illustration, but you should remember that the list is *not* completed in *Step One* before going on to *Step Two*. You will be adding to the observations throughout the entire study. Don't be concerned that the observations be sequential. If you are half way through the chapter, and have a fresh thought about verse 1, note it right there. Don't worry about trying to squeeze it in at the top of the page.

1 PETER 2 — OBSERVATIONS

(I) • Verse 1—To follow this advice is to become alienated from the world, for this is how the world acts. Not to follow it is to be alienated from God.

(C) • Verse 3—Psalm 34:8.

(O) • Verses 1, 11—Sanctification is one of the emphases of 1 Peter. It must be in three directions: (1) toward God

(1:13)—hope, have faith, appropriate God's grace; (2) toward others (2:1)—related to the last six of the Ten Commandments; and (3) toward self (2:11)—these are sins that primarily hurt the person committing them.

(O) ● Verses 4-8—Three quotes from the Old Testament are used to explain the use of *stone* in reference to Jesus Christ (Isaiah 28:16; Psalm 118:22; Isaiah 8:14).

(O) ● Verses 9-10—Who are we? We are a . . .

—*Chosen people*—the word *chosen* is also used in 1:2. We have been chosen to obedience (1:2), and we have been chosen for service (2:9). Sanctification is our goal and obedience is the process.

—*Royal priesthood*—in verse 5 it was a *holy* priesthood; here it is a *royal* one, with the imagery probably taken from Melchizedek, the king-priest in the Old Testament (Genesis 14).

—*Holy nation*—collectively we are the people of God and form a unique nation, one that has holiness as its hallmark. Our goal is not to be like the world, but to be like Jesus Christ.

—*Peculiar people* (KJV)—we are a people especially suited for God to possess. The older expression *peculiar* means "to bring about or obtain for oneself." God has obtained us to be a people for Himself.

(A)   —We were not always those four things, so we should praise God because He has changed us:

1. From darkness to light—from sin to glorious salvation.

2. From being no people to God's people—from insignificance to purpose and meaning.

3. From receiving no mercy to having mercy in abundance—we do not have to face judgment for our sins.

(A) • Verse 13—"every authority instituted among men." We must obey every law that does not violate God's laws whether the government is favorable or hostile, and we do it for the Lord's sake (see Acts 4:19; 5:25).

(O) • Verses 15, 19-20—the *two reasons* given in this section for submission and serving are: (1) demonstrate to the world that God's call is to a life of good and not evil; and (2) God is pleased with such conduct, since it is a reflection of the character of Jesus Christ (see verses 21-25).

(O) • Verses 13, 15—the two commands given in this section are *submit* and *serve*.

(O) • Verses 13-14, 18—the two groups to whom we are to submit and whom we are to serve are the *government* and *employers*.

(O) • Verses 13-20—possible outline for this section: "Submissive Servants—the Example of the Believer to the World."
1. Divine Despotism (verse 16)—proper perspective
2. Demonstration (verse 17)—proper attitude
3. Divine Directive (verses 13, 18)—proper life style
4. Two Groups (verses 13-14, 18)
5. Two Reasons (verses 15, 19-20)

(O) • Verse 25—we are very much like straying sheep, but Christ has brought us back to Himself. He is shown to be:

—*the Shepherd*—one of the oldest descriptions of God in the Bible (see Isaiah 40:11). He took care of His sheep—His people—even better than a shepherd in Judea took care of his sheep—the animals.

—*the Overseer*—this word means one who presides over, guards and protects. This is what Christ is to His people (see Matthew 28:20).

The observations in this section will vary in length, depending on how much time you are able to give to the study. Don't become discouraged if you don't "observe" much the first few times you do the study. With practice your observations will increase in number and in depth.

(I) *Step Two*—Take another sheet of paper and divide it in two parts, leaving ⅔ of the space on the left and ⅓ on the right. On the *far* left, write numerals down the page according to the number of verses in the chapter (25 for 1 Peter 2). On the left ⅔ of the sheet, verse by verse, state the key thought, that is, the main teaching, subject, or thought the writer is communicating in the content of the verse. (At times you may have difficulty verbalizing the key thoughts of certain verses, such as 1 Peter 2:1.)

On the remaining ⅓ of the sheet, try to combine the key thoughts of the verses into summary key thoughts. Try to feel the flow of the writer's argument. As you combine verses, it will become apparent where the paragraph divisions in the chapter are located.

It is important to note the flow of ideas in a passage—the relationship of the verses to one another. Sometimes the writer makes a general statement, then explains it with examples (see 2 Timothy 3:1-5). At other times he may list a series of ideas and then summarize with a general statement (see James 2:14-17). Or he may give a command, warning, or advice and back them up with reasons, purposes, or proofs. Try to determine what it is the writer is doing in the presentation of his material. Note the way he moves from one idea to the next. See Figure 1 for an example of 1 Peter 2.

(I) *Step Three*—Take a third sheet of paper and place it next to the sheet used in *Step Two*. You are now ready to begin tying the chapter together.

Looking at your *Summary of Key Thoughts* (right ⅓ of the

1 PETER 2 — KEY THOUGHTS AND SUMMARIES

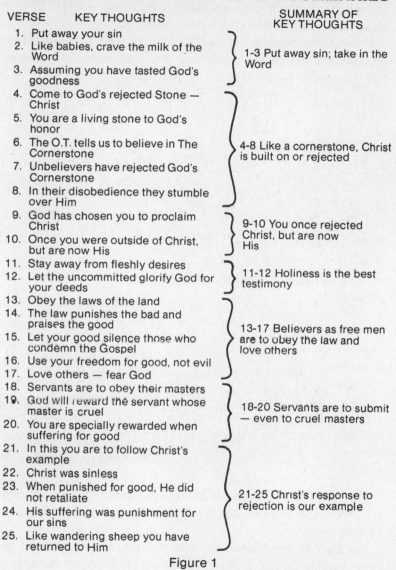

VERSE	KEY THOUGHTS	SUMMARY OF KEY THOUGHTS
1.	Put away your sin	
2.	Like babies, crave the milk of the Word	1-3 Put away sin; take in the Word
3.	Assuming you have tasted God's goodness	
4.	Come to God's rejected Stone — Christ	
5.	You are a living stone to God's honor	
6.	The O.T. tells us to believe in The Cornerstone	4-8 Like a cornerstone, Christ is built on or rejected
7.	Unbelievers have rejected God's Cornerstone	
8.	In their disobedience they stumble over Him	
9.	God has chosen you to proclaim Christ	9-10 You once rejected Christ, but are now His
10.	Once you were outside of Christ, but are now His	
11.	Stay away from fleshly desires	11-12 Holiness is the best testimony
12.	Let the uncommitted glorify God for your deeds	
13.	Obey the laws of the land	
14.	The law punishes the bad and praises the good	
15.	Let your good silence those who condemn the Gospel	13-17 Believers as free men are to obey the law and love others
16.	Use your freedom for good, not evil	
17.	Love others — fear God	
18.	Servants are to obey their masters	
19.	God will reward the servant whose master is cruel	18-20 Servants are to submit — even to cruel masters
20.	You are specially rewarded when suffering for good	
21.	In this you are to follow Christ's example	
22.	Christ was sinless	
23.	When punished for good, He did not retaliate	21-25 Christ's response to rejection is our example
24.	His suffering was punishment for our sins	
25.	Like wandering sheep you have returned to Him	

Figure 1

previous sheet), divide the chapter into its paragraphs. These are easily determined by the natural breaks in the writer's flow of thought.

Write a key thought for each paragraph. The key thought for each paragraph will be a combining of all summary statements on that paragraph. Likewise, the key thought of the chapter will be a summary of the key thought of your paragraphs. What you are doing here is funneling the passage in such a way as to distill its essential meaning (see Figure 3). The key thought for the paragraph is the distilled essence of that paragraph in one sentence and the key thought of the chapter is the distilled essence of the chapter in one sentence. Make each of these sentences as brief as possible without sacrificing the main truth.

You can take each paragraph and put subpoints under it. This is especially helpful if the paragraph(s) tend to be long. This is an optional part of *Step Three*.

1 PETER 2 — OUTLINE

I. Verses 1-10—By studying the Word of God, the Christian is to reflect the character of Christ, who is God's cornerstone, rejected by men.
   A. Strip off the world; drink in the Word (verses 1-3)
   B. Stone of stumbling or salvation (verses 4-8)
   C. Showcase of contrast (verses 9-10)

II. Verses 11-25—Christ set an example for the Christians on how to respond to a world that does not know Him.
   A. Sanctified living is the best testimony (verses 11-12)
   B. Submission—the Christian's example to the world (verses 13-20)
   C. Submission—Christ's example to the believer (verses 21-25)

(A) *Step Four*—Choose from the possible applications the one God would have you work on: stating the problem, an example of the problem, the solution, and the specific things God would have you do to apply the solution.

1 Peter 2—Application

- Verse 13—"Submit yourselves for the Lord's sake to every authority instituted among men." The Lord has spoken to me regarding my habitually exceeding the speed laws. When I drive my auto, I almost always go faster than the speed limit.

    For example, the other day I was on my way downtown and caught myself with one eye looking ahead and the other behind, to see if I would be caught speeding by the police. I know the Lord would have me slow down.
- More often than not, I speed because I am late for an appointment. This happens because of laziness on my part. To make application, I will:
    1. Ask the Lord's forgiveness.
    2. Declare myself on this issue to my family and friends, and ask that they remind me when I exceed the law.
    3. Leave early for every appointment, so I won't have the pressure of disobeying the "authority instituted among men."

Do not go on to the Advanced section until you have mastered these four basic steps.

Advanced Analytical Study

If, after doing these four steps for a period of time, you want to add to your study, you can do two things. One is to read Chapters 8–11 and implement those parts of observation, interpretation, correlation, and application that apply to these four steps of the basic study. The other is to add further steps to your study. Be bold and imaginative in this. Try new things. Methods are designed to help you, not enslave you. Put aside what doesn't work for you and add what does. Remember, the objective of Bible study is to determine the meaning of the writer at the time he wrote it, and apply this truth to your life. Everything else is methodology to help you in this quest.

The following are five other steps you can add if and when you feel ready.

(I) *Step Five*—Select the pivotal idea in the passage. This is the word or phrase around which the thought of the passage moves. Ask yourself, *Is the flow of the passage in the direction of exhortation to action, or teaching doctrine?* If action, then concentrate on the verbs. The pivotal idea is likely to be found there. If the flow of the passage is on teaching doctrine, then concentrate on the nouns.

On a separate sheet of paper make two columns. List the key verbs in one and the key nouns in the other, verse by verse. Study these lists and determine if the thrust of the chapter is in the direction of action or doctrine.

Look for the appropriate verb or noun (or perhaps phrase) that is amplified in some respect in each paragraph of the passage. This is the pivotal idea. If there is more than one that qualifies, then choose the best one.

After studying these parallel bits in Figure 2, you can see that 1 Peter 2 is an exhortation to action. From the important verbs listed, the key ones are circled. Peter's exhortation is to follow His (Christ's) example (verse 21). "Follow His Example," then, is the pivotal idea of the passage.

(I) *Step Six*—The *key thought of the passage* is the essence of the passage in one sentence. The key thought of each paragraph is how the writer develops that passage. This was determined in *Step Three.* By now you have discovered that finding the *pivotal idea (Step Five)* is helpful in determining the *key thought of the pas-*

1 PETER 2 — PIVOTAL IDEA

VERSE VERBS	NOUNS
1. rid (yourselves)	malice, deceit, hypocrisy, jealousy, slander
2. crave, (grow)	babies, milk (Word, S.C.), salvation
3. taste	Lord, good
4. come	Stone
5. are being (built) offering, acceptable	stones, house, priesthood, sacrifices
6. trusts	cornerstone
7. believe, rejected	stone, builders, capstone
8. causes, makes, stumble	stone, rock, message
9. you are, (declare)	people, priesthood, nation, darkness, light
10. were not, (now) are	people, God, mercy
11. abstain	(sinful) desires, soul
12. live (see)	(good) lives, deeds
13. submit	authority, king
14.	governors
15.	
16.	
17. show . . . respect, love, fear	
18. (submit) (yourselves)	slaves, masters
19. bears up	commendable, God
20. suffer	
21. (you) were called, (follow)	Christ, example
22.	
23.	
24.	
25.	Shepherd, Overseer

Figure 2

sage, which we will elaborate on here in *Step Six.* This whole process is illustrated in Figure 3.

THE FLOW OF THE WRITER'S ARGUMENT

Key Thought of each Verse

Summary Key Thoughts
(a group of verses)

Key Thoughts of Paragraphs

The Pivotal Idea

Key Thought of
the Whole
Passage

Figure 3

The *key thought of the passage* should then be developed as the eminent truth of the passage. In doing so, state the *key thought of the passage* at the beginning and end of your eminent truth. The development of the key thought of the passage is the articulation of the writer's message and follows the flow of the passage (see Figure 3 above). You can have only *one* key thought to the passage. Each person doing a study may state it in his own words, but it should become immediately apparent in a comparison of key thoughts written by various people that they are all studying the same passage. A correct application of the above six steps should lead everyone to the same conclusion. This is illustrated in Figure 4.

I Peter 2 — Key Thought of the Passage

The Christian is called on to follow the example of Christ into a life of submission and suffering at the hands of a hostile world.

EMINENT TRUTH

The Christian is called on to follow the example of Christ and live a life of submission and suffering at the hands of a hostile world.

The holiness of Jesus Christ was such a contrast to a sinful world that men either had to conform to Him or destroy Him Peter uses the illustration of a cornerstone. The cornerstone properly laid insured that the building would be straight and solid Prior to Christ all "buildings" (lives of people) were crooked. The contrast wasn't seen till Christ the perfect "building" appeared He was rejected and crucified (verses 4-8).

Christ's suffering and rejection was *caused* by the sinfulness of man and *resulted* in the salvation of man. His death on the cross (verse 24) paid the penalty for sin and brought a solution to man's problem.

All of this was possible, however, because Christ understood His role and was submissive to it (verses 22-23). So we also must understand our roles and be submissive to them Our holiness (verses 1, 9, 11, and others), like Christ's, evokes a negative reaction from a sinful world (verse 20). Thus sinful men persecute us just as they did Him. Our response must be to *serve* and *submit*. This example will aid in God's plan of redemption (verses 12, 15). In short, we are to *follow His example* (verse 21).

The Christian is called on to follow the example of Christ into a life of submission and suffering at the hands of a hostile world

Figure 4

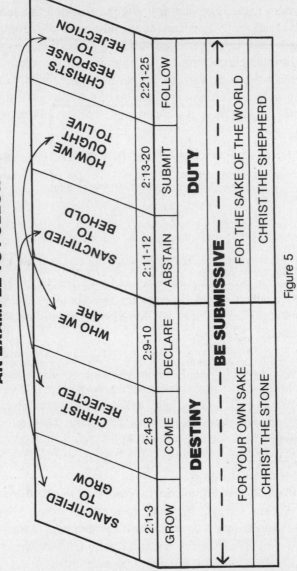

Figure 5

(I) *Step Seven*—Write a title for each paragraph and then for the whole chapter (or passage). The purpose of a title is *identification*. It is a tool to help you recall the passage and its contents. Here is where you can show your creativity, and may want to use something catchy.

---

1 PETER 2—TITLE
"An Example to Follow"

Figure 6

(C) *Step Eight*—Charting a passage is a way of relating the part to the whole and comparing the various parts with one another. Read Chapter 5, which explains the various techniques for charting, and chart the passage you have just studied. See Figure 5 for an example.

(O) *Step Nine*—For the truly ambitious, a ninth and final step you may incorporate is to memorize the passage. Though such a task is hard work, it pays rich rewards. As you review the passage, fresh observations and insights will come to mind which you can add to your *Observation* section *(Step One)*. The following suggestions are for your consideration.

1. Memorize from only one translation. Use the one from which you are studying.

2. Place the verses on cards—one verse per card—putting the verse on one side and the reference on the other. (Blank cards specifically designed for this may be obtained from your local Christian bookstore, or by writing Customer Services, NavPress, P.O. Box 20, Colorado Springs, Colorado 80901.)

3. Review, *Review,* REVIEW. Few things are as frustrating as memorizing a portion of Scripture and then forgetting it. Review is hard work, but keep current in it.

4. Memorize the passage *before* you begin your study. This will help you in every step you employ. It will tie the passage into a unit and give you the ability to have the whole in mind as you study it verse by verse.

Do not allow the methodology to overwhelm you. For example, in the five advanced steps, choose only those with which you feel comfortable. In time you may want to design a new step and use it. There is nothing sacred about methodology. Its value lies in its ability to help you become a more proficient student of the Word of God.

4 The Synthetic Method of Bible Study

SYNTHETIC STUDY

The broad, overall study of a book of the Bible.

The synthetic method of Bible study approaches each book of the Bible as a unit and seeks to understand its meaning as a whole. The objective is to get a broad, panoramic view of the book. It does not concern itself with details but the overall scope of the book.

In the analytical method you looked at the text through a microscope. In the synthetic method you look at it through a telescope. What did the writer, moved by the Holy Spirit, have in mind as he wrote? What is the key thought or big idea in the book? How does he make his point? These are the kinds of questions that are germaine to the synthetic method.

This method is probably the most difficult of all the Bible study methods, but can also prove to be the most rewarding.

As in every method of Bible study, you will incorporate four basic parts:

(O) OBSERVATION
(I) INTERPRETATION
(C) CORRELATION
(A) APPLICATION

Next to each step in the study you will note one of the above four letters. These are meant to alert you to the part employed in that step. Further information on how to approach each of these four parts may be found in Chapters 8–11.

Basic Synthetic Study

For the purpose of illustration, the Book of Romans will be synthesized in walking through the procedure.

(O) *Step One*—Read through the book carefully. Take a sheet of paper and mark *Observations* on the top. This will be used throughout the entire study. Include on this sheet:

1. Observations—Note the key thoughts or main arguments that flow through the book. List the important words. Note such things as places, events, and important names. List things you may want to study later.

2. Problems—When you are unable to follow the thinking of the writer, note when this occurs and exactly what it is you don't understand.

3. Cross-references—Note any important events or quotes the writer uses from other parts of the Bible. For example, Romans 10:18-21 refers to a series of quotes from the Old Testament (Psalm 19:4; Deuteronomy 32:21; Isaiah 65:1-2). An understanding of the context of each of those quotes will help you discover the flow of Paul's argument in the Book of Romans.

4. Possible Applications—Several of these will come to your attention as you read and reread the book. Note these for use later in your study.

Figure 7 is a sample list of observations taken from the Book of Romans. They are all listed on one page, but it should be remembered that the *Observations* are *not* completed in *Step One* before going on to *Step Two*. Rather, use this sheet throughout the entire study and add to it as you go along.

(I) *Step Two*—Read the book through a second time, involving yourself in a process of intensive exploration. Your objective is to unravel the writer's argument. As you read, list under your *Observations* the key thoughts or major themes of the book. Try to put them in your own words. Don't let the chapter and verse divisions destroy the unity of the book, for these divisions were not there when the writer penned his book originally. Be sure to do this reading in one sitting.

(The illustration of *Step Two* is included in *Step One* in Figure 7.)

(I) *Step Three*—Read the book carefully a third time. Ask the Holy Spirit to enable you to approach it with a fresh mind. With a pen in your hand complete your reading in one sitting.

As you read this time, look for the main theme or big idea the writer is communicating. This is the key thought of the book—the organizing principle that gives the book its unity.

Is there any particular place in the book where the key thought is mentioned? Does any one verse or passage state the idea more succinctly than any other? If so, note this.

As you compare this key thought with the themes listed in *Step Two*, the unity should become apparent. Write the key thought out in your own words.

ROMANS — Observations

VERSE   OBSERVATIONS

1:18   Paul begins his epistle by establishing the fact of man's sin. He deals first with the world at large (1:18-32), then the moralist (2:1-16), and finally the Jew (2:17 – 3:9).

3:21-26   Here we see the solution to our problem—the death of Christ—a beautiful, logical fiow in Paul's teaching.

2:7   What does this mean? Is Paul here saying that a person can *work* his way to heaven?

3:1
(A)   The Jews had a tremendous advantage. So do I as a man born in a Christian heritage. I should list all the advantages I have that much of the world does not.

4:1   Why does Paul talk about Abraham after Christ?

5:12-21   What is the gist of Paul's argument in this passage? What is he seeking to communicate?

6:1-4   A beautiful picture of our identification with Christ in His death, burial, and resurrection.

Whole   Outline:
1. Man's need (1:1 – 3:20)
2. God's solution (3:21 – 5:21)
3. Implication for Christians (6:1 – 8:39)
4. Implication for Jews (9:1 – 11:36)
5. Application (12:1 – 16:27)

9:3
(A)   Paul wished himself "accursed" from Christ for his kinsmen. Do I have that kind of love for people?—a real challenge!

11:1-32   Paul seems to indicate that there will be a future for Israel? Is this for the nation or just certain individuals? What does "ALL" in verse 26 mean?

12:19
(A)   "Avenge not yourself"—I find that I tend to be vindictive toward people who I feel have wronged me.

13:2   Does this passage imply that the thirteen colonies were wrong in declaring their independence from Britain in 1776?

14:1-23   This is a passage on Christian liberties. It has far-reaching implication for the church today. Note the question and answer method Paul uses in communicating.

Figure 7

ROMANS—KEY THOUGHT

Romans 1:16-17—*The just shall live by faith.*

(C) *Step Four*—Read the entire book a fourth time. Approach your reading as though you are exploring the book for the very first time. Don't "breeze" through it. Again, do this reading at one sitting. Be sure and set aside adequate time so as not to be interrupted.

This time through, develop a broad outline of the book. Be more interested in the flow of the writer's thinking than the chapter divisions. Resist the temptation to use the outline found in many study Bibles'. This is *your* exploration, so get your own outline.

Title the various divisions in your outline and write a title for the book.

ROMANS—OUTLINE

A Christian Catechism

I. Doctrine, 1:1–5:21
   A. Introduction, 1:1-17
   B. Man's Problem, 1:18–3:20
   C. God's Solution, 3:21–5:21

II. Implication, 6:1–11:36
   A. Believers, 6:1–8:39, . . .
      1. and sin, 6:1-23
      2. and the law, 7:1-25
      3. delivered, 8:1-39
   B. Jews, 9:1–11:36
      1. A sovereign choice, 9:1-33
      2. A universal message, 10:1-21
      3. A future for Israel, 11:1-36

III. Application, 12:1–16:27
   A. The Believer and the Church, 12:1-21
   B. The Believer and the World, 13:1-14
   C. The Believer and Christian Liberty, 14:1–15:7
   D. Future Plans and Closing Remarks, 15:8–16:27

(O) *Step Five*—Summarize the historical background on the book. You can derive much of this information from the book itself; for some of it you will have to consult Bible study aids, such as, *Zondervan Pictorial Encyclopedia of the Bible* (5 volumes), *Eerdmans Bible Handbook,* and *Halley's Bible Handbook.*

Try to determine the following:

1. Who wrote the book? How is the writer presented in the book? What does he reveal about himself?
2. To whom was the book written? Where did they live? What was the geography like and what kind of people were they?
3. When and where was it written? What circumstances and environment surrounded the writer as he wrote?
4. Why was the book written? What was on the writer's mind when he sat down to write? Were there any special problems that occasioned the writing? Is the book designed to communicate a particular thing?

ROMANS—BACKGROUND

1. The letter begins by claiming to be written by Paul (1:1). When the writer describes his ministry later on (Chapter 15), it sounds like Paul. The ideas, style of the letter, and vocabulary all support the claim that Paul wrote it.

   The church fathers and others through the centuries all refer to Paul as the writer.

   Having never visited Rome on his missionary journeys, Paul communicates a warmth and acceptance of the Romans (1:4-12); he states that his contact with them will be *mutually* edifying.

2. Many theories exist as to how the Church at Rome got started (such as, the Apostle Peter founded it), but the best is that it was started by Jews from Rome converted on the day of Pentecost (see Acts 2). Many Jews lived in Rome, having been taken there when Palestine was conquered by Rome in 63 B.C.

3. Paul says he has finished the first phase of his ministry and is ready to move on into Spain (see 15:22). He wants to visit Rome on his way, traveling first to Jerusalem.

   Phoebe is mentioned in this letter (16:1), and she was from Corinth. This, along with other evidence, indicates that Corinth was the city from which Paul wrote Romans. It was written during his third journey, about A.D. 57-58.

4. Since Paul had never ministered in Rome, there were no special problems that confronted him. He wanted to introduce himself to the church and gain their support for his further missionary activity in Spain.

   Some say he wanted to reconcile differences that existed between the Jews and Gentiles, but more probably he simply wanted to set forth a compendium of his thoughts on the theology of the gospel.

(A) *Step Six*—Choose from the possible applications listed in your *Observations* the one on which God would have you work. Suggestions on how to do this are found in Chapter 11.

Do not go to the Advanced section until you have mastered these six basic steps.

Advanced Synthetic Study

If, after doing these steps for a period of time you want to add to your study, you can go two routes. One is to read Chapters 8–11 and implement those parts that apply to these steps. The other is to add further steps of your own. Be bold and imaginative. Try new things. Method is designed to help you, not enslave you. Put aside what doesn't work for you and add what does. The objective of Bible study is to determine the meaning of the writer at the time he wrote it, and apply this truth to your life. Everything else is methodology to help you in this quest. Three more steps are suggested here.

(I) *Step Seven*—Study the format of the book to determine the style the writer uses. The following are examples of what to look for in the book you are studying.

1. Topical—Here the writer deals with certain topics. The Gospel of Matthew is an example. Matthew sets forth the life of Christ in topical fashion.

2. Chronological—Here the writer relates a sequence of events and a story unfolds. An example of this style are in the books of 1 and 2 Kings, which originally were one book.

3. Apologetic—Here in polemic form the writer argues his point. Galatians is a beautiful example of this. Paul dispenses with the usual niceties in his introduction and gets right down to business.

4. Interrogative—Here the writer, in making his point, jabs with probing questions. This is the style used by Malachi.

5. Logical—Here the writer systematically moves in such a way so as to lead us to his conclusion. This is Paul's style in the Book of Romans. He begins with the universal fact of sin, systematically destroying any argument for self-recovery in the process, and leads us to the foot of the cross. His method is that of using questions and answers, much like the techniques used in catechism instruction.

(C) *Step Eight*—Chart the book. This will prove to be a helpful step in viewing the book as a unit and comparing the parts with one another. For assistance in how to do this, turn to Chapter 10. Study the example in Figure 8.

(I) *Step Nine*—Determine the place of the book in the Bible as a whole. Each book has its own unique contribution to the whole of the Bible. What would be missing if this book were omitted?

ROMANS – A CHRISTIAN CATECHISM

	Doctrine			Implication	Application
Theme	SIN	SALVATION	SANCTIFICATION	SELECTION	SERVICE
Subject	MAN (Unbeliever in Sin)	GOD (God the Son)	MAN-GOD (HIS) (Believer in Sin)	GOD (God the Father)	MAN
By Faith	LIFE BY FAITH				SERVICE BY FAITH
Slave	Slave to Sin		Slave to God		Slave Serving God
HIS Righteousness	HIS Righteousness IN LAW	HIS Righteousness IMPUTED	HIS Righteousness OBEYED	HIS Righteousness IN ELECTION	HIS Righteousness DISPLAYED
Salvation	The Need of Salvation	The Way of Salvation	The Life of Salvation	The Scope of Salvation	The Service of Salvation

Section divisions:

Verses	Section	Theme
1:1-17	Introduction	SIN
1:18-2:16	The Unbeliever and Sin	SIN
2:17–3:20	The Unbeliever and the Law	SIN
3:21-31	The Unbeliever Delivered	SALVATION
4:1-25	Deliverance in the OT III. — Abraham	SALVATION
5:1-21	The Doctrine of Imputation Elaborated	SALVATION
6:1-23	The Believer and Sin	SANCTIFICATION
7:1-25	The Believer and the Law	SANCTIFICATION
8:1-39	The Believer Delivered	SANCTIFICATION
9:1-33	A Sovereign Choice	SELECTION
10:1-21	A Universal Message	SELECTION
11:1-36	A Future for Israel	SELECTION
12:1-21	The Believer and the Church	SERVICE
13:1-14	The Believer and the World	SERVICE
14:1–15:7	The Believer and Christian Liberty	SERVICE
15:8–16:27	Future Plans and Closing Remarks	SERVICE

Figure 8

Romans—Its Contribution

Many believe Romans to be the greatest of the New Testament books. It certainly is the most thorough presentation of the "whole counsel of God." It forms the basis of the great theological works written through the ages and it was the major book of the Protestant Reformation.

In contrast to the other religions of the world, which are religions of achievement, Christianity is a religion of rescue. Romans is the clearest presentation of this fact of all the New Testament documents.

Conclusion

Ideally the synthetic method should be used in conjunction with the analytic method. View the book as a whole, then look at its parts, and finally reexamine the whole. Diagramed, it would look like this:

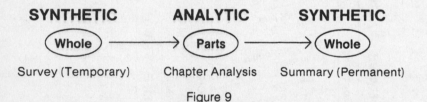

SYNTHETIC   **ANALYTIC**   **SYNTHETIC**

(Whole) ———→ (Parts) ———→ (Whole)

Survey (Temporary)   Chapter Analysis   Summary (Permanent)

Figure 9

Applying this method means you do a synthetic study first, as described in this chapter. Then do a chapter by chapter analysis of the book described in the preceding chapter. Finally, repeat the synthetic study of the book. This final study will either confirm or invalidate the first synthetic study.

If you elect to do this, be careful to approach your second synthetic study with an open, fresh mind. Put your first study aside and don't refer to it till you are all done. Then bring it out for purposes of comparison.

This is a step that should only be taken by a seasoned Bible student. Do not tackle more than you can handle, as it leads to frustration, discouragement, and ultimately quitting. If, as you implement these steps, you find you are doing too much, back away from the new material. You are not in competition with anyone. Later, if you feel up to it, give it another try. If you decide never to try, fine!

5 The Topical Method of Bible Study

TOPICAL STUDY

The tracing of a selected topic through the Bible or a portion of it.

In Paul's Epistle to the Romans he introduces a number of different topics and weaves them together into the message he is communicating. Examples of these topics are faith, grace, justification, Holy Spirit, and sin. His treatment of each of these topics is not complete, but it does give you some insights into how God feels about them.

This is true for all the writers of the Bible. Each touches on a host of topics in making his point.

51

In the topical method of Bible study you "chase" a selected topic through the Bible. How far you chase it will depend on the time you have and your overall objective. For the average student, the larger the topic the more narrow the study will have to be.

For example, the study of *sin* in the Bible would promise to be a gargantuan task. Even a study of *Jesus' teaching on sin* would be huge. Either you will have to avoid subjects of this size, or narrow them down still further, like, *John's teaching of sin in his first letter*.

A smaller topic can be treated much more broadly. If, for example, you decide to study the word *victory* in the Bible, you can search all 66 books, and find that in the whole Bible it only appears 11 times.

Sometimes the topic being studied has synonyms: law, statutes, commands, ordinances, precepts, testimonies are all used interchangeably in the Psalms. For this reason, a topical or cyclopedic index can often prove more useful than a concordance. The *Thompson Chain Reference Bible* is excellent for this, as is *The NIV Topical Study Bible*. *Strong's* and *Young's* concordances are two exhaustive ones from which to choose. *The New Nave's Topical Bible* is still another.

As in the Verse Analysis method, to draw attention to the four basic parts of Bible study, a letter indicating the part you are doing is noted next to each of the steps.

    (O) OBSERVATION
     (I) INTERPRETATION
    (C) CORRELATION
    (A) APPLICATION

Basic Topical Study

For purposes of illustration, we will use the word *hospitality* as our topic for study.

(C) *Step One*—Choose the word to be studied and the boundaries of the study, such as a book, section of Bible, or the whole Bible. Write out the purpose or objective of the study. Using a Bible study aid such as those listed above, locate the references to be included in your study. On a sheet of paper list these references vertically using the left hand side of the sheet.

HOSPITALITY—TOPIC, PURPOSE, AND REFERENCES

Topic to Be Studied: HOSPITALITY
Purpose of the Study: To learn the biblical concept of hospitality, so that we might use our home as the Bible teaches.
References:
> Matthew 25:35
> Luke 7:44-46
> Luke 11:5-8
> Romans 12:13
> 1 Timothy 3:2
> Titus 1:8
> Hebrews 13:2
> 1 Peter 4:9

(O) *Step Two*—Take a sheet of paper and mark *Observations* on the top. This will be used throughout the study. Include on this sheet:

1. Observations—Note any and every detail you notice. Bombard the references with questions such as: who? what? where? when? why? and how? Note the nouns, verbs, and other key words.

2. Problems—Write out what you don't understand about the references and topic. Don't say, "I don't understand Ephesians 4:8." Rather, elaborate on what it is you don't understand. Some of your questions will resolve themselves as you continue your study. Others will be resolved only by referring to outside sources such as your pastor or a commentary. Some of your questions may never be answered.

3. Possible application—you will observe several of these in the course of your study. Note them on this sheet with an (A) in the margin. At the conclusion of your study you will return to these possible applications and select the one on which the Holy Spirit will have you focus.

HOSPITALITY—OBSERVATIONS

(O) • *Definitions:* Hospitality is "the reception and entertainment of strangers" *(The Open Bible).*

Hospitable as entered in the dictionary listing is between *Hospice,* a place for a stranger to rest and lodge, and *Hospital,* a place to care for the sick. It means: "Given to generous and cordial reception of guests" *(Webster's New Collegiate Dictionary).*

Hospitality is "hospitable treatment, reception, or disposition" *(Webster's New Collegiate Dictionary).*

(O) • Matthew 25:35—Jesus' judgment on the nations for their acceptance or rejection of Him and His brethren in the context of provision.

—The bare essentials are listed: food, drink, shelter, clothing, and fellowship.

—Why is the emphasis placed on strangers? The church was dispersed and the traveling believer could find acceptance and provision in the context of the local body of believers; therefore, the saints were to expect strangers. Also they never knew when they might be entertaining angels (Hebrews 13:2).

(A)   —My tendency is to entertain those I *know,* rather than provide for the stranger.

(O) • Luke 7:44-46—Jesus contrasts the entertaining host and the hospitable stranger. The host did not provide any courtesies to his guest, while the stranger provided water, greeting, and anointing.

—Jesus reveals that a person's motives are reflected in whether hospitality is given out of love or obligation.

—What are the courtesies of hospitality in my culture today? A welcome greeting, something to drink, communicating an interest in the guest, food, and other amenities.

—Contrast Simon to Martha and Mary, who eagerly received Jesus into their home (Luke 10:38; John 12:2).

(O) • Luke 11:5-8—There is a cost in meeting the needs of others: inconvenience (the hour was late and the family settled for the night), time, and provision.

—Because of a friendship (relationship), the person felt free to go to him for help in a time of need.

—Hospitality is meeting the needs of others, not merely entertaining guests as our culture portrays. Cultural entertaining to show off our skills as cooks, tidy homekeepers, or the array of such things as china, silver, and art objects, is opposite of the biblical teaching on hospitality.

(O) • Romans 12:13—The providing of needs and the commitment to hospitality are listed together.

—The believers are singled out as the recipients.

—Synonyms: given, committed, addicted (1 Corinthians 16:15 KJV).

—Hospitality isn't a decision making procedure but the reflection of a life style. The home isn't regarded as an ivory tower of retreat for themselves but a hospice for service to others.

(O) • 1 Timothy 3:2—What does it mean to be given to hospitality? The word *given* connotes more than something you take or leave, but a way of life, a life style.

> —In Genesis 18, Sarah and Abraham were not expecting guests, yet as the strangers approached, Abraham *ran* to meet them, greeted them by *bowing* to them, gave them *water* to wash their feet, and then had Sarah prepare a full meal. They went out of their way to make the strangers welcome. The cost to them was time, effort, and provisions. Yet there was no hesitation on their part, but an eager giving of themselves (see 2 Corinthians 8:5).

(O) • Titus 1:8—Church leaders must love hospitality.

> —Hospitality cannot be separated from people and a concern and interest in them. It means giving myself to others because I am concerned for them.

> (O) —In John 4, we see Jesus as a tired, hungry traveler. Yet He gave Himself to the Samaritan woman by talking with her, answering her questions, and offering her living water that would satisfy the deepest needs of her life. What a contrast to the response of the disciples, who were shocked that he would even speak to her!

> (O) —2 Kings 4:8-10—A Shunammite couple with financial means prepared a room with a table, stool, lamp, and bed for the traveling prophet Elisha, so he might have a place to stay.

(A) • Hebrews 13:2—It is easy to become so involved in my own activities and friends that I neglect the stranger, such as visitors who attend church without my greeting them. If I did my part along with the rest of the congregation, "official greeters" wouldn't be necessary.

—Do angels still visit today?

—What are the Bible's accounts of people entertaining angels and not realizing who they were?
  • Genesis 18:2-15—Abraham
  • Genesis 19:1-22—Lot
  • Judges 6:11-24—Gideon
  • Judges 13:1-21—Samson's mother and father

—The angelic visitations were to convey a message, yet in each account they were entertained not because they were angels but because the people opened their homes and lives to strangers.

(O)(C) • 1 Peter 4:9—Because hospitality involves giving, the admonition of 2 Corinthians 9:7 applies: "Each person should give what he has decided in his heart to give, not reluctantly or under compulsion, for God loves a cheerful giver."

—Hospitality should reflect a heart attitude of eagerness, not the fulfillment of a duty. If I grasp the privilege of ministering to others by being hospitable, it removes the obligation and allows the Spirit of God to minister to others through me, which then becomes the reflection of a life style.

(I) *Step Three*—On the sheet used in *Step One* write out the *key thought* for each reference listed. The key thought is the distilled essence or main idea of the verse stated in your own words.

While doing *Step Three,* you should list many of your *observations* suggested in *Step Two.*

Hospitality—Key Thoughts

Topic to Be Studied: HOSPITALITY
Purpose of the Study: To learn the biblical concept of hospitality, so that we might use our home as the Bible teaches.
References:

Matthew 25:35—acceptance and provision for the stranger
Luke 7:44–46–to provide the courtesies of hospitality
Luke 11:5–8—cost involved in meeting others' needs
Romans 12:13— providing needs; committed to hospitality
1 Timothy 3:2— church leaders must be committed to hospitality
Titus 1:8—a lover of hospitality
Hebrews 13:2— entertain strangers; some have hosted angels
1 Peter 4:9—be hospitable without grudging

(C) *Step Four*—Arrange the verses into categories. The *key thoughts* listed in *Step Three* will help you select your categories. Ask yourself questions like, *What are the main categories suggested by these verses? How would I outline this subject to another person?* Some verses will fit under more than one category.

Hospitality—Categories

Attitudes of hospitality
    1 Peter 4:9; Titus 1:8; 1 Timothy 3:2; Romans 12:13
Definition of hospitality
    Matthew 25:35; Luke 7:44-46; Romans 12:13
Costs and rewards of hospitality
    Luke 11:5-8; Hebrews 13:2

(C) *Step Five*—Outline the categories created in *Step Four*, listing the major divisions and important subdivisions. Place the key verses next to each division and subpoint.

Work for logical order and simplicity of structure. Don't make it complicated. Generally speaking, the simpler you make it the more you understand it. Constantly keep in mind the purpose of the study.

HOSPITALITY—OUTLINE

I. Hospitality defined (Romans 12:13; Matthew 25:35-40)
II. Hospitality demonstrated (Luke 7:44-46)
   A. Attitudes toward hospitality (Titus 1:8, 1 Peter 4:9; 1 Timothy 3:2)
   B. Costs and benefits of hospitality (Luke 11:5-8; Hebrews 13:2)

(I) *Step Six*—Write out the *key thought* for each major division, remembering that the key thought is your stating the main idea in one sentence. Then write a key thought for the whole study. This becomes the "big idea" or theme of the study. In the process, you narrow down the material (as in a funnel) from the key thought of each verse to the key thought of the whole.

HOSPITALITY—KEY THOUGHTS OF THE WHOLE STUDY

I. Hospitality defined:
   Being sensitive to the needs of people around me, including the stranger, and providing the necessary aid to meet those needs.
II. Hospitality demonstrated:
   By fulfilling the common courtesies in my culture so the guest knows he is welcome.
   A. An attitude of commitment and love for hospitality is essential.
   B. Time, effort, and provisions are part of the cost, but the benefits can be an unexpected heavenly guest.

Key Thought for the Whole Study: Hospitality is committing myself to others, including the stranger, and communicating a genuine interest in them by extending cultural courtesies and providing for their needs.

(A) *Step Seven*—Choose from the possible applications listed in your *Observations* the one on which God would have you work.

HOSPITALITY—APPLICATION

I attend a large church where it is easy to become lost among the people. I don't go out of my way to greet people I don't recognize. I merely go on my own way.

This is contrary to the Bible's teaching of having a life style of being hospitable.

I will try to greet those around me following the worship service, introduce myself, and inquire if they're visitors. I'll welcome them and ask if I can be of any service to them (such as, finding a Sunday School class).

Advanced Topical Study

The following additional steps are optional and should only be tried after you have gained proficiency in the first part of the study. This cannot be overemphasized: don't try to tackle too much at once. Add to your methodology slowly. You are seeking to develop life-long habits of Bible study.

(I) *Step Eight*—Take the key thought of your study and write several paragraphs elaborating on the central truth. View this key thought as the pivotal point of your elaboration. Never stray far from it. The purpose here is to nail down the basic truths or principles found in the study.

HOSPITALITY—ELABORATING ON THE KEY THOUGHT

Hospitality is committing myself to others, including the stranger, and communicating a genuine interest in them by extending cultural courtesies and providing for their needs.

Hospitality is a commitment in that it is not merely entertaining but a way of life—a lifestyle. Entertaining is something you choose to do or don't do depending on your will, but hospitality is an openness of life and home. It is giving of yourself to others in an attitude of commitment, not obligation.

Hospitality is communicating to your guest an interest in him by extending common courtesies in keeping with our culture. This might include a warm handshake, the offering of a beverage, time to converse (without mentally being preoccupied as you listen), and the invitation to a meal or lodging if it is appropriate to the time of day and circumstances.

The guest may have needs other than physical (such as, food and drink). These may include acceptance or a problem which needs to be discussed. Hospitality includes fellowship with genuine interest in seeking to minister to the needs of the other person.

Because hospitality involves giving, there is a cost involved. It could be in time, effort, or material things, yet the cost is only one aspect of hospitality. The other is the reward of hospitality. This may or may not be evident immediately. God is a giving God and when His children participate in His nature, He rewards them, sometimes with a "heavenly" guest.

Therefore, by committing myself to others, including the stranger, and communicating a genuine interest in them by extending cultural courtesies and providing for their needs, I am obeying the biblical admonition of being hospitable.

(C) *Step Nine*—Referring to the material found in Chapter 10, make a chart on your topical study. This will be a helpful step in viewing the study as a whole and seeing how the parts relate to one another. The type of topical study you have done will influence the kind of chart you select.

HOSPITALITY – CHART

BIBLICAL HOSPITALITY	CULTURAL ENTERTAINING
Reflection of a lifestyle	Fulfilling an obligation
Sharing what you have	Showing off what you have
Stranger is welcome	The well-known person is welcome
Home as a hospice	Home as an ivory tower

Figure 10

(I) *Step Ten*—Refer to outside material on the topic you studied and add or alter any part of your study. This last step is a helpful "check" on your conclusions, especially if you plan on any public presentation of your study.

6 The Biographical Method of Bible Study

This is a "fun" kind of Bible study, for you have an opportunity to explore the characters of people the Holy Spirit has placed in the Bible and learn from their lives. Paul, writing to the Corinthians, said, "These things happened to them as examples and were written down as warnings for us, on whom the fulfillment of the ages has come" (1 Corinthians 10:11).

A great deal of material has been written on some of the people in the Bible. When you study people like Jesus, Abraham, and

Moses, you may want to narrow down your study to areas such as, "The life of Jesus as revealed in John's Gospel," "Moses during the Exodus," or "What the New Testament says about Abraham." Constantly work at keeping your Bible studies to manageable size.

The same reference materials suggested in Chapter 5 are useful here.

As in the Verse Analysis method, a letter indicating the part you are doing has been noted next to each of the steps to draw attention to the four basic parts of Bible study.

(O) OBSERVATION
(I) INTERPRETATION
(C) CORRELATION
(A) APPLICATION

Basic Biographical Study

For the purpose of illustration, we will use Rahab in this study.

(C) *Step One*—Choose the person you want to study and set the boundaries of the study (for example, "The life of David before he became king"). Using a concordance or cyclopedic index, locate the references that have to do with the person you are studying. Read these several times, and write a summary for each.

RAHAB—REFERENCES

Joshua   2:1—a harlot living in Jericho
          2:3—the king of Jericho asks about the spies from her
          2:4—she hid the spies and lied to the king
          2:5—she purposely distracted the men of the city
          2:6—she hid the spies under flax
          2:8-9—she acknowledged that the Lord had conquered Jericho

2:10—the rumor of the Exodus and victory over the Amorites

2:11—the fear of her people and the fact that the Lord was God of all

2:12-13—she asked for safety for herself and her family

2:14—the spies make her a promise

2:15—she provided their escape route

2:16—she gave them a plan for safety

2:17-20—the spies plan for her safety

2:21—the sign of her commitment

6:22-23—Rahab's rescue along with her family

Matthew 1:5—Rahab's place in the genealogy of Jesus Christ

Hebrews 11:31—by faith she didn't die because she received the spies

James 2:25—she was justified by her action of sending the spies away

(O) *Step Two*—Take a sheet of paper and mark *OBSERVATIONS* on the top. Use this sheet throughout the study. Include on this page:

1. Observations—Note any and every detail you notice about this person. Who was he? What did he do? Where did he live? When did he live? Why did he do what he did? How did he accomplish it? Note details about him and his character.

2. Problems—Write out what you don't understand about this person and events in his life.

3. Possible application—Mark several of these during the course of your study, and write an (A) in the margin. At the conclusion of your study, you will return to these possible applications and select the one on which the Holy Spirit will have you focus.

(No illustration is included here, for the process is the same as *Step Two* under the *Topical Method of Bible Study,* pages 53-57.)

(O) *Step Three*—In paragraph form, write a brief sketch of the person's life. Include the important events and characteristics stating the facts without interpretation. Keep the material as chronological as possible.

RAHAB—A SKETCH OF HER LIFE

Rahab was a harlot in the town of Jericho, which was situated across the Jordan River in the land of Canaan. She, along with other members of her community, had heard how God had allowed the Israelites to cross the Red Sea on dry land and how they had also defeated the two kings of the Amorites.

When the spies came to her door she received them in peace and hid them from the king of Jericho, who was seeking their lives. She lied to the king that they were not there and sent the men of the city on a false chase after them.

She requested of the spies safety for herself and her family testifying to them that she believed the Israelite God to be the God of heaven and earth based on what she had heard of His acts.

The spies promised her safety if she wouldn't reveal their whereabouts and have all her family in her house when they conquered Jericho. Proof of their mutual commitment was a scarlet cord hanging from her window.

Her life was spared at the fall of Jericho and later she is found as the great great grandmother of King David and thus in the lineage of Jesus Christ.

The New Testament also records her faith and justification by her act of receiving the spies.

(I) *Step Four*—List the strengths and weaknesses of the person. Why did God consider him/her great? When did he or she fall short?

RAHAB—STRENGTHS AND WEAKNESSES

Strengths: Based on very little knowledge (a rumor), Rahab staked her whole life and the lives of her family on what she heard. She *applied* what she knew. God considers this greatness—to believe Him and act on what you have. Her people had the same information, yet they didn't believe.
Weaknesses: She was a liar and a traitor to her country.

(I) *Step Five*—Choose the key verse for his/her life. This is the verse or passage that more than any other sums up the direction of that person's life. State the crowning achievement or contribution of that life.

RAHAB—KEY VERSE

"By faith the prostitute Rahab because she welcomed the spies, was not killed with those who were disobedient" (Hebrews 11:31).

Her faith was exercised while she was a prostitute and God counts her great at that stage of her life, not following her acceptance into the Jewish community. She acted on the little knowledge she had by hiding the spies and believed that Jehovah was the true God of heaven and earth.

(I) *Step Six*—In one sentence, state the key thought regarding the person's life. This may be positive or negative. Here you are trying to sum up the person's life in one sentence. There should be a correlation between this key thought and the key verse in *Step Five.*

RAHAB—KEY THOUGHT

Rahab was willing to take great risks with God on the basis of little information, and God considered this true greatness.

(A) *Step Seven*—Choose from the possible applications listed in your *Observations* the one on which God would have you work.

RAHAB—APPLICATION

It is easy to fall into the habit of reading the Bible to gain new insights and miss the life-changing aspects of application. I am guilty of this.

Since the key to a changed life is applying the Word of God to my life, not increasing my knowledge, I will pray and commit myself to apply a truth of Scripture each time I read the Bible.

Advanced Biographical Study

The following steps may be added if and when you feel they will help in your biographical studies. They are optional and should only be included progressively as you gain confidence and proficiency.

(O) *Step Eight*—Trace the historical background of the person. Use a Bible dictionary to augment this step only when necessary. The following questions should stimulate your thinking.

1. When did the person live? What were the political, social, religious, and economic conditions of his time?
2. Where was the person born? Who were his parents? Was there anything unusual surrounding his birth and childhood?
3. What was his vocation? Was he a teacher, farmer, or in some other occupation? Did this influence his later ministry? How?
4. Who was his spouse? Did they have any children? What were they like? Did they help or hinder his life and ministry?
5. Chart the person's travels. Where did he/she go? Why? What was accomplished?
6. How did the person die? Was there anything extraordinary in his life?

RAHAB—HISTORICAL BACKGROUND

Jericho, the City of Palms, was in the land of Canaan. It was on a caravan route between Egypt to the south and Babylon to the north. Canaan consisted of small kingdoms, each with fortified cities and a king (see Joshua 9:1-2). Jericho was fortified with a double wall, and Rahab's house was on that wall.

The Canaanites were the descendants of Ham (see Genesis 19:18-25), and their worship consisted of idolatry, fertility rites, and human sacrifices to Baal.

From the time the residents of Jericho heard of the Exodus, they lived in fear. The men of the city had hearts that "melted" within them.

According to the Bible account, the flax had been harvested since it was on the roof to dry, thereby setting the story in the end of March or first of April.

Later Rahab married Salmon and had a son, Boaz. Boaz married the Gentile Ruth, after whom the Old Testament book is named. Their son Obed bore Jesse, who was the father of Israel's greatest king, David.

(I) *Step Nine*—Write a couple of paragraphs on the person's philosophy of life. What motivated him or her? What were his or her attitudes? What were his or her life objectives? What did the person want out of life and did he or she get it?

RAHAB—PHILOSOPHY OF LIFE

Rahab's philosophy of life was to believe that the God of the Israelites must be the true and living God. She had heard of the miracles He had performed for His people. While her countrymen lived in fear, she lived in faith, believing that God had already conquered Jericho. Her faith motivated her to receive the spies, hide them, and help them escape. She also wanted safety for herself and her family, which she received. She acquired a permanent place in the history of Israel and in the lineage of Jesus Christ.

(C) *Step Ten*—Referring to the material in Chapter 10, make a chart on this person. Make it chronological, marking the various phases of his or her life. If you desire, make another chart showing his or her relationship to others who entered his or her life. Figure 11 is an illustration of the life of Rahab in chart form.

RAHAB - CHART

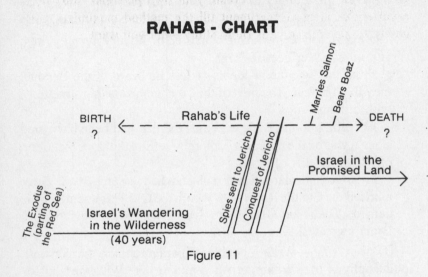

Figure 11

(C) *Step Eleven*—Compare and/or contrast the person with others in the Bible. The person compared may be a contemporary, or if it is someone like Moses or Abraham, the comparison may be made with Christ.

RAHAB—COMPARISON

An interesting comparison to Rahab is Lot's wife. She had a family relationship with Abraham and was aware of God's promises to him. Yet when the angels came to deliver her from the destruction of Sodom and gave specific commands not to look back, she didn't believe. This unbelief resulted in her judgment as she turned into a pillar of salt.

Chapters 8–11 have been added to further stimulate your mind in expanding your biographical study and making it an even greater challenge to you. Just as it isn't necessary to include all of the above eleven steps in your study, so also don't feel that you need to incorporate all the suggestions in Chapters 8–11. They simply give you an opportunity to create your own personal study from a variety of ideas. Experiment till the method maximizes your ability to glean from your Bible study what you want.

SECTION

II Improving Your Bible Study Skills

7 Improvement Is for Everyone

Section II will help you improve the skills that you have already learned and launch you into developing your own methods of doing Bible study. Before you use the methods suggested here, however, make sure you are familiar with the methods described in Section I of this book. After you have done the Bible studies described there for some time, using those methods, refer to this part.

The contents of this section will help you go into greater depth into the four major essentials or parts of Bible study—observation, interpretation, correlation, and application. As you begin to sense the need for some additional help in a particular part of your Bible study, or want some new ideas, refer to the appropriate part.

This section will teach you new concepts of Bible study as well as new methods. Take sufficient time to understand any new concepts thoroughly. You will want to employ these in any of the methods you use, i.e., analytical, synthetic, topical, etc.

The suggestions in this section are only a sampling of the hundreds that are available. Use your own creativity to develop new methods, but before you do, take time to learn the methods presented. True creativity follows structure.

8 Observation: The Role of a Detective

OBSERVATION
The recording of what may be seen in a selected method of Bible study.

Webster's New Collegiate Dictionary defines observation as the "act of recognizing and noting a fact or occurrence"; it means to be mentally aware of what one sees. The purpose of observation in Bible study is to saturate yourself with the content of the passage of Scripture, to become as familiar as possible with all that the biblical writer is saying and implying.

Accuracy is important in observation. Not everything you read will be of equal value in ascertaining the meaning of the passage. So you will have to learn to discern what is important and what is not. Practice and concentration are the two ingredients that will sharpen your expertise.

Jesus' last words of instruction to His disciples were to prepare them for the time when He would no longer be physically with them. He assured them that "the Counselor, the Holy Spirit, whom the Father will send in my name, will *teach* you all things and will remind you of everything I have said to you" (John 14:26). A little later on in the same conversation He said, "But when He, the Spirit of truth, comes, He will *guide* you into all truth" (John 16:13).

A prayerful dependence on the Holy Spirit is key to all aspects of Bible study, and especially to observation. Diligence, openness, dependence, an eagerness to learn—all these must characterize the student as he begins digging in the Word.

How do you begin observing? Where do you start? Take a piece of paper (8½" x 11" will do fine) and begin to record all you see. No item or idea is insignificant. Write it down so your mind can free itself to look for new things. The following suggestions are not necessarily given in the order of their importance. You will want to pick and choose from them depending on your level of proficiency and the type of material you are studying. Some suggestions will be more applicable to a character study, for example, than to an analytic study.

Have the Right Mental Attitude

You have already learned that a basic requirement for making good observations is a prayerful dependence on the Holy Spirit. As you have worked on making good observations, you have probably become aware that more is required than just that attitude. Five more requirements are necessary as well.

1. *Observation requires an act of the will.* You must have the will and the desire to be aware of what is in the biblical text, then to perceive and recognize what is there. You must have the determination to know and to learn. For example, when you meet people for the first time, do you remember their names? If not, it is likely that you have not purposed in your mind that you are going to learn their names. Learning begins with an act of the will—you must want to learn.

2. *Observation requires a persistence to know.* Learning is never easy. It requires diligence and discipline. You cannot have an effective disciple without him or her being a disciplined person. One of the keys in persisting in your personal Bible study is to see that the results are really worth the effort and the work that you have put into it. Take time to reflect on the results that have taken place in your life over the past six months because you have been doing Bible study faithfully.

3. *Observation requires patience.* In a day when you have instant communication, instant everything, there is a tendency to want an instant education. True learning, however, takes a great deal of time. You cannot take shortcuts in the learning process. The so-called short cuts are in fact only short circuits; they lead to ineffective results. In personal Bible study as well as in everything else in the Christian life, the process is as important as the product.

4. *Observation requires diligent recording.* As you look over the observations you recorded in some of your previous Bible studies, you will probably notice that there are some that you have completely forgotten. You will remember only a small portion of the observations you had made. So it is best for you to record all the observations you make in your personal Bible study diligently. In doing so, you will again see the importance and value of having a study Bible where you can keep a record of your good observations for the next time you study that portion of Scripture.

5. *Observation requires caution.* Observation is only the first step in studying the Bible—interpretation, correlation, and application must follow. Three warnings must be heeded.
   a. Don't lose yourself in the details; divide your time proportionately for all parts of the passage under study.
   b. Don't stop with observations, but go on to ask questions and seek meaningful answers.
   c. Don't give equal weight to everything; carefully discern what is more important.

Use the Six Basic Questions

1. *WHO?* List all the people involved. In 1 Thessalonians 1 you will note that Paul talks about *we, you,* and *they.* In verse 1 the *we* included Paul, Silas, and Timothy. The same verse also suggests that *you* refers to the believers in the city of Thessalonica. Verse 7 reveals who is included in the *they*—those in the provinces of Macedonia and Achaia.

2. *WHAT?* What happened? What ideas are expressed? What are the results? In 1 Thessalonians 1 Paul is discussing the effects of the gospel. The Thessalonians' labor was not in vain: lives were changed (verse 5). The Thessalonian believers assumed responsibility for sharing the Good News with others (verse 8). Paul could see from his "spiritual grandchildren" the results of his ministry to the Thessalonians (verses 9-10).

3. *WHERE?* Where does this take place? What is the geographical setting? Here a good Bible dictionary will prove helpful: Zondervan's *New International Dictionary of the Bible* is a good investment if you don't already own a similar volume. As you investigate the background of this city, you discover that it was rebuilt and given its name in 315 B.C. at the time of Alexander the Great. It was named after Alexander's step-sister. Located in the northeastern corner of the Thermaic Gulf (here you will want to consult your maps), it straddled the Egnation Way, a famous road in Macedonia used by the Romans. The city had the best natural harbor in Macedonia. During Paul's time it was the capital of that province. Many similar observations could be made.

4. *WHEN?* When did this take place? What was the historical background? Consulting your Bible dictionary once again, you discover that Paul founded the church in Thessalonica on his second missionary journey (see Acts 17:1-9). After ministering in this city, Paul and his team worked their way south through the Greek provinces of Macedonia and Achaia ending up in Corinth. It was from that city that Paul wrote 1 Thessalonians in about A.D. 54.

5. *WHY?* Why did this happen? What is the purpose or stated reason? Continuing to use 1 Thessalonians as our example, we find by reading the historical account of Paul's second journey (Acts 17–18) that he was plagued by a group of unbelieving Jews. These men followed Paul from city to city causing trouble. Persecutions of the new Christians inevitably followed. Timothy was sent back to Thessalonica to see how the believers fared and to encourage them in their Christian lives. Timothy returned with a positive report and Paul followed up with this letter. His purpose in writing was to communicate his confidence in them, assure them of the hope of the resurrection (a particularly precious doctrine during times of persecution), and exhort them to holy living.

6. *HOW?* How are things accomplished? How well? How quickly? By what method? Paul followed up his ministry to the Thessalonians by sending Timothy back to see them and then writing this letter. Though Paul had ministered there but a short time, the Thessalonian believers had become committed disciples of Christ.

Discover the Form or Structure of the Passage Under Study

As you observe the contents of a passage you are studying, you will also want to become aware of the form it takes. How God says something is as important as what He says. You should ask yourself questions like, *How does the writer deal with the content? What form or structure does he use?* Some examples you may notice are:

- The writer asks four questions and answers them.
- The writer lists seventeen things we are to avoid.
- The writer gives us five commands we are to obey.
- The writer makes three declarative statements and then supports them.

The writer of a section of Scripture may place his content in the form of poetry, narrative, parable, logical argument, discourse, practical advice, history, drama, or some other forms. The way that the content of God's Word unfolds reveals the mind and method of the writer in communicating God's truth, and gives you further insight and feeling into the meaning of the passage under study. Some other things to look for as you examine structure are:

- Use of cause and effect (as in 1 Thessalonians 1)
- The movement from particulars to generalities (as in 1 Thessalonians 2), or from generalities to particulars (as in 1 Thessalonians 5)
- Use of Old Testament references in the New Testament (as in Romans 10)
- Use of illustrations in the text of the main argument or narrative (as in Galatians 4)
- Use of the current events of the times (as in Luke 13:1-5)

Some of the methods writers employ to relate their messages are:

1. *Relating the way things are*—1 Thessalonians 1 is a good example of this. Paul is communicating certain truths in this passage, but he does that by reviewing a sequence of events they all had in common. We might paraphrase this chapter as follows: "I came to you, preached the gospel, and you responded. This response manifested itself in your sharing the gospel with those near you. Their response to the gospel assured me that you were serious in your commitment to Christ."

2. *Admonition or exhortation*—Paul's letter to the Galatians illustrates this. The Galatians had bought the message of the Judaizers. Paul exhorts them to consider the implications of following what he considers grievous error. In Galatians 2:1-14 Paul relates *the way things are* as he does in 1 Thessalonians 1, but this is parenthetical and illustrative of the main argument he is setting forth. Commands to obey and errors to avoid are the kinds of things to look for in this type of passage.

3. *Teaching*—Jesus' dissertation commonly referred to as the Sermon on the Mount (Matthew 5–7), and Paul's Epistle to the Romans are examples of the teaching style of communication. The

message is timeless in that the author is not addressing a current situation as Paul does in his letter to the Galatians. In Romans, Paul uses a common technique of teaching: asking questions and then answering them. For example, he asks the question, "What advantage, then, is there in being a Jew, or what value is there in circumcision?" (Romans 3:1). Then he proceeds to answer his own questions, much like a catechism.

4. *Parables*—These are frequently used by Jesus as a poignant way of driving home spiritual truth. With parables, the student seeks to discover the main point being made and must be careful not to allow his imagination to carry him to conclusions not intended by the story. Particularly with parables, it is possible to observe too much.

5. *Narrative*—Large portions of the Bible take this form of writing. Genesis, Exodus, most of Numbers, Joshua through Esther, most of the Gospels and Acts are all narrative in form.

6. *Other methods*—Practical advice is found in Proverbs and various poetic styles in the Psalms, other poetical books, and many of the prophetical books. As you begin your study, note the form or structure carefully, for it will greatly assist you in identifying the means used by the writer in communicating his message.

Find the Key Words

In some passages that you study, the key word jumps out at you and is readily apparent. *Love* in 1 Corinthians 13 and *faith* in Hebrews 11 are examples of this. Most of the time, however, it requires diligent work to discover the key words in a passage.

While Webster's dictionary is helpful in defining the English words of a Bible passage, it is inadequate in giving the literal meanings of Hebrew or Greek words or phrases. To check the definition of a biblical word, the average person must rely on other resources. Often a Bible dictionary will give a more thorough and comprehensive description of a word or topic.

Other background material which will prove helpful in defining

New Testament words are W. E. Vine's *An Expository Dictionary of New Testament Words* and M. R. Vincent's *Word Studies in the New Testament. Girdlestone's Old Testament Synonyms* is a good reference for Old Testament word studies. Good commentaries, explaining the literal meaning of biblical words and phrases, will also be helpful. Without a command of either the Hebrew or Greek languages, you can profit in your study of the Scriptures from the excellent scholarship and research available in a few well chosen books.

Let us take 1 Peter 1 as our example. In the *King James Version,* Peter says, "that the trial of your faith" (verse 7). As you compare the word *trial* with the *Revised Standard Version,* you note that it is replaced with the word *genuineness.* The *New International Version* uses the phrase *proved genuine. The NIV Exhaustive Concordance of the Bible* will give you the Greek word and the other places in the Bible where that same Greek word is used: Luke 14:19; 1 Corinthians 3:13; 2 Corinthians 8:22; 1 Thessalonians 2:4; and James 1:3; 12. And you find the word is used in a variety of ways.

Tracing the meaning of this Greek word *dokimos,* you find it means, "A test, the means of proof, the result of the contact of faith with trial, and hence the verification of faith" (Vincent's *Word Studies*). This is a key idea, not only in 1 Peter 1, but in the whole of his first epistle. These dispersed Christians were suffering for their faith. The difficulties were not without benefit, however. They revealed that their faith in Christ was genuine. Like gold purified by fire, the suffering Christian is "tested in battle and found to be pure and reliable." *Suffering* is one of the major themes in 1 Peter and *trial* (KJV) is a key word in understanding that suffering.

In Romans 3 words like *propitiation, justified, remission, redemption, righteousness,* and *forbearance* (KJV) are all key in understanding the meaning of this passage.

If you feel that your level of understanding of words such as these is small, and that such study is, at best, difficult, don't feel as though you are alone. These illustrations are meant to be suggestive of how you can go about studying a passage. Use what you feel comfortable with and leave the rest. At a later time when you feel comfortable with the tools you are using in your study, you will be ready to go back and add a few more.

Consider Comparisons and Contrasts

Two kinds of observations to make in your personal Bible study are comparisons and contrasts. Comparisons show how things are alike; contrasts show how things are different. Make a special effort to find contrasts and comparisons in the passage you are studying. If there are none in that passage, try to find other Scriptures which will give you contrasts and comparisons with the section you are studying.

To help you in making observations of comparison and contrast, look for words like "even so," "as . . . so . . .," and "likewise." These are not the *only* words that provide comparisons, but they almost always do so. When you find a comparison, spend sufficient time thinking through the things being compared. Then record as many ways as possible in which they are alike.

Figure 12 — Comparison

Contrasts may be more difficult to find because the range of intensity can vary from distinct contrasts to mild differences. Look for things which are similar in one respect and dissimilar in another. Key words to look for are "but," "nor," and "not."

Figure 13 — Contrast

In this observation exercise you will especially want to use cross-references. As you read a story or statement in the Scriptures, consider things which are similar in certain respects but different in others. Observing these contrasts will help you discern the overall truth of the Word of God.

In his letter to the Thessalonians, Paul makes two comparisons between his ministry and the role of parents with children. He compares his activities among them as being that of "a mother caring for her little children" (1 Thessalonians 2:7), and that he dealt with them "as a father deals with his own children" (2:11). Considering the characteristics of a mother, you might think about infant care, tenderness, caring for babies individually, and feeding them on schedule. Considering the role of the father, you would think of discipline, concern, instruction, and giving direction. Making these observations will give you additional insight into Paul's character and his relationship to the Thessalonians.

Several contrasts also appear in this letter. Paul stated, for example, that his preaching was "not trying to please men *but* God" (2:4). Later, as he was exhorting them, he said, "Let us not be like others who are asleep, *but* let us be alert and self-controlled" (5:6).

The Book of Hebrews frequently makes use of comparisons and contrasts. Figure 14 is a chart made from such a treatment of Christ and Aaron in Hebrews 7.

CONTRASTS BETWEEN THE TWO PRIESTHOODS
(Hebrews 7)

Chapter Divisions	MELCHIZEDEK/CHRIST	Contrasts in Verses	LEVI/AARON
7:1-3	WHO MELCHIZEDEK WAS		
7:4-10	RECEIVED TITHES FROM ABRAHAM	4	PAID TITHES TO MELCHIZEDEK THROUGH ABRAHAM
	GAVE A BLESSING	6	RECEIVED A BLESSING
	LIVES FOREVER	8	DIED
7:11-19	FREE FROM AN IMPERFECT LAW	11	MARRIED TO AN IMPERFECT LAW
	PRIESTHOOD UNCHANGED BY VIRTUE OF HIS LIFE	12/16	PRIESTHOOD CHANGED BY VIRTUE OF HIS TRIBAL HERITAGE
	COULD MAKE PEOPLE PERFECT	19	COULD NOT MAKE PEOPLE PERFECT
7:20-22	WITH AN OATH	20	WITHOUT AN OATH
7:23-25	ONE PRIEST	23/24	MANY PRIESTS
	EVER LIVETH	23/24	DEATH
	ABLE TO SAVE	25	UNABLE TO SAVE
7:26-28	SEPARATE FROM SIN	26/27	SINNER
	OFFERED HIMSELF ONCE	27	OFFERED SACRIFICES (animals) MANY TIMES
	PERFECT	28	WEAK
	GOD/MAN	28	MAN

Figure 14

Investigate the Use of Old Testament References

The only Scriptures people had in the early days of the church were the writings of the Old Testament. The advent of Jesus Christ was the fulfillment of what the Old Testament had promised. Because of this fact, New Testament writers constantly dip back into the Old Testament to show how Jesus is the Messiah or to relate the implications of this fact to the lives of people.

The Book of Galatians is a beautiful example of this. Paul, reasoning from the Old Testament, convinced those in the province of Galatia that Jesus was the Christ. Then the Judaizers followed his ministry, arguing from the same Old Testament that people coming to Christ had to follow Old Testament laws, such as circumcision, in order to be saved. In his letter, Paul argues back that the Old Testament itself teaches that these laws that the Judaizers were pressing should no longer be kept. Paul's selection and use of Old Testament references is absolutely masterful in proving this difficult point.

Note the Progression of an Idea or Thought Chain

Thought chains graphically associate similar ideas. You will need a study Bible you can mark and some colored pencils. Look through a passage for similar thoughts. Then using one color for similar ideas, draw a circle around each one. Using the same color, connect the circles with thin lines and give the chain a title. Use different colors to make other chains of associated thoughts.

Now consider chain titles to see how they fit together to make one theme of the passage. In Figure 15 only one chain has been worked out. It is the "Character of the Minister." Other chains might be titled "Effect of the Ministry" and "Concern for Young Christians." These lead to the theme, "How to Minister to Young Believers."

1 THESSALONIANS 2:1

Paul's Ministry in Thessalonica

2 You know, brothers, that our visit to you was not a failure. [2]We had previously suffered and been insulted in Philippi, as you know, but with the help of our God we dared to tell you his gospel in spite of strong opposition. [3]For the appeal we make does not spring from error or impure motives, nor are we trying to trick you. [4]On the contrary, we speak as men approved by God to be entrusted with the gospel. We are not trying to please men but God, who tests our hearts. [5]You know we never used flattery, nor did we put on a mask to cover up greed—God is our witness. [6]We were not looking for praise from men, not from you or anyone else.

[7]As apostles of Christ we could have been a burden to you, but we were gentle among you, like a mother caring for her little children. [8]We loved you so much that we were delighted to share with you not only the gospel of God but our lives as well, because you had become so dear to us. [9]Surely you remember, brothers, our toil and hardship; we worked night and day in order not to be a burden to anyone while we preached the gospel of God to you.

[10]You are witnesses, and so is God, of how holy, righteous and blameless we were among you who believed. [11]For you know that we dealt with each of you as a father deals with his own children, [12]encouraging, comforting and urging you to live lives worthy of God, who calls you into his kingdom and glory.

Figure 15

In 2 Timothy 1, Paul talks about not being ashamed of the gospel. Note his progression of thought:

- Verse 8—"Do not be ashamed . . ."
- Verse 12—"I am not ashamed . . ."
- Verse 16—"Onesiphorus . . . was not ashamed / . ."

A more technical illustration of this may be seen in the idea of *imputation* used by Paul in the Book of Romans:

- Romans 3:21-31—the imputation of Christ's righteousness to the sinner
- Romans 4—imputation illustrated in the life of Abraham
- Romans 5:12-21—the imputation of Adam's sin to mankind
- Romans 6-8—the outworking of imputation in the life of the believer

Be Alert for Proportions

The law of proportions is one of the keys to maintaining a balance of emphasis in your personal Bible study. Make sure that you are observing such proportions as importance of the subject, people involved, the time element, and the subject matter itself. The following chart of the Book of Acts will help you observe the time element as it is found in the book.

Chapters	1	2	3-8	9-12	13-14	15	16:1-18:22	18:23-21:16	21:17-28:31
Time Span	50 days	1 day	2 years	9 years	1½ years	few days	2½ years	4 years	5 years

Figure 16

Observe also how much of Paul's first letter to the Thessalonians deals with the second coming of Jesus Christ. The topic is mentioned in each chapter and discussed at length toward the end of the letter (see 1 Thessalonians 1:10; 2:19; 3:13; 4:13-18; 5:1-11). Also notice the references Paul made to his unblamable conduct and behavior before the people in Thessalonica. These proportion observations can give you a clue to Paul's major emphases in writing that first epistle.

Record Repetitions

As you do your Bible study, take particular note of the repetition of words, phrases, and expressions in the passage being studied. You can do this by making a chart of the repetitions in the passage. The benefit of this method is not in filling out the chart, but in enabling you to ask the right questions after you have seen the repetitions in the passage. An example from 1 Thessalonians 3 may be seen below in Figure 17.

WORD OR PHRASE	NUMBER OF REPETITIONS	VERSES USED
FAITH	5	2, 5, 6, 7, 10
AFFLICTION	3	3, 4, 7

Figure 17

Observing that the word *faith* appears five times in this section, you might ask, "Why is faith mentioned so often?" Seeing the repetition of the word *affliction,* you might conclude that faith is increased by the right response to affliction.

In almost every passage you will study, there will be words or phrases that will be repeated. Look for them and examine them carefully. Determine why they are repeated and how they are related.

Observation also includes the opposite aspect of repetition—omission. As you study a given passage, think to yourself, *What words or phrases would I have included in writing this?* Then continue your observation by asking questions like, "If these thoughts and ideas are omitted, why are they omitted?" "Is there a substitute the author used?" "What is that substitute?" Obviously, it is much more difficult to observe omissions than to see repetitions, but omissions must be carefully noted.

For example, a notable omission in the Book of Acts is the complete absence of the word *love.* On the other hand, the results of love, unity and oneness, are mentioned often.

Visualize the Verbs

Another key to making good observations is discerning the action
or movement of a passage. In grammar, action is carried by verbs.
They tell us what is being done, and reveal the movement or flow
of a passage.

Underline all the verbs in the passage you are studying, then list
them on your Bible study worksheet. After you have underlined
them all, examine them carefully. What kind of action do the verbs
portray? Are most of them active or passive? Does the subject
influence the action or is it being acted on? Do the verbs indicate
that the passage is basically a narrative or poetry? Are there any
quotations? Are the verbs imperatives—do they give commands?
Which verbs are repeated? What is the significance of their usages?

For example, in Hebrews 11 the verbs are active, indicating that
the believer has a vital role in the life of faith. He must respond to
what God is doing in his life.

In Ephesians 1:3-14 the verbs are passive and indicate that the
believer is acted on. Observing the use of verbs in this passage
gives us the clue that the emphasis is on what is done for the
believer rather than what he does or must do.

The following illustration from 1 Thessalonians 1 shows the
underlining process (Fig. 18).

Picture the Illustrations

Have you ever been struck by how many verbal illustrations there
are in the Bible? Many of the writers God used to record His Word
talked in pictures. Jesus used this device often as He called His
followers vines, sheep, fishers of men, farmers, and many other
such expressions.

As you study, pay particular attention to finding illustrations
being used by the writer of the passage you are observing. Some
illustrations are obvious, like the vine and the branches in John 15.
Others are not so obvious, but Scripture abounds in illustrations

1 Thessalonians

1 Paul, Silas[a] and Timothy,

To the church of the Thessalonians, who are in God the Father and the Lord Jesus Christ:

Grace and peace to you.

Thanksgiving for the Thessalonians' Faith

[2]We always <u>thank</u> God for all of you, <u>mentioning</u> you in our prayers. [3]We continually <u>remember</u> before our God and Father your work produced by faith, your labor <u>prompted</u> by love, and your endurance <u>inspired</u> by hope in our Lord Jesus Christ.

[4]Brothers <u>loved</u> by God, we <u>know</u> that he has <u>chosen</u> you, [5]because our gospel <u>came</u> to you not simply with words, but also with power, with the Holy Spirit and with deep conviction. You <u>know</u> how we <u>lived</u> among you for your sake. [6]You <u>became</u> imitators of us and of the Lord; in spite of severe suffering, you <u>welcomed</u> the message with the joy <u>given</u> by the Holy Spirit. [7]And so you <u>became</u> a model to all the believers in Macedonia and Achaia. [8]The Lord's message <u>rang out</u> from you not only in Macedonia and Achaia—your faith in God <u>has become known</u> everywhere. Therefore we do not need <u>to say</u> anything about it, [9]for they themselves <u>report</u> what kind of reception you <u>gave us</u>. They <u>tell</u> how you <u>turned</u> to God from idols <u>to serve</u> the living and true God, [10]and <u>to wait</u> for his Son from heaven, whom he <u>raised</u> from the dead—Jesus, who <u>rescues</u> us from the coming wrath.

Figure 18

and word pictures. In James 3 alone, there are at least nine different illustrations (and comparisons and contrasts).

Once you observe an illustration, think through on how it clarifies the subject of the passage. Try to think of other illustrations that Scripture uses to present this subject. Then compare and contrast your illustration with these. For example, Paul's use of a thief in the night illustrates the need for being prepared (1 Thessalonians 5:2); a woman with child illustrates suddenness (5:3); and a breastplate of faith illustrates being equipped (5:8).

If there are no illustrations in the passage you are studying, which is highly unlikely, then look for illustrations and examples in other portions of Scripture relevant to the passage under study.

Examine the Explanations

An explanation is anything that is used to illustrate, clarify, illuminate, describe, or demonstrate. An explanation may be one verse long or a whole chapter.

To understand an explanation clearly, you must follow the logic of the writer. What point is he trying to make? How is he trying to make it? How does he present it?

Sometimes the Scriptures explain a question that is not stated but implied. Often a statement in one verse will cause you to ask a question, and the following verse will then answer your question. Be sure to note this kind of tie-in between verses and paragraphs.

For example, Paul said, "We maintain that a man is justified by faith apart from observing the law" (Romans 3:28). A natural question which may come out of observation on this statement might be, "Could people in the Old Testament be saved?"

In the next two paragraphs (Romans 4:1-8), Paul explains how Abraham and David were both justified by faith without the deeds of the law. This helps explain the earlier statement, but don't presume that the paragraphs of Romans 4 were written primarily to explain your question on Romans 3:28.

Be Sensitive to Connecting Words and Conjunctions

Someone once said that the little two-letter word *if* connotes the difference between law and grace. It certainly connotes condition, and when speaking of what God wants to do in the lives of people is an immediate indication of whether the people's response will affect what God promises to do. For example, God said to the nation of Israel, "Now if you obey me fully and keep my covenant, then out of all nations you will be my treasured possession" (Exodus 19:5). This did not come about because Israel did not obey.

Other important connectives include *therefore,* which introduces a summary of ideas or the results of some action; *because, or, for,* and *then* are words that often introduce a reason or result; *but* lets you know there is a contrast that follows; and *in order that* is a phrase often used to set forth a purpose. Stay alert for these in your study.

Be Willing to Change Your Viewpoint

In order to change your viewpoint, you will have to eliminate preconceived ideas. Do not allow these to control or even color your thinking about the Word of God. Read your study passage as though you were an impartial observer. In his first letter to the Thessalonians, Paul levels several accusations at a particular group of people (1 Thessalonians 2:14-16). At first glance, out of some preconceived ideas you might have, you might envision these people as being vicious and cruel. But the fact is that this group was well respected and well thought of in their society. With this in mind, you may need to change your viewpoint and reread this passage making new observations.

One of the more interesting ways to change your viewpoint is to put yourself in another person's shoes. How would you feel if you were the author of this epistle? (When Paul wrote Ephesians, he was in prison.) How would you as a recipient understand the message? (Paul rebukes his recipients in 1 Corinthians.) What

would a third party at the scene think of the situation as he listened
to Paul? (Silas and Timothy were with Paul when he wrote 1
Thessalonians.) What would strict Jews think of Paul's letter to the
Galatians? Or strict Romans of James' letter? You need to learn to
observe from different perspectives.

Mark Your Bible as You Read

You should have a study Bible with wide margins that you can use
to record your observations. (Many are available on the market
today—check with your local bookstore or the American Bible
Society.) As you make observations on a passage you have chosen
to study, mark it in the text and in the margins. You may use some
or all of the following devices: brackets, parallel diagonal lines in
the margin, circles, vertical lines in the margins, arrows, inked in
words and/or phrases, marked through words and/or phrases,
underlining (see the section *Visualizing the Verbs* earlier in the
chapter). Also you may create your own symbols, marks, and
system.

In marking a study Bible (not a good reading Bible made of
India paper) you can use pen and ink, ballpoint, and fine and
course felt-tip pens. To mark *through* words and phrases for
emphasis use a light highlighter felt-tip pen to allow you to read the
words through it. Use india ink in marking a fine Bible. Some
examples follow in a marked-up copy of 1 Thessalonians 2:1-12.
(Fig. 19.)

Summary

Do not become discouraged if your observations do not immediately bear the fruit you desire. It is hard work and, like any
other skill, takes time to develop. Nor should you feel like a failure
if you are unable to apply all these suggestions to your Bible study.
They have been given to serve as a set of "handles" for you to get a
grip on *observation*. Some of these "handles" won't apply to
every passage.

1 THESSALONIANS 2:1

Paul's Ministry in Thessalonica

2 You <u>know</u>, brothers, that our visit to you was not a failure. We had previously suffered and been insulted in Philippi, as you know, but with the help of our God we dared to tell you <u>his gospel</u> in spite of strong opposition. [3]For the appeal we make does not spring from error or impure motives, nor are we trying to trick you. [4]On the contrary, we speak as men approved by God to be entrusted with <u>the</u> gospel. We are not trying to please men but God, who tests our hearts. [5]You know we never used flattery, nor did we put on a mask to cover up greed—God is our witness! [6]We were not looking for praise from men, not from you or anyone else.

[7]As apostles of Christ we could <u>have been a burden</u> to you, but we were gentle among you, like a mother caring for her little children. [8]We loved you so much that we were delighted to share with you not only the <u>gospel</u> of God but our lives as well, because you had become so dear to us. [9]Surely you remember, brothers, our toil and hardship; we worked night and day in order not to be a burden to anyone while we preached the <u>gospel of God</u> to you.

[10]You are witnesses, and so is God, of how holy, righteous and blameless we were among you who believed. [11]For you know that we dealt with each of you as a father deals with his own children, [12]encouraging, comforting and urging you to <u>live</u> lives worthy of God, who <u>calls</u> you into his kingdom and glory.

Handwritten margin notes: See Acts 16 · Contrast · ← · Key: Sharing our lives with others ←

Figure 19

You will find prayerful reflection to be indispensable. Be imaginative. Put yourself in the role of the writer or the people you are studying. How did they respond? How should they have responded? Seek to feel things as they must have felt them. Dialogue with them.

Also, be patient. If, after your study, you find you have overlooked an important *observation,* remember that others never stop discovering new and fresh insights from passages with which they have lived for many years.

9 Interpretation: The Role of a Decision Maker

INTERPRETATION
Understanding the meaning of what has been observed in Bible study.

Observation seeks to answer the question "What does it *say?*" Interpretation seeks to answer the question "What does it *mean?*" The dictionary defines interpretation as "The act or process of explaining; to clarify the meaning of; to offer an explanation." In this part of the Bible study, you are seeking to clarify the *meaning* of the passage and understand the writer's *meaning* as he communicated these words to the people of his day.

Foundational to this step in Bible study is the application of the 24 rules of interpretation found on pages 147–221. They form the ground rules for understanding the Bible. You should review them periodically, for the value of your Bible study will be in direct proportion to their application.

Interpretation follows observation. It is analogous to drawing the net around a school of fish you have just caught. It is an exciting part of your Bible study, for it is a time in which you come to some conclusions. The individual insights that made up your observations are now brought together into a coherent whole.

The three parts to the interpretive process are purpose, key thought, and flow.

Purpose

Here your objective is to determine why the writer is bringing up the subject. Paul, writing to the church at Rome, said, "For everything that was written in the past was written to teach us" (Romans 15:4). What the Holy Spirit has included in the Bible is there in order that we might learn from it. Determining the *purpose* of the book, passage, poem, story, or whatever else is the first step in interpretation.

As you do a synthetic study of Galatians, for example, you learn that Paul's purpose for writing that letter was to communicate that a person is justified by faith in Jesus Christ apart from the works of the law.

Sometimes the purpose is fairly easy to discover, as is the case with the Gospel of John. John states his purpose for writing: "These are written that you may believe that Jesus is the Christ [the Old Testament Messiah], the Son of God, and that by believing you may have life in his name" (John 20:31).

The purpose of the writer of Hebrews beginning with a comparison of Jesus Christ to angels (Chapters 1–2) is to establish the fact that God's revelation to man in the person of Christ is through no mere angel. Rather, He is the eternal Creator God of the universe.

In the Old Testament, when God wanted to speak authoritatively to His people, He frequently sent an angel. Jesus is infinitely better than the angels.

As you study the narration of an event, seek to discover its purpose. Why did Elijah retreat into the wilderness after his spectacular victory at Mount Carmel? (See 1 Kings 18–19.) Why did God keep Israel at Mount Sinai for such a long time after the Exodus? (See Exodus 19–40.) Similar questions should be asked in your study of Bible topics and biographies.

Key Thought

The *key thought* is the "big idea," theme, or distilled essence of the book, passage, topic, or person you are studying. As much as possible, state the key thought in one sentence. Make it a complete sentence with a subject and predicate. Generally speaking, the longer and more complicated the theme, the less you understand what it is. A good rule of thumb is to try to limit your key thought to about 20-30 words. The purpose of the theme is to state the main truth or spiritual principle as clearly and as succinctly as possible. Generally there is only one theme to a passage, not many. It may be stated in different ways, but the core should remain the same.

A possible theme for 1 Peter 2 might be stated as follows: "The believer is called to follow the example of the rejected Christ into a life of submission and suffering at the hands of a hostile world."

In a study of the life of Rahab and why she was considered great in God's sight, the theme might be stated as follows: "The reason for Rahab's inclusion in God's Hall of Fame [Hebrews 11] is found in her willingness to take great risks for God on the basis of little knowledge."

Or let us say you are studying the training of the 12 disciples in the years of Jesus' public ministry. What was the *main* thing Jesus sought to impart to them? Your topical study would reveal that the "big idea" Jesus sought to communicate was *faith*. The articulation of your key thought would center around this idea of faith.

If a group was doing a study on what Jesus sought to impart to the disciples, all should conclude that faith was the main truth, though the wording of that truth might vary from person to person.

Flow

How did the writer get to where he is? How did he arrive at the theme? Determining the flow is the third step in the process of interpretation. It is the movement of the argument, narrative, or teaching. In a topical study the flow is expressed in the natural unfolding of the topic.

Maybe you decide to study the topic of *prayer*. Because it is such a large topic you elect to narrow it to what the Gospel of John teaches about it. The flow is answered in such questions as: "How does John handle the subject of prayer?" "Is it by teaching, example, or combination?" "Through whose life or lives is it seen?"

In another area, you might ask: "How does Jesus go about teaching His disciples faith?" "Is there any pattern?" "Does He combine teaching and experience?"

These three aspects of interpretation, *purpose, key thought,* and *flow* are seen in each of the types of Bible study. It is at the same time both an interesting and an important part of your study. Attack it in a spirit of expectation.

10 Correlation: The Role of a Coordinator

One dictionary defines *correlation* as: "To bring two or more things into relation with one another; the act of relating." This is an exciting and highly rewarding aspect of Bible study. In scope it will range from relating one verse to another, to relating one paragraph to another, and to relating the various chapters of a book to one another.

Since the Bible is truth, and all truth due to its divine origin is unified, it is important to relate various truths to one another. It makes the Scriptures coherent and helps the student to be consistent with what the rest of the Bible says on any given subject.

Some basic ways of correlating your study are through cross-references, paraphrases, outlines, and charts.

Cross-references

This expression of correlation is to compare a word, verse, idea, event, or story with another portion of Scripture. Often the content of one passage will help clarify the content of another. At times you will want to cross-reference the thought with another thought found within the passage you are studying. At other times you will look for the cross-reference outside the passage, but within the book. Then too, there will be times when you will want to go outside the book you are studying into another portion of the Bible.

Several types of cross-references are available for your use.

Word cross-references—At times in your study you will discover an important word that you may want to cross reference. It may appear important to the passage and you may want to investigate it further. The person Melchizedek is such an example (Hebrews 5:6). Cross-referencing from within Hebrews, you find him discussed at some length in Chapter 7. Outside of Hebrews, he is introduced in Genesis 14:18 and briefly mentioned in Psalm 110:4.

This kind of cross-reference becomes strategically important in your topical and biographical studies.

Parallel cross-references—These are verses or thoughts that say virtually the same thing. Often the wording and context are slightly different, giving you fresh insight on the subject you are studying. The Gospels and some of Paul's epistles are places where this type of cross-reference is readily used. Paul wrote to the Ephesians, "Speak to one another with psalms, hymns, and spiritual songs. Sing and make music in your heart to the Lord" (Ephesians 5:19). You may cross reference that with his exhortation to the Colossians: "Let the word of Christ dwell in you richly as you teach and counsel one another with all wisdom, and as you sing psalms, hymns and spiritual songs with gratitude in your hearts to God" (Colossians 3:16). Comparing the context of these two statements is a fascinating study in and of itself. The parable of the sower in Matthew 13:3-23 may be cross referenced with the parallel accounts in Mark 4:3-20 and Luke 8:4-15.

Corresponding cross-references—The New Testament writers frequently quote from the Old Testament. A study of the context of the passage quoted is often helpful in understanding the point the author is making. When Jesus was in Nazareth, the town in which He was raised, He read from the Scroll of Isaiah in the local synagogue (see Luke 4:16-30). When you cross reference Luke 4:18 with Isaiah 61:1-2, you note that Jesus ends His quotation of Isaiah *halfway* through verse 2. Why does He do this? He does this because the Isaiah passage includes both of His comings—the first in humility and the second in glory—and He was at that time in Nazareth only in His first advent.

Another type of corresponding cross-reference is where another portion of Scripture refers to the same event. For example, Paul said, "You know, brothers, that our visit to you was not a failure" (1 Thessalonians 2:1). When did this occur? Luke tells in the Book of Acts (see Acts 17:1-10).

Idea cross-references—These are the most helpful cross-references in the analytical study. Here you endeavor to capture the thought of the author in the verse or paragraph being studied and compare it with a similar thought elsewhere in the Bible. The key thought of 1 Peter 1:23, for example, is that a person needs to be born again by the eternal Word of God. When cross referenced with John 3:1-8, you find Jesus saying that a person needs to be born again, but by the Holy Spirit. Why the difference? That is, why does Peter say it is by the Word and Jesus by the Spirit? Because you cannot know the living God apart from the Bible and you cannot know the Bible apart from the Spirit of the living God. The two are inseparable, and for this reason may be interchanged (see also Hebrews 4:12-13).

Contrasting cross-references—Contrasting examples in the Bible help you pinpoint proper action as well as bringing into balance a proper understanding of what the Bible teaches on a subject. Perhaps it will be helpful to illustrate both.

Contrast how Jesus handled temptation in Matthew 4 at the beginning of His ministry with how Adam handled it in Genesis 3. The "first Adam" met Satan and was defeated; the "second Adam" met Satan and was victorious.

In Paul's first letter to the Corinthians he makes an interesting comment. "I say this as a concession, not as a command" (1 Corinthians 7:6). Some may conclude that what follows was Paul's idea, and not from the Lord. A contrasting cross-reference brings important balance to this statement. Paul had previously told them, "This is what we speak, not in words taught us by human wisdom but in words taught by the Spirit, expressing spiritual truths in spiritual words" (1 Corinthians 2:13). Here Paul reminds us that even that which is spoken by "concession" is what the Holy Spirit is teaching.

A number of good sources of cross-references are available to you today. If you are cross-referencing a word, use a good concordance such as *Strong's Exhaustive Concordance of the Bible* or *NIV Exhaustive Concordance*. Many Bibles have excellent lists of cross-references in the margins next to the verses or in an abbreviated concordance in the back of the Bible. *The Treasury of Scripture Knowledge* is probably the best source of cross-references. It lists 500,000 difficult cross-references and includes every book in the Bible.

Don't fall into the trap of relying completely on these helps rather than thinking for yourself. Often cross-references that give you the most satisfaction are those you will have thought of yourself.

Personal Paraphrase

Another form of correlation is the paraphrase—stating the content of the section you are studying in contemporary language by relating it to itself. Some modern paraphrases provide good examples of this form of correlation. The following excerpts are from *The New Testament in Modern English, Revised Edition* by J. B. Phillips and *The Living Bible* by Kenneth Taylor.

---

1 Thessalonians 2:7-8 (PH)

"Our attitude among you was one of tenderness, rather like a nurse caring for her babies. Because we loved you, it was a joy to us to give you not only the Gospel of God but our very hearts—so dear had you become to us."

1 Thessalonians 2:7-8 (LB)

"But we were gentle among you as a mother feeding and caring for her own children. We loved you dearly—so dearly that we gave you not only God's message, but our own lives too."

Figure 20

Scripture Versions

When you are being creative in your personal paraphrasing, do not stray from the basic content of the passage you are studying. Your paraphrase must express the thought of the writer, though in different words.

Detailed Outline

Some people enjoy using a detailed outline for their correlation of a passage within itself. This type of outline includes every idea mentioned in the section you are studying without omitting any details. Such an outline of 1 Thessalonians 1:1-5 appears in Figure 21.

I. PAUL'S GREETING (1:1)

A. From: Paul, Silvanus, and Timothy

B. To: The Church of the Thessalonians — in God and Christ

C. Greeting: Grace to you and peace

II. PAUL'S PRAYER AND GOSPEL MINISTRY (1:2-5)

A. Paul's prayer for the Thessalonians (vv. 2,3)

  1. Always giving thanks for them

  2. Constantly remembering their:

    a. Work of faith

    b. Labor of love   } in Christ

    c. Steadfastness of hope   in the presence of God

B. Paul's Gospel Ministry to the Thessalonians (vv. 4-5)

  1. God loved the Thessalonians and chose them

  2. The Gospel came:

    a. In Word

    b. In Power

    c. In the Holy Spirit

    d. With full conviction

  3. Paul's manner of living was for their sake

Figure 21

Charts

This method of correlation maximizes your opportunity to be creative in your Bible study. For this reason it is for many the most fun and rewarding. The chart is also one of the most effective ways of grasping the unity of a passage, book, or topic. Its purpose is to give you a "bird's eye" view of the principal thoughts, so you can relate them to one another.

The chart is simply one of the many possible tools you may want to use in Bible study. It is not a substitute for your outline or other forms of examination; it can be a helpful augmentation. In fact, your chart will utilize your outline and will be one of the last things you do.

A variety of ways may be used to make a chart. Your selection of the type will depend on what you are trying to accomplish.

Horizontal Charts

These charts are most helpful in seeing the whole of your study of a passage or book, in comparing various elements in your study, and in making a topical grid. They are versatile, allowing for many possibilities of development and do not follow any rigid rules. Use your creativity and draw them in such a way that they will serve you.

SURVEY CHARTS—These charts enable you to see the whole of your study at one glance, whether it be a passage or a whole book. Take a sheet of paper (8½" x 11" is a good size) and draw a line the long way down the middle. Divide that line according to the number of sections in your study outline. Place your titles (of the outline) in the upper section with the references, and note the correlations in the lower section. Remember, you are trying to relate the parts to the whole visually. Keep the chart neat and orderly, but be creative. You can draw these charts on passages (chapters) and whole books, small or large.

The simplest survey chart is on a chapter, as illustrated in Figure 21. Each section on the chart contains a paragraph and the divisions are indicated by the verse numbers in the corners. Write your paragraph titles at the top of each section, then list the key thoughts that led you to those titles under them; you may want to tie related thoughts together with arrows. Finally, record your con-

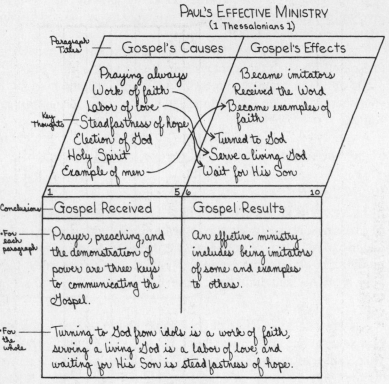

Figure 22

clusions—for each paragraph and for the whole passage—in the bottom section of the chart. Figure 22 is another variety of a survey chart on a chapter—1 Thessalonians.

Survey charts of whole books may also vary in complexity. Figure 23 illustrates a simple chart of 2 Timothy 2; Figure 24 is also a simple chart; Figure 25 shows more detail on the Book of 1 Peter; and Figure 26 is a very detailed chart on the Epistle to the Hebrews.

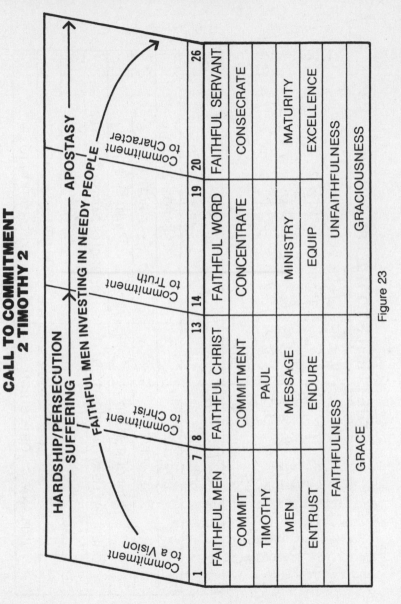

Figure 23

THE EPISTLE TO THE EPHESIANS

PREDETERMINED PURPOSE	PRAYER FOR UNDERSTANDING	PURPOSE APPROPRIATED	PRAYER FOR APPLICATION	PERSONAL RESPONSIBILITIES	PRAYER
1:1-14	1:15-23	2:1 — 3:13	3:14-21	4:1 — 6:18	6:19-20

Doctrine	Application
DOCTRINE	APPLICATION
POSITION	RESPONSIBILITY
PASSIVE	ACTIVE
WHAT CHRIST DID	WHAT WE DO
CHURCH'S HEAVENLY POSITION	CHURCH'S EARTHLY CHALLENGE
INDIVIDUAL	CORPORATE
GOD'S ACTIONS	OUR PROPOSED REACTIONS
EXPLANATION OF POSITION	EXHORTATION TO LIVE

Figure 24

1 PETER
"SYLLABUS FOR SUFFERING SAINTS"
"HOW TO HOLD UP, NOT FOLD UP"

GRACE AND PEACE

SALVATION	SUBMISSION	SUFFERING
Introduction (1:1-2) Plot Permanent vs. Passing	Introduction (2:11-12)	Conclusion (5:12-14)
THE PRIVILEGES OF SALVATION (1:3-12)	IN THE STATE (2:13-17) CIVIL	AS A CITIZEN (3:13-4:6)
THE PRODUCTS OF SALVATION (1:13-25)	IN THE HOUSEHOLD (2:18-25) SOCIAL	AS A SAINT (4:7-19)
THE PROCESS OF SALVATION (2:1-10)	IN THE FAMILY (3:1-7) DOMESTIC	AS A SHEPHERD (5:1-7)
	Summary (3:8-12)	AS A SOLDIER (5:8-11)
DOCTRINE IS DYNAMIC!	THE CHRISTIAN'S LIFE-STYLE!	THE CHISEL TO SHAPE THE SOUL!
1:3 2:10	2:11 3:12	3:13 5:11
THE DESTINY OF THE CHRISTIAN	THE DUTY OF THE CHRISTIAN	THE DISCIPLINE OF THE CHRISTIAN
Our Relationship to God	Our Relationship to Others	Our Relationship to Circumstances
Our Belief	Our Behavior	Our Buffeting
Our Relationship	Our Responsibility	Our Rejoicing

GRACE AND PEACE

Figure 25

THE EPISTLE TO THE HEBREWS
A COMPARISON OF CHRIST TO THE OLD TESTAMENT
CHRIST: THE FULFILLMENT OF OLD TESTAMENT MESSIANIC PROMISES

CHRIST THE PERFECT HIGH PRIEST

CHRIST THE PERFECT WAY

Reference	Comparison / Theme	Section Title	Key Statement	Warning
1:1-14	than Angels	THE PERSON AND WORK OF CHRIST	Created the Universe	
2:1-18	than Angels	THE PERSON AND WORK OF CHRIST	Redeemed Men	Heed the Word of God 2:1-4
3:1-19	than Moses	THE POSITION OF CHRIST	Built the Church	Don't Be Hardened in Unbelief 3:12-14
4:1-16	Rest	THE PROVISION OF CHRIST	Provided Acceptance	
5:1-14	than Aaron	THE PERFECT PRIESTHOOD OF CHRIST	Demonstrated Obedience	
6:1-20	Assurance (HE IS BETTER)	THE PROMISES OF CHRIST	Provided a Hope	Maturity Affects Assurance 5:11—6:12
7:1-28	Priesthood	THE PERFECTION OF CHRIST	Intercedes Continuously	WARNINGS
8:1-13	Covenant	THE PLACE OF CHRIST'S MINISTRY	Established a Covenant of Grace	WARNINGS
9:1—10:18	Sacrifice	THE PRIESTLY MINISTRY OF CHRIST	Sacrificed Himself	WARNINGS
10:19-39		ENDURANCE OF FAITH	Provided a New and Living Way	Don't Reject Christ 10:26-31
11:1-40	A BETTER FAITH	EXPLANATION AND EXAMPLES OF FAITH	Gave Promises	
12:1-29	A BETTER FAITH	ENCUMBRANCES OF FAITH	Is by Our Side	Heed the Word of God 12:25-29
13:1-25	A BETTER FAITH	EXPRESSIONS OF FAITH	Is the Same Always	

Summary divisions:

Preeminence of Christ	Preeminence of Christ's Priesthood	Practical Teaching and Exhortation
What Have We?	We have such a High Priest	Having, therefore, let us . . .
INSTRUCTION		EXHORTATION
A NEW COVENANT		AN OLD FAITH
SUPERIOR PERSON	SUPERIOR MINISTRY	SUPERIOR LIFE
What Christ Did — His Person		What We Do — Our Response

Figure 26

COMPARATIVE CHARTS—These charts are used to sort out a mixture of information for the purpose of comparison and contrast. To make your chart, take a sheet of paper (8½" x 11" preferably) and divide it into the desired number of squares. Horizontally state the things to be compared; vertically state the people or events. Figure 28 illustrates this type of chart by comparing the journeys of the Apostle Paul, while Figure 29 charts his imprisonments. (These two charts are not filled in—you can do that sometime— but illustrate the concept.)

A TOPICAL GRID—Many passages of Scripture deal with one particular topic. For example, 1 Corinthians 13 is about love, 1 Corinthians 15 about the resurrection, and 2 Peter 2 about false teachers. The themes of these chapters are usually best stated in a word or phrase, rather than a sentence. Figure 27 illustrates a topical grid on 2 Thessalonians 2.

TOPIC: FOLLOW-UP   CHAPTER: 2 THESSALONIANS 2

Verse	Positive Characteristics	Negative Attitudes	Relationships	Activities
4	approved by God; entrusted with Gospel	not speaking to please men		
5		no flattering speech; not greedy.		
6		no glory seeking; not asserting authority		
7	gentle		a nursing mother	caring for them
8	having fond affection, very dear to them			imparting lives

Figure 27

PAUL'S JOURNEYS

Journeys	Scripture	Dates	Places Visited and Length of Stay	Churches Established and the Date	Men Traveling with Paul	Letters Written and Dates
1						
2						
3						

Figure 28

PAUL'S IMPRISONMENTS

Imprisonments	Scripture	Dates	Men Paul Appeared Before	Reason for Imprisonment	Men Sent out by Paul and Where Sent	Men with Paul	Letters Written and Dates
Caesarean							
First Roman							
Second Roman							

Figure 29

In the left hand column list the references that will break the chapter up into smaller portions. The smaller portions may be paragraphs, sentences, or individual verses.

Next, determine what you want to investigate about this topic and list these categories horizontally. Some of them are illustrated in Figure 27. This type of chart will correlate the whole chapter for you.

Vertical Charts

These charts also may be used in different ways: to correlate the content of a chapter or section of a book, to compare and contrast people and events, and to sort out chronological events. Again, you should use your creativity to draw them in such ways that they will be most useful to you.

PASSAGE DESCRIPTION—To correlate the content of a chapter or passage, first divide the chapter you are studying into paragraphs. Mark down the beginning verse and the ending verse of each paragraph on your chart. For example, in 1 Thessalonians 1 you will find two paragraphs, verses 1-5 and verses 6-10.

1 THESSALONIANS 1	
PARAGRAPH 1 — vv. 1-5 v. 1	PARAGRAPH 2 — vv. 6-10 v. 6
v. 5	v. 10

Figure 30

The next step is to write in key thoughts from the paragraph in the block allotted to it. Avoid interpretation at this point; just record what you observe.

1 THESSALONIANS 1	

PARAGRAPH 1 — vv. 1-5
v. 1 — Paul greets the
    Thessalonians
    — Paul prays
    — Paul brought the
    Gospel to them
 	
v. 5
	PARAGRAPH 2 — vv. 6-10
	v. 6 — The Thessalonians . . .
	    — became imitators
	    — became examples
	    — spread their faith abroad
	    — turned to God
	
	v. 10

Figure 31

The third step is to title your paragraphs. Consider the key thoughts you have written in your chart rather than rereading the biblical text. After you have considered what you wrote for the first paragraph of 1 Thessalonians 1, you might title it, "The Gospel Received." Other possibilities might be "Paul's Ministry" or "The Enlivening Message."

1 THESSALONIANS 1	
THE GOSPEL RECEIVED	THE GOSPEL RESULTS

PARAGRAPH 1 — vv. 1-5
v. 1 — Paul greets the
    Thessalonians
    — Paul prays
    — Paul brought the
    Gospel to them
 	
v. 5
	PARAGRAPH 2 — vv. 6-10
	v. 6 — The Thessalonians . . .
	    — became imitators
	    — became examples
	    — spread their faith abroad
	    — turned to God
	
	v. 10

Figure 32

COMPARATIVE CHART—A vertical chart may be used to make comparisons and contrasts. Figure 13 in Chapter 8 is an illustration of this as the ministry of Christ was contrasted with that of Aaron.

CHRONOLOGICAL CHART—This type of chart is particularly helpful in sorting out chronological events in various periods of Bible history. If you, like many, have difficulty following the sequence of events in Israel's history during the period of the divided kingdom, a chart might help you understand those times. After the reign of Solomon (1 Kings 12), Israel was divided into the southern kingdom (Judah) and the northern kingdom (Israel). The division occurred about 931 B.C. The northern kingdom of Israel ended with its deportation at the hands of Assyria in 722 B.C. while Judah ended in 586 B.C. with the Babylonian captivity.

To chart the chronology of this period, place the dates vertically, with 931 at the top of the page, working down through 586 (it may take more than one sheet of paper). Horizontally place the information you want to correlate. Write in the kings of Judah and Israel, the number of years they reigned, their character (whether good or bad), and the active prophet(s) during their reign. Figure 33, a partial chart of the period, includes those elements and shows you how it may be drawn. You may also add other elements, such as, the relationship of each king to his predecessor, how each king died, and the Scripture references. You can add or delete as you want.

Pyramid Charts

This type of chart is useful in arranging your material to show movement from the specific to the general and vice versa.

Peter opens his first letter with these words: "Praise be to the God and Father of our Lord Jesus Christ! In his great mercy he has given us new birth into a living hope through the resurrection of Jesus Christ from the dead, and into an inheritance that can never perish, spoil or fade—kept in heaven for you" (1 Peter 1:3-4). The progression of his thought is charted in Figure 34.

PERIOD OF THE DIVIDED KINGDOM

DATE	JUDAH		YRS REIGN	GOOD/BAD	ISRAEL		YRS REIGN	GOOD/BAD	PROPHET
931	Rehoboam	931	17	bad	Jeroboam	931	22	bad	
925									
920									
915	Abijam	913	3	bad					
910	Asa	911	41	good	Nadab	910	2	bad	
905					Baasha	909	24	bad	
900									
895									
890					Elah	886	2	bad	
885					Zimri	885	7 days	bad	
880					Omri	885	12	bad	
875	Jehoshaphat	873	25	good	Ahab	874	22	bad	
870									
865									
860									
855	Jehoram	853	8	bad	Ahaziah	853	2	bad	
850					Jehoram	852	12	bad	
845	Ahaziah	841	1	bad					
840	Athaliah	841	6	bad	Jehu	841	28	bad	
835	Joash	835	40	good					
830									
825									
820									
815					Jehoahaz	814	17	bad	
810									
805									
800									
795	Amaziah	796	29	good	Jehoash	798	16	bad	

Figure 33

Figure 34

The whole book of 1 Peter has four major themes: sanctification, suffering, salvation, and submission. The Holy Spirit is sanctifying the believer, which builds a contrast between him and the life style of the non-Christian. The unbeliever's reaction is to persecute the Christian. The Christian's response of submission brings about the salvation of the non-Christian. You can chart all that in the manner of Figure 35.

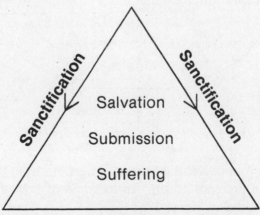

Figure 35

Whenever you have a progression of thought that flows from the general to the specific, this type of chart can be used effectively.

Illustrative Charts

This method of charting is the most creative of all the methods and also the most difficult to describe or explain. You are familiar with the proverb, "A picture is worth a thousand words." In this type of charting, you seek to draw the truths together in picture form.

Paul pictures God as being sufficient to meet all our needs (Philippians 4:13, 19). One possible way of illustrating this is shown in Figure 36.

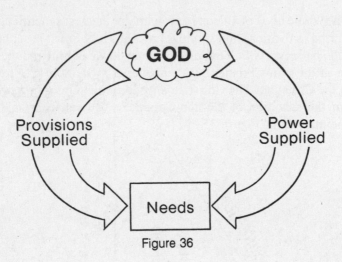

Figure 36

Romans 6–8 details the believer's freedom from the penalty, power, and presence of sin. An example of how this may be charted is found in Figure 37.

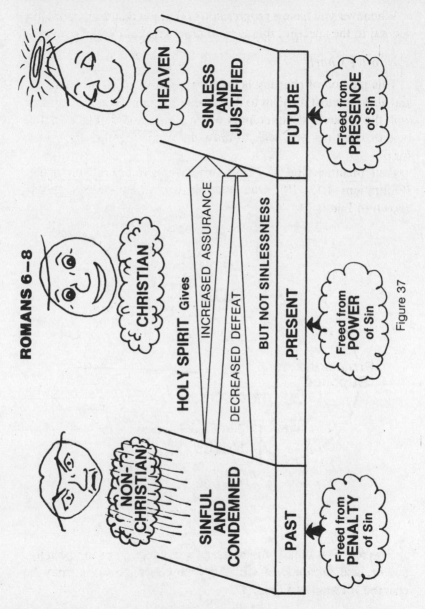

ROMANS 6—8

HOLY SPIRIT Gives

INCREASED ASSURANCE

DECREASED DEFEAT

BUT NOT SINLESSNESS

NON-CHRISTIAN

CHRISTIAN

HEAVEN

SINFUL AND CONDEMNED

SINLESS AND JUSTIFIED

PAST

PRESENT

FUTURE

Freed from PENALTY of Sin

Freed from POWER of Sin

Freed from PRESENCE of Sin

Figure 37

You can incorporate many creative approaches into your study as long as you include the content of the passage under study. Two examples of illustrative charts from 1 Thessalonians 1 are shown in Figures 38 and 39.

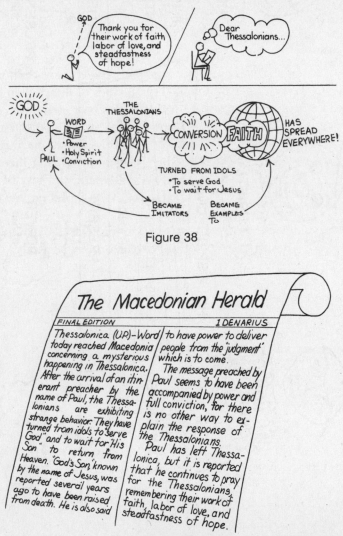

Figure 38

Figure 39

Combination Charts

At times you will want to combine the various methods of charting. Figure 40 is a chart giving an overview of Hebrews 7. It combines the *horizontal* and *illustrative* methods. Another is shown in Figure 41, in which the *horizontal* and *vertical* elements are combined.

Summary

The need to be creative in this aspect of Bible study cannot be overemphasized. So experiment. Try all kinds of things, combining what you have learned here with some of your own ideas. Use colored pens for contrast and keeping track of the movement of your ideas. Remember, your objective is to correlate the various truths in your study to one another, and in so relating them to discover new truth. Don't be intimidated by the newness of the approach or the variety of methods. Start with a portion you can handle, and go from there.

Let your creative instincts take over. Remember, the methodology is to help *you* get a grasp on the passage under study.

THE PERFECTION OF CHRIST
HIS IS A BETTER PRIESTHOOD
Hebrews 7:1-28

HIS PERSON		HIS PROMISE		HIS PERFORMANCE	
Credentials of Melchizedek	Consideration of His Greatness	Change Needed in the Old Order	Covenant Established by an Oath	Contrasting Abilities in the Priesthoods	Christ's Sacrifice of Himself
7:1-3	7:4-10	7:11-19	7:20-22	7:23-25	7:26-28
BETTER ORDER		BETTER COVENANT		BETTER PRIEST	
WHO HE WAS		WHY HE CAME		WHAT HE DID	
BECAUSE HE IS FROM MELCHIZEDEK		HE IS NOT LIMITED BY SINAI		HE IS NOT LIMITED BY THE ALTAR	

Figure 40

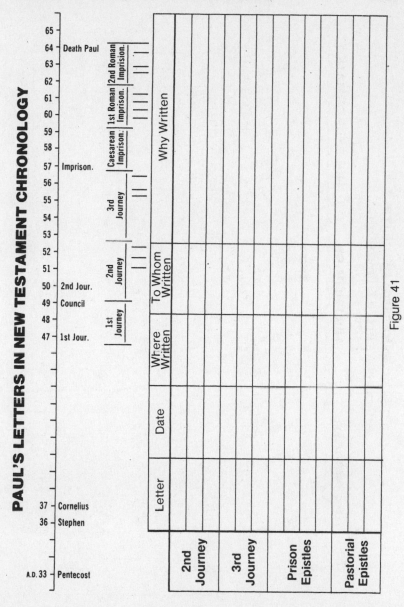

Figure 41

11 Application: The Role of an Implementor

APPLICATION
Implementing what has been studied to daily Christian living.

Throughout the centuries, the application of God's Word constantly expresses itself as *the* major need in Christianity. Even in Bible times God again and again rebuked His people for failure to make application of His truths. James put it this way: "Do not merely listen to the Word, and so deceive yourselves. Do what it says" (James 1:22).

Learning is far easier than applying. If you find this to be true in your own life, you are no different than most Christians. Yet God insists on your working at applying His truths to your life.

Rule Six under the principles of interpretation states, "The primary purpose of the Bible is to change our lives, not increase our knowledge." In this part of your Bible study program you are prayerfully endeavoring to bring your life more completely into conformity with God's standards.

In making a personal application it is important to distinguish between emotion and volition. Often applying God's Word is an emotional experience. However, *action* and not just feeling is what God wants. Jesus' parable of the two sons makes this point quite clear (see Matthew 21:28-32). The father asked the first son to work in the vineyard, but he refused to go. Later he changed his mind and obeyed his father. The second son readily agreed to go when asked, but never showed up for work. "Which of the two did what his father wanted?" was the question Jesus asked (Matthew 21:31). You would agree that it was the first. Ideally the Lord wants both your emotions and volition, but it is when you *do* what God wants that you make application.

Procedure for Making Applications

The following seven steps are a helpful mechanical procedure for making applications.

1. *Use the Principle of Observation.* Include in your observation section of Bible study "possible" points of application as you discover them. (These have been illustrated in each of the observation sections of the five methods of Bible study.) Mark them with a colored pen or put (A) in the margin so you can identify them. List as many possible applications as you can, for you will find that every passage is "loaded" with them. Ask the Holy Spirit to help you dig them out. InterVarsity Press, in their little booklet titled *Quiet Time,* offers six suggestions—all in the form of questions—that are helpful in stimulating your mind as to possible applications. They are:

- Is there any example for me to follow?
- Is there any command for me to obey?
- Is there any error for me to avoid?
- Is there any sin for me to forsake?
- Is there any promise for me to claim?
- Is there any new thought about God Himself?

2. *Follow the Rules of Interpretation.* A proper application can only be made after you have correctly interpreted the passage. This principle is elaborated on in Rule Six, Corollary 2 in the second section of this three-part book, *Interpreting the Bible.* There may be many applications of a passage, But only one correct interpreation.

Remember, too, a literal interpretation is always best unless the text demands otherwise. Rule Ten in *Interpreting the Bible* may be reviewed for an elaboration of this point.

3. *Be Selective.* Prayerfully review the possible applications you have listed in the observation section of your study. Select the one you feel the Holy Spirit would have you work on now. Don't try to choose more than one as this can prove to be counter-productive. If you try to apply too many, you will become frustrated and unable to apply any. It is like someone throwing a dozen eggs to you. Trying to catch them all can cause you to miss them all. Select one, make sure you catch it, and let the rest go by.

The process is subjective simply because it is between you and the Lord. If your heart is open and teachable, He will reveal what He wants you to apply.

4. *Be Specific.* Resist the temptation to address yourself to generalities. Put your finger on the heart of the problem and press.

For example, "Philippians 2:5—'God would have me to be more like Jesus'" is too general.

On the other hand, the following is a more specific way of making an application. "When Paul said that Jesus took on Himself 'the very nature of a servant' (Philippians 2:7), I realized that I have not been serving my family as I should. I sit around and let my wife and children wait on me and find myself resenting it when I have to go out of my way to do anything for them.''

5. *Be Personal*. How easy it is to use pronouns such as "we," "us," "they," and "our" when making application. How hard it is to talk in terms of "I," "me," "my," and "mine." This is not "our" problem; it is "my" problem. When writing your applications, stick to the first person singular pronouns.

6. *Write Out Your Application*. As an integral and essential part of your study, the application should be written out. It is hard on pride to verbalize on paper areas of personal application, but you will find it extremely helpful in your quest to do business with God. Writing it out affords an opportunity to go back and check your progress against what you specifically vowed before God you would do.

7. *Set Up a Check-up Procedure*. Sometimes your application will require one specific thing like returning a book you borrowed months before, or apologizing to someone for a wrong you did. At other times your application will require time. It may be a habit God wants you to break, or a series of steps you may have to take like paying installments on a large overdue bill. Then too there will be times when the Holy Spirit will give you a long-range project to work on such as working on an attitude or a virtue.

For example, you are studying the life of Moses and note as a possible application Numbers 12:3, "Now the man Moses was very *meek,* above all the men which were upon the face of the earth." You look up the word *meek* to obtain a precise definition and find it means, "Enduring injury with patience and without resentment" *(Webster's)*. The Holy Spirit speaks to you about your unwillingness to let people take advantage of you without a fight. You list specific illustrations when this has been true in your life, but you also realize that a proper application is going to take a major re-working of your attitude.

This type of an application may require a year to work on—not to the exclusion of any further applications during the year—but certainly as the major area on which you will be working. Numerous short-range applications may need to be made throughout the year, but this is the major long-range one.

The longer an application takes, the more difficult it is to check up on the progress. Also, applications dealing with attitudes and motives are harder to measure than those dealing with specific points of action. All of this must be taken into consideration when seeking ways to check up on yourself.

Returning to the application of meekness taken from the life of Moses, a possible plan of attack would be:

- "I will memorize Numbers 12:3 and review it daily throughout the year."
- "I will write *meek* on a card and tape it to the mirror in the bathroom, so that daily I will be reminded of my need to work on this. Each morning I will review Numbers 12:3 and pray about its application in my life for *that* day."
- "I will share this need with my spouse and with [a friend], who knows me well. Once a month I will talk over my progress with them and ask for a frank evaluation."

Example of a Typical Application

Following is an example of an application that might be written from a study of Philippians 3.

The passage—"In my study of Philippians 3 the Holy Spirit convicted me of my gluttony through verses 18-19: 'For, as I have often told you before and now say again even with tears, many live as enemies of the cross of Christ. Their destiny is destruction, their god is their stomach, and their glory is in their shame. Their mind is on earthly things.'"

An example—"The other day we were over to the home of Mrs. Jones for dinner and she had prepared the most delicious fried chicken I had ever seen. I overate totally. I knew at the time I was doing it, and felt uncomfortable and embarrassed afterward. I simply love good food.''

The solution—''I must 'put a knife to my throat.' When I eat, especially in the home of another, I will take but *one* helping and a moderate one at that.''

The specific steps—''To insure that I follow through on this application, I covenant before God that I will:

"1. During grace before each meal, silently ask the Lord to enable me to eat moderately.

"2. Ask my spouse to kick me under the table each time I become immoderate as a gentle reminder of my vow before God.

"3. Write a note of apology to Mrs. Jones for the way I behaved at her table. This will be hard, but it will reinforce my determination never to do it again.''

Summary

By its very nature, an application is a personal thing. The above are suggestions on how you can put "shoe leather" on your desire to apply the Scriptures. The third section, ''Applying the Bible'', pages 256–335, gives more practical helps. The bottom line, however, is a change in your character. This change must originate from within. The Holy Spirit will give you wisdom and the courage of your convictions as you apply His Word.

12 Two Plans for Long-Range Bible Study

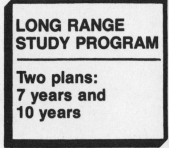

LONG RANGE STUDY PROGRAM

Two plans:
7 years and
10 years

This suggested program is arranged for 45 weeks of study each year. A two-week synthetic study is scheduled for each book of the Bible—an introductory survey study before and a concluding summary study after. (This means that seven weeks are allowed for a five-chapter book like 1 Thessalonians.). *Topical* and *Biographical* studies are *italicized*. The order of topical studies assumes a person has already been fairly well grounded in basic doctrines through question-and-answer studies. Old Testament chapter studies are underlined.

This program is not meant to be a rigid one, and you may adjust it as you feel you need for your own study program. Interchange books, topics, biographies, and Old Testament chapters, adding or deleting as you think best.

First Year	Weeks
1 Thessalonians	7
1 John	7
Philippians	6
Salvation	2
Witnessing	2
Follow-up	2
Gospel of Mark	18
Biographical: Daniel (Daniel 1–6)	1

Second Year	**Weeks**
Colossians	6
Jesus Christ (deity, death, resurrection)	3
1 Timothy	8
Biographical: Timothy (use a concordance)	1
Gospel of John	23
Prayer	2
Biographical: Josiah (2 Kings 22–23; 2 Chronicles 34–35)	1
Isaiah 52:13–53:12	1

Third Year	
Galatians	8
The Holy Spirit and the Lordship of Christ	3
Ephesians	8
Biographical: Barnabas (use a concordance)	1
Romans	18
Exodus 20	1
2 Timothy	6

Fourth Year	
The Word of God	2
Titus	5
Biographical: Gideon (Judges 6–8)	1
Obedience	1
Biographical: Joseph (Genesis 28–50)	2
Acts	30
Exodus 12	1
Pacesetting	1
Genesis 3	1
World Vision	1

Fifth Year

	Weeks
1 Peter	7
Suffering	1
Joshua 1	1
1 Corinthians	18
Biographical: Elijah (1 Kings 17–22; 2 Kings 1–2)	1
The Will of God	2
Hebrews	15

Sixth Year

2 Thessalonians	5
Stewardship and Generosity	2
Genesis 22	1
Love	2
Psalm 1	1
The Second Coming of Christ	3
Psalm 2	1
Biographical: Hezekiah (2 Kings 18–20; 2 Chronicles 29–32; Isaiah 35–39)	2
Gospel of Luke	26
The Church, Church Growth, and Other Christian Works	2

Seventh Year

James	7
The Tongue	1
Temptation and Victory	1
Purity	1
Biographical: Elisha (2 Kings 1–13)	1
2 Peter	5
Repentance	1
Sin	2

	Weeks
Satan	2
Psalm 23	1
Psalm 37	1
2 Corinthians	15
1 Samuel 17	1
2 Samuel 7	1
Discipline and Diligence	1
Good Works	1
Proverbs 2	1
Psalm 78	1
2 John	1

Seven-year Summary:

23 New Testament Books (Mark through 2 John)	249
24 *Topical Studies*	41
9 *Biographical Studies*	11
14 Old Testament Chapters	14
Seven Years at 45 Weeks per Year	315

Eighth Year

3 John	1
Jude	1
Humility	1
Honesty	1
Revelation	24
Judgment and Hell	2
Biographical: Nehemiah (Nehemiah 1–13)	2
Genesis 1	1

	Weeks
Genesis 12	1
Philemon	1
Redeeming the Time	1
Biographical: Peter (use a concordance)	5
Judges 7	1
1 Kings 18	1
Job 1	1
Job 2	1

Ninth Year

Gospel of Matthew	30
Correction and Rebuke	1
2 Kings 17	1
Psalm 40	1
Numbers 14	1
Faithfulness—God's; Man's Required	2
Psalm 103	1
Deuteronomy 4	1
Joshua 3	1
Jonah	6

In the Tenth Year you may begin again, selecting from the previous nine, or you may add any other Old Testament books, topics, and biographies that you desire.

How to Interpret the Bible

13 Interpretation Is for Everyone

This book has been written for those who enjoy studying the Bible and wonder if they are doing it correctly. You no doubt have heard it said, "Everyone has his own interpretation of the Bible," or, "The two things people can never agree on are religion and politics."

If such assertions are true, then Christianity is meaningless and the Bible has no message for us. If an individual can make the Bible say what he wants it to say, then the Bible cannot guide him. It is merely a weapon in his hands to support his own ideas. The Bible was not written with that purpose in mind.

Most books on the subject of biblical interpretation are quite lengthy and involved. Produced for those familiar with Hebrew,

Aramaic, and Greek, the languages in which Scripture was originally written, they seek to treat the subject in a thorough and scholarly way. For example, they contain detailed explanations of allegories, similes, metaphors, and other language uses. They explore trends in theology, such as the impact of neoorthodoxy on the church or the effect of liberalism in denying the supernatural.

This book presents basic biblical laws of interpretation in simple terms, and in so doing provides a functional tool for every Christian who wants to understand and apply Scripture.

Every person lives his life with certain basic assumptions. These assumptions vary from one situation to another. For example, if you were to fly to Japan, you would have to assume at least four things:

1. The pilot knows how to fly the aircraft.
2. The plane will arrive safely.
3. The immigration people in Japan will honor your passport.
4. You will be able to accomplish your intended purpose for going.

In our study of the laws or rules for interpreting the Bible, we must also assume certain things:

1. The Bible is authoritative.
2. The Bible contains its own laws of interpretation, which, when properly understood and applied, will yield the correct meaning to a given passage.
3. The primary aim of interpretation is to discover the author's meaning.
4. Language can communicate spiritual truth.

These assumptions will appear frequently in the principles listed in this section. Some are rules as well as assumptions and will appear as such.

These assumptions make a significant difference in the whole approach to Bible study. To study, interpret, and be able to apply the Bible *correctly* are the goals of every conscientious Christian. Before noting how these four assumptions and the subsequent principles affect the study of Scripture, it is worth noting that there are four basic parts in studying the Bible correctly. They are:

• **OBSERVATION,** which answers the question, "What do I see?" Here the Bible student approaches the text as a detective. No detail is unimportant; no stone is left unturned. Every observation is carefully listed for further thought and comparisons.

• **INTERPRETATION,** which answers the question, "What does it mean?" Here the interpreter bombards the text with questions such as, "What did these details mean to the people to whom they were given?" / "Why did he say this?" / "How will this work?" / "What is the major idea he is seeking to communicate?"

• **CORRELATION,** which answers the question, "How does this relate to the rest of what the Bible says?" The Bible student must do more than just examine individual passages. He must coordinate his study with what else the Bible says on the subject. An accurate understanding of the Bible on any subject takes into account *all* the Bible says about that subject.

• **APPLICATION,** which answers the question, "What does it mean to me?" This is the goal of the other three steps. An expert in the field said it succinctly, "Observation and interpretation without application is abortion." The Bible is God speaking. His Word demands a response. That response needs to be nothing less than obedience to the revealed will of God.

These four parts of Bible study are guided by the ground rules of interpretation. The psalmist said, "I seek you with all my heart; do not let me stray from your commands. I have hidden your word in my heart that I might not sin against you" (Psalm 119:10-11). His words echo the heart cry of the dedicated Christian, whose goal is to so saturate himself with God's Word that he begins to think and react in a Godlike way. To do this, the Bible student must so familiarize himself with these ground rules that they become part of his Scripture investigation.

The rules of interpretation are divided into four categories: General, Grammatical, Historical, and Theological.

General Principles of Interpretation (Chapter 14) are principles that deal with the overall subject of interpretation. They are universal in nature rather than being limited to special considerations, which are listed in the other three sections.

Grammatical Principles of Interpretation (Chapter 15) are principles that deal with the text itself. They lay down the ground rules for understanding the words and sentences in the passage under study.

Historical Principles of Interpretation (Chapter 16) are principles that deal with the background or context in which the books of the Bible were written. Political, economic, and cultural situations are important in considering the historical aspect of your study of the Word of God.

Theological Principles of Interpretation (Chapter 17) are principles that deal with the formation of Christian doctrine. They are, of necessity, "broad" rules, for doctrine must take into consideration all that the Bible says about a given subject. Though they tend to be somewhat complicated, they are nonetheless important, for they play a profound role in shaping that body of belief you call your convictions.

14 General Principles of Interpretation

In matters of religion the Christian submits either consciously or unconsciously to one of the following as his ultimate authority: Tradition, Reason, or the Scriptures. The official, historical position of the Roman Catholic Church has been to make tradition the final court of appeal. The doctrine of the virgin Mary is an example. What the Bible teaches about Mary is interpreted in accordance with how the Catholic Church has traditionally viewed her.

Rationalism has occupied center stage in much of Protestantism. Liberalism and Modernism are terms coined to describe this approach. For them, the conclusion that the mind draws is the final court of appeal. What the human mind cannot accept as reasonable is rejected. Likewise, reason is left to decide what is fundamental to a faith in God. For example, a person embracing this approach may conclude that belief in the virgin birth of Christ is neither rational nor essential, and the biblical teaching can therefore be denied.

The evangelical Christian looks to the Bible as his final court of appeal. Belief in Jesus' virgin birth is embraced because the Bible teaches it. What the church has believed concerning the virgin Mary must be interpreted by the Scriptures and not vice versa.

This is not to suggest that there is no validity in each of the three forms of authority. Adherents to each of the above systems of thought would readily agree to the importance of each of the others. In case of conflict, however, the question is, which vote counts? If tradition, reason, and Scripture differ as to how to view Mary and the virgin birth of Christ, which authority is the final arbitrator? *The first law of interpretation says the Bible is the final court of appeal.*

The subject of biblical authority is often tied to the question of the inspiration of the Scriptures. A person cannot submit to the Bible as his authority if it is not the inspired Word of God. The same issue arose during the ministry of Jesus Christ on earth. He taught "as one who had authority" (Matthew 7:29). But on what was His authority based? How can we know if He truly is the Christ as He claims to be?

In answer to these probing questions, Jesus said, "If a man chooses to do God's will, he will find out whether my teaching comes from God or whether I speak on my own" (John 7:17). "If you will *do* what I ask you to do, then you will *know* if what I am saying is right or not," is what Jesus basically said. If you will *do,* then you will *know*. Doing comes before knowing. Commitment comes before knowledge. Hundreds of years ago St. Augustine put it this way, "I believe; therefore I know."

Authority has to do with the will, with obedience, and with doing. Inspiration concerns the intellect, understanding, and knowledge. The question of inspiration must follow authority. Just as it is only after you do what Jesus asks you to do that you know that He is the Christ, so also only after you have submitted yourself to the authority of the Bible and obeyed it will you know that it is the inspired Word of God.

The demand that commitment come before knowledge is not unique to the Christian faith. It is common, everyday experience for all people. In the introduction we talked about the use of assumptions. We used the illustration of going to Japan. By making those assumptions you simply made a commitment before you knew what would happen. You didn't *know* the authorities would let you into Japan. You *assumed* they would, and *committed* yourself to that assumption before you *knew*.

Expanding the illustration, let us say you go to the pilot before takeoff and inquire about the safety of the huge aircraft.

"Will it really get me to Tokyo?" you ask.

"Certainly," the captain assures you.

You probe further. "But what about the airplane that went down in the Pacific a number of months ago. Can you *guarantee* that the plane will arrive in Japan safely?"

"No," says the captain, "I can't guarantee it. But climb aboard and when we arrive (if we arrive), you will know."

That is commitment before knowledge. You are willing to commit yourself and take the risk because it is a long swim to Japan.

Therefore in Bible study you begin with the issue of authority. It and the question of inspiration which naturally follows are answered when you submit to the Word of God. You may study inspiration as a separate topic, but you only *know* the Bible to be the inspired Word of God as you place yourself under its authority.

* * *

As you seek to submit yourself to what the Scriptures say, it is important to understand that authority in the Bible is expressed in various ways.

1. *A person acts in an authoritative manner, and the passage explains whether the act is approved or disapproved.* For example, in the Garden of Eden, " 'You will not surely die,' the serpent said to the woman" (Genesis 3:4). We know this to be wrong because Adam and Eve in fact did die.

King David wanted to build a temple for God, so Nathan said to him, "Whatever you have in mind, go ahead and do it, for the Lord is with you" (2 Samuel 7:3). Nathan in an authoritative way told David what to do, but we read that his advice was wrong and that God did *not* want David to build the temple (verses 4-17).

After the Jerusalem Council (Acts 15), the Apostle Peter visited the church in Antioch of Syria and ate with the Gentiles. Paul said of Peter, "Before certain men came from James, he used to eat with the Gentiles. But when they arrived, he began to draw back and separate himself from the Gentiles because he was afraid of those who belonged to the circumcision group [Jewish Christians]" (Galatians 2:12). We know that his act of separating from Gentile Christians was wrong, for Paul rebuked him for it and then explained why it was wrong.

2. *A person acts in an authoritative manner and the passage does not indicate approval or disapproval.* In this case the action must be judged on the basis of what the rest of the Bible teaches on the subject. For example, Abraham and Sarah go to Egypt because of a famine in Canaan (Genesis 12:10-20). Fearful that Pharaoh might kill him in order to take beautiful Sarah for himself, Abraham said to his wife, "Say you are my sister, so that I will be treated well for your sake and my life will be spared because of you" (12:13). Was this a cowardly thing for Abraham to do? The passage does not say. You are left for your conclusion to your own understanding of what the rest of Scripture has to say on the subject.

You will have to decide in your mind whether Abraham was wrong in his actions or not, and this is precisely what interpreting the Bible is all about. This book will not seek to give you the "correct" interpretation, but will simply help you choose for yourself the correct basis for coming to your conclusions.

After Lot lost his wife when God destroyed Sodom and Gomorrah, he and his two daughters went to live in a cave in the mountains above Zoar. Fearful that they would never marry and thus die childless, the two daughters took matters into their own hands. On two successive nights they made their father drunk, and then they had sexual intercourse with him, one on each night. They became pregnant and bore sons, Moab and Ben-ammi, by their father (see Genesis 19:30-38).

Yet Peter said that Lot was a righteous man. "If he [God] condemned the cities of Sodom and Gomorrah by burning them to ashes, and made them an example of what is going to happen to the ungodly; and if he rescued Lot, a righteous man, who was distressed by the filthy lives of lawless men . . ." (2 Peter 2:6-7). Was what happened in the cave of Zoar a righteous act? The passage does not say. The Scriptures do, however, have a great deal to say about the kind of behavior that took place in the cave of Zoar, and the action can be judged on the basis of those many teachings.

3. *God or one of His representatives states the mind and will of God.* These are often in the form of commandments. For example, Jesus said, "A new commandment I give you: Love one another. As I have loved you, so you must love one another. All men will know that you are my disciples if you love one another" (John 13:34-35).

Some commands, however, are for immediate circumstances and are not meant to be universally applied. God said to Noah, "So make yourself an ark of cypress wood; make rooms in it and coat it with pitch inside and out" (Genesis 6:14). Jesus said to two of His disciples, "Go to the village ahead of you, and at once you will find a donkey tied there, with her colt by her. Untie them and bring them to me'' (Matthew 21:2). Because God told Noah to build an ark, it does not mean we must feel it is the will of God that we build arks; nor do we go around untying donkeys and bringing them to Jesus. The context and nature of the command indicates whether or not it is to be universally applied.

All Scripture is authoritative, but there are parts you are not to follow. You must be careful, however, not to use fancy logic to avoid doing what you know the will of God to be for you.

Secular man is drifting farther and farther from the biblical absolutes. This in turn puts pressure on the church to take a fresh approach to the biblical commands regarding such things as divorce and a wide variety of moral questions. More often than not this fresh approach is nothing more than the gross immorality that caused the fall of Sodom and Gomorrah. Such trends originate in an unwillingness to submit to the authority of the Bible.

For the Christian, the Bible is and will always remain authoritative.

RULE TWO

The Bible interprets itself; Scripture best explains Scripture.

The Bible tells us that one of the first interpreters of God's Word was the devil.

"Now the serpent was more crafty than any of the wild animals the Lord God had made. He said to the woman, 'Did God really say, "You must not eat from any tree in the garden"?' The woman said to the serpent, 'We may eat fruit from the trees in the garden, but God did say, ''You must not eat fruit from the tree that is in the middle of the garden, and you must not touch it, or you will die. 'You will not surely die,' the serpent said to the woman. 'For God knows that when you eat of it your eyes will be opened, and you will be like God, knowing good and evil' '' (Genesis 3:1-5).

Earlier God had said, "You are free to eat from any tree in the garden; but you must not eat from the tree of the knowledge of good and evil, for when you eat of it you will surely die" (Genesis 2:16-17). Satan did not deny that God said those words. Rather he twisted them, giving them a meaning they did not have. Such error takes place by omission and addition.

Omission—quoting only that part which suits you while leaving out the rest. There are two types of death in the Bible, physical and spiritual. Physical death is the separation of the soul from the body. Spiritual death is the separation of the soul from God. When God told Adam, "You will surely die" (Genesis 2:17), He was referring to both spiritual and physical death. When the serpent said to Eve, "You will not surely die" (3:4), he was purposely omitting the fact of spiritual death.

Addition—saying more than the Bible says. In her conversation with Satan, Eve quotes what God told her husband. But she adds to His Word the phrase, "And you must not touch it" (Genesis 3:3). You can twist Scripture by making it say more than it, in fact, says. Usually the motive is a desire to make God's command unreasonable and thus unworthy of being obeyed.

* * *

When you study the Bible, let it speak for itself. Neither add to it, nor subtract from it. Let the Bible be its own commentary. Compare Scripture with Scripture.

For example, Isaiah says, "Therefore the Lord himself will give you a sign: The virgin will be with child and will give birth to a son, and will call him Immanuel" (Isaiah 7:14). In Hebrew the word translated in many versions as "virgin" can actually be translated either "young woman" or "virgin." This same verse is quoted by Matthew in reference to the virgin birth of Jesus Christ (Matthew 1:23). In Greek, however, the word has only *one* meaning, "virgin." In other words, Matthew interprets the word for us and we translate Isaiah's expression as "virgin."

We will usually apply this rule to the great truths of the Bible rather than to specific verses. Such a truth is *assurance of salvation*. Individual verses can be quoted on both sides of the question of whether or not we can lose our salvation. Paul said to the Galatians, "You have fallen away from grace" (Galatians 5:4). Some Christians reading this would conclude that it is possible to lose your salvation having once obtained it.

On the other hand, Jesus said, "My sheep listen to my voice; I know them, and they follow me. I give them eternal life, and they shall never perish; no one can snatch them out of my hand. My Father, who has given them to me, is greater than all; no one can snatch them out of my Father's hand" (John 10:27-29). A thorough study of the topic of *assurance of salvation*, comparing Scripture with Scripture, however, indicates that the believer can have assurance that he is saved on the basis of the finished work of Christ.

A further application of this rule is in the use of cross-references in your Bible study. When studying a chapter or a paragraph, the context is the primary place you will look for the interpretation. Cross-references are useful, but you should try to cross-reference the *thought* of the verse rather than just a word or phrase.

For example, in studying the crucifixion of Christ from Matthew 27:27-50, you will be cross-referencing verse 35, "When they had crucified him, they divided up his clothes by casting lots." Good cross-references would include Psalm 22:18, which is the Old Testament verse quoted here. Also Mark 15:24, Luke 23:34, and John 19:23-24, all of which are references to the Crucifixion from the other Gospels. Secondary cross-references would be Joshua 7:21, 1 Kings 11:29, and Daniel 7:9, which refer to the word *clothes*.

In all of these examples the principle remains the same—let Scripture explain Scripture. The Bible will interpret itself if studied properly.

RULE THREE

Saving faith and the Holy Spirit are necessary for us to understand and properly interpret the Scriptures.

When Jesus was in Galilee by the seaside, the multitudes gathered around Him, drinking in His incredible words as He explained to them the mysteries of the kingdom of heaven. He finished the parable of the sower with these words, "He who has ears, let him hear" (Matthew 13:9). Jesus then interpreted the parable only to His disciples with this explanation: "For this people's heart has become calloused; they hardly hear with their ears, and they have closed their eyes. Otherwise they might see with their eyes, hear with their ears, understand with their hearts and turn, and I would heal them" (Matthew 13:15).

People have two sets of eyes and ears. One set sees and hears things physically, the other spiritually. The Apostle Paul commenting on this said, "The god of this age has blinded the minds of unbelievers" (2 Corinthians 4:4). The god of this world, Satan, does his utmost to prevent people from perceiving spiritual truth.

The dedicated Christian reads a passage and its truth is self-evident to him. It is so simple and so obvious when he explains it clearly to his non-Christian friend, but that friend fails to grasp its significance. Try as he may, the Christian cannot communicate the simple truth. It is as though there is a barrier of understanding between them.

Through the years Christians have been aware of this problem. Writing to the Corinthians, Paul described it this way: "The man without the Spirit does not accept the things that come from the Spirit of God, for they are foolishness to him, and he cannot understand them, because they are spiritually discerned" (1 Corinthians 2:14).

We see a striking example of this at the raising of Lazarus from the dead. Jesus' good friend had been dead four days and decay

had already set in. Friends had gathered to console Mary and
Martha, the sisters of Lazarus. Then Jesus arrived. The stone was
rolled away and Jesus shouted loudly, "Lazarus, come out!"
(John 11:43) Still in his graveclothes, Lazarus walked out of the
tomb in obedience to the command of Christ.

As John recorded this event, he said, "Therefore many of the
Jews who had come to visit Mary, and had seen what Jesus did, put
their faith in him. But some of them went to the Pharisees and told
them what Jesus had done. Then the chief priests and the Pharisees
called a meeting of the Sanhedrin" (John 11:45-47). Some saw it
as it was, a miracle of God. Others viewed this same event with
entirely different eyes. They saw it as a threat to their own beliefs,
goals and objectives.

It is easy to stand aghast at such crass unbelief. But before we
judge too harshly, we might remind ourselves that this is the result
of a spiritual battle. Satan seeks to blur our spiritual vision in like
manner. The Bible says, "We have not received the spirit of the
world but the Spirit who is from God, that we may understand what
God has freely given us" (1 Corinthians 2:12). We must study the
Bible with a deep sense of dependence on the Holy Spirit, realizing
that He is the One who "will guide you into all truth" (John
16:13).

It is possible to claim the Bible as your authority and still be
spiritually blind. You may have had the experience of being
approached by someone from the Jehovah's Witnesses, the Mormons, or some other cult. These people are quick to tell you that
their faith is based on the Bible, but you do not have to speak with
them long before you realize that they have failed to interpret the
Bible properly. Rather, they have twisted its meaning to substantiate their own positions.

This problem of using the Bible as your authority while being
blinded to its true meaning is not limited to the cults. Many of the
worst atrocities through the centuries have been committed in the
name of Christ. In the early twelfth century, in response to the

church's call, thousands gathered under the banner of the cross to free the Holy Land (Palestine) from the Muslims. It was not uncommon for the zealots in these crusades (as they were called) to massacre whole communities of Jews and pagans, even impaling infants by throwing them into the air and catching them on their spears.

During the Civil War in America the Bible was used both to denounce and to support slavery. It is reported that one of Abraham Lincoln's generals said to him during the fierce conflict, "I hope God is on our side."

The president replied, "Sir, I am not half as concerned that God is on our side as I am that we are on God's side."

Seeing things from God's point of view is a ministry of the Holy Spirit to those who have not only trusted Him for salvation but for enlightenment as well. Though being a Christian is no guarantee that you will accurately interpret every passage in the Bible, it is foundational for properly understanding spiritual truth.

RULE FOUR

Interpret personal experience in the light of Scripture and not Scripture in the light of personal experience.

As you read through the New Testament, you discover that it contains two main types of literature—narrative and instructional or teaching. (Most of Revelation and parts of the Gospels can be classified as prophetic.) The narrative portions trace the life of our Lord Jesus in the four Gospels and the history of the early church in the Book of Acts. The letters or epistles are largely written to instruct members of these early churches on how to live the Christian life.

When studying the instructional portions you discover the writer does not say that because such and such a thing happened, therefore this must be true. Rather, he asserts just the opposite. Because this is true, a particular thing happened. For example, the New Testament does not teach that because Jesus rose from the dead He is therefore the Son of God. Rather, because He is the Son of God, He rose from the dead.

The events that unfold throughout the Bible are interpreted on the basis of what God states to be true and never vice versa. We do not conclude that the world was wicked because God destroyed it with a flood in the days of Noah. Rather, the Bible says that because the world was wicked God said He would destroy it and did.

Throughout the Book of Acts the narrative of what happened in the lives of first century believers unfolds. You do not draw doctrinal conclusions from these events unless they include preaching. Rather, you interpret these events in the light of the doctrinal passages. There are several instances when people in the Acts record encountered the Holy Spirit. When you analyze all the varied experiences, it becomes obvious that you cannot form doctrine from these encounters. On the Day of Pentecost Peter and the disciples spoke in tongues, and people of different language groups were all able to understand the gospel in their own languages. "Utterly amazed, they asked: 'Are not all these men who are speaking Galileans? Then how is it that each of us hears them in his own native language?'" (Acts 2:7-8).

When Peter went to Samaria to look in on the ministry of Philip, the new converts had not yet received the Holy Spirit. "Then Peter and John placed their hands on them, and they received the Holy Spirit" (Acts 8:17). There is no mention of any speaking in tongues following this occurrence.

After Paul's conversion on the road to Damascus, Ananias came to him and laid hands on him. Paul was filled with the Holy Spirit and was baptized (Acts 9:17-19).

In the city of Ephesus Paul met some men who had been baptized only with "John's baptism"—a baptism of repentance. Paul preached Jesus to them, and they believed and were baptized.

"When Paul placed his hands on them, the Holy Spirit came on them, and they spoke in tongues and prophesied" (Acts 19:6). We are not told what language these men spoke, but it probably was different from that spoken at Pentecost. The situation was different. It was most likely an unknown tongue, requiring an interpreter such as Paul mentions in his letter to the Corinthians (1 Corinthians 14).

The teaching portions of the New Testament speak about the use of tongues by believers. The significant passage on this teaching is 1 Corinthians 12–14. Note that this passage addresses itself to the use and control of tongues without mentioning the practice of tongues as in Acts. In other words, Paul says, "Here is the correct doctrine regarding tongues—make sure your own experience complies with it." He does not say that because a certain phenomenon was experienced in the church, a certain doctrinal truth may be drawn from it.

Your personal experiences—whatever they may be—must be taken to the Scriptures and interpreted. Never the other way around. "Because I have had this experience, the following must be true" is not sound procedure in interpreting the Bible.

None of this suggests that there is no value in experience. Quite the contrary. Experience attests to the validity of the doctrine. The resurrection of Jesus Christ substantiates the fact that He is the Son of God. You know that your salvation is true because of what you have experienced. But you do not form the doctrine of salvation on the basis of your experience. You take your experience to the Scriptures to find out what has taken place in your life.

We often see in the Bible that a statement is made and an experience follows to prove its validity. For example, we find the following test to see if the man claiming to be a prophet really is one: "If what a prophet proclaims in the name of the Lord does not take place or come true, that is a message the Lord has not spoken. That prophet has spoken presumptuously. Do not be afraid of him" (Deuteronomy 18:22).

Ahaziah, the son of Ahab and Jezebel, was king over Israel, the northern kingdom. Because of his sin, Elijah the prophet prophesied that he would die. King Ahaziah sent soldiers to arrest Elijah. "Elijah answered the captain, 'If I am a man of God, may fire come down from heaven and consume you and your fifty men!' Then fire fell from heaven and consumed the captain and his men" (2 Kings 1:10). Elijah's prophetic statement was followed by its fulfillment, proving that Elijah was a true prophet of God. His statement was followed by the experience.

Personal experience is an important part of the Christian life, but you must be careful to keep it in its proper place. Though you learn from experience, you do not judge the Bible on the basis of it.

It is easy to forget this in so many areas in life. For example, suppose you have had difficulty with deficit spending. The Lord speaks to you about this and you feel He would have you abolish all forms of buying on credit. You work hard, economize, and pay off all your creditors. This revolutionizes your life. You are now free from debt and convinced that you should never return to installment buying. Up to this point all is well.

But then you go one step further and suggest that anyone owning credit cards or buying on time is violating a biblical command. To prove your point you quote, "Let no debt remain outstanding" (Romans 13:8). You have now broken this important rule of interpretation. You have interpreted the Bible in the light of your own experience and demanded that others should follow this interpretation.

The Scriptures blend beautifully with life's experiences. The more time you spend in Bible study, the more this truth becomes imprinted in your life. It seems that the biblical authors had *you* in mind when they penned their words, so pointed and alive are the applications.

It is precisely for this reason that you must exercise care in not reversing this rule. You allow the Word of God to interpret and shape your experiences rather than interpreting Scripture from your experiences.

RULE FIVE

Biblical examples are authoritative only when supported by a command.

As you read through the Bible it becomes obvious that you are not to follow the example of every person you meet. You need not follow the example of Moses and confront the leaders of Egypt. You are not to follow the example of King David and commit adultery and murder. Nor are you to follow the example of the Apostle Peter in denying Christ.

These illustrations may seem to be oversimplified, but the Bible is full of many examples that *are* worthy of imitation. Are you not obligated to follow these? Yes, if the example illustrates a biblical command. No, if the example is not supported by such a command.

Jesus Christ is the perfect Man. If ever there is a life worth copying it is His. As we look at His perfect life, if we find it is not necessary to follow all His examples, it will logically follow that this will be true for the rest of the Bible.

Jesus wore a long robe and sandals. Usually He walked. When He did ride, it was on a donkey. He never married and never left the country of His birth (except as an infant when His parents fled to Egypt to escape from King Herod and a brief visit to Syro-Phoenicia). It becomes immediately apparent that you are not expected to follow His example in areas such as these.

For instance, to follow Jesus' example in His remaining single would mean that Christians are not to marry; yet the Bible has a great deal to say about the marital relationship, commending it highly and using it as an illustration of the whole Christ-Church relationship.

Jesus was a man of great love and compassion. You know you are to follow His example in this because He said, "A new commandment I give you: Love one another. As I have loved you, so you must love one another. All men will know that you are my disciples if you love one another" (John 13:34-35).

Examples from the life of Jesus or from the lives of His followers that are *not* supported by commands do have some value:

1. *A biblical example can verify what you think the Lord is
leading you to do.* You may feel, for instance, that God would
have you remain single the rest of your life. Since most people
marry, you may feel pressure from others in this direction. But
your conviction that the Lord would have you never marry is
biblically supported by the fact that Jesus never married.

2. *A biblical example can be a rich source of application for
your life.* Suppose you are reading the Gospel of Mark and pause to
meditate on this account, "Very early in the morning, while it was
still dark, Jesus got up, left the house and went off to a solitary
place, where he prayed" (Mark 1:35). After thought and prayer
you feel the Lord would have you spend time with Him each day
early in the morning. This would be an appropriate application and
would undoubtedly benefit your spiritual life.

To take this application, however, and try to apply it to other
people would be taking an example from the Bible and treating it as
a command. The Scripture does command us to pray; Paul urged,
"Pray continually" (1 Thessalonians 5:17). And the Bible does
exhort us to spend time in the Word, "Let the Word of Christ dwell
in you richly as you teach and counsel one another with all
wisdom, and as you sing psalms, hymns and spiritual songs with
gratitude in your hearts to God" (Colossians 3:16). No command
of Scripture says that this should be done early in the morning,
even though this is when Jesus did it, and may be the best time for
you.

Each individual must draw his own application from those
biblical examples that are not followed by a command. The commandments of the Bible are, of course, authoritative for all people.
But biblical examples, unless supported by a command, are not.

* * *

A corollary to this principle is also true:

The believer is free to do anything that the Bible does not prohibit.

An obvious example of this principle may be seen in the present-day activities of the church. A local congregation may build a new sanctuary, develop a large Sunday School, begin a Boys Brigade work, or start a Christian day school. The Scriptures do not have examples of these, much less commands to do them, yet such actions are entirely permissible. The Bible sets boundaries on what *cannot* be done, not on what can be done. All things are lawful unless specifically prohibited.

Such a clear prohibition applies in the area of premarital and extramarital sex. Paul says that such people "will not inherit the kingdom of God" (see 1 Corinthians 6:9).

The Holy Spirit uses the Bible to guide and direct our lives. As we follow His leading and expose ourselves to the great truths of the Scriptures, we take upon ourselves more and more the character of Jesus Christ. The Bible calls this process sanctification. And in sanctification the Lord gives us great freedom—freedom in the exciting adventure of becoming Christlike.

As we study the Bible, we must exercise care that we do not restrict this freedom either for ourselves or for others. To quote the great Puritan divines of a by-gone day, "The Bible is our only rule for faith and practice."

> **RULE SIX**
>
> **The primary purpose of the Bible is to change our lives, not increase our knowledge.**

When He superintended the writing of the Bible, the Holy Spirit intended that we who read the Scriptures learn and apply what is taught. The Scriptures themselves state this as their intended purpose.

When Paul wrote his first epistle to the Corinthians, he drew from the experience of Israel during the Exodus to make his point. Israel lusted in the wilderness for things they didn't have.

Commenting on this to the church in Corinth, Paul said, "Now these things occurred as examples, to keep us from setting our hearts on evil things as they did" (1 Corinthians 10:6).

Two of the ways you can learn a lesson are through personal experiences and through the experiences of others. Some lessons in life you can learn only by living through them. But some lessons are too expenseive to learn that way. The wise person will learn them by observing the lives of others.

The unbelief of Israel during the Exodus cost that nation forty wasted years of wandering in the wilderness. Paul says to the Corinthians that God recorded this for us so that we would not make the same tragic mistakes. In a most remarkable way the Lord shows us in the pages of the Bible the failures and shortcomings (as well as the strengths) of His people so that we can learn from them. "Learn from their strengths and avoid their weaknesses," seems to be the Holy Spirit's message to us.

We must understand before we can apply, but understanding without application does not make a person godly. Satan knows the Bible well. No doubt he could pass any examination in theology offered him. He has even memorized Scripture, which he demonstrated when he quoted from the Psalms during the temptation of Jesus.

"Then Jesus was led by the Spirit into the desert to be tempted by the devil. After fasting forty days and nights, he was hungry. The tempter came to him and said, 'If you are the Son of God, tell these stones to become bread.'

"Jesus answered, 'It is written: "Man does not live on bread alone, but on every word that comes from the mouth of God."'"

"Then the devil took him to the holy city and had him stand on the highest point of the temple. 'If you are the Son of God,' he said, 'throw yourself down. For it is written: "He will command his angels concerning you, and they will lift you up in their hands, so that you will not strike your foot against a stone"'" (Psalm 91:11-12).

"Jesus answered him, 'It is also written: "Do not put the Lord your God to the test."'

"Again, the devil took him to a very high mountain and showed him all the kingdoms of the world and their splendor. 'All this I will give you,' he said, 'if you will bow down and worship me.'

"Jesus said to him, 'Away from me, Satan! For it is written: "Worship the Lord your God, and serve him only."'" Then the devil left him, and angels came and attended him" (Matthew 4:1-11).

"Even the demons believe that—and shudder," is the way James put it (James 2:19). The Bible was not given to us so that we could be as smart as the devil; it was given to us so that we could become as holy as God. Peter has written: "He has given us his very great and precious promises, so that through them you may participate in the divine nature and escape the corruption in the world caused by evil desires" (2 Peter 1:4).

Paul advised Timothy, "All Scripture is God-breathed and is useful for teaching, rebuking, correcting and training in righteousness, so that the man of God may be thoroughly equipped for every good work" (2 Timothy 3:16-17). All Scripture was given with this end in mind—that it shape our lives. You must be careful, though, when seeking to apply "all Scripture" to remember two things. They may be stated as corollaries to this rule.

✳ ✳ ✳

1. Some passages are not to be applied in the same way they were applied at the time they were written.

Suppose you are reading through the Book of Leviticus, seeking to make an application to your life, and you read, "These are the regulations for the guilt offering, which is most holy: The guilt offering is to be slaughtered in the place where the burnt offering is slaughtered, and its blood is to be sprinkled against the altar on all sides" (Leviticus 7:1-2). A wrong application would be to do the same thing the Old Testament priests did: offer an animal sacrifice.

The New Testament tells us that Jesus Christ "abolished in His flesh the enmity, even the law of commandments contained in ordinances" (Ephesians 2:15 KJV). You might possibly apply this Leviticus passage by purposing to reflect on how great a price the Savior paid to have every one of your sins forgiven, using the Old Testament sacrificial system as a point of reference.

The Bible offers another possible application: "Through Jesus, therefore, let us continually offer to God a sacrifice of praise—the fruit of lips that confess his name. And do not forget to do good and to share with others, for with such sacrifices God is pleased" (Hebrews 13:15-16).

2. When you apply a passage it must be in keeping with a correct interpretation.

For example, our Lord is coming down from the Mount of Transfiguration when He meets some of His disciples trying to heal an epileptic (Matthew 17:14-16). Since they are unable to do it, the boy's father turns to Jesus for help. Jesus casts out the unclean spirit and the frustrated disciples later ask why they were unable to do it. Jesus replies, "Because you have so little faith. I tell you the truth, if you have faith as small as a mustard seed, you can say to this mountain, 'Move from here to there' and it will move. Nothing will be impossible for you" (17:20).

If you were burdened for a loved one who had a terminal disease, you might read this passage, and, wanting to make an application, reason that only your lack of faith was keeping you from healing him. You try to heal him, but the person dies. So you blame yourself and think, *Maybe it is because of sin in my life that I was unable to heal him.*

Probably sin and unbelief were not your problem. You simply misinterpreted the passage. Earlier, Jesus had specifically instructed His disciples, "Heal the sick, raise the dead, cleanse those who have leprosy, drive out demons. Freely you have received, freely give" (Matthew 10:8). They were rebuked for their lack of faith because they had been commanded by the Lord to heal and had been endowed with appropriate power to do so. God did not give such a specific command to you.

Every part of the Bible is applicable to you. Correct interpretation, however, is essential before you seek to make application. Failure to do so may lead to unnecessary misunderstanding and heartache. Take care to interpret the passage correctly, then prayerfully make the application.

RULE SEVEN

Each Christian has the right and responsibility to investigate and interpret the Word of God for himself.

This principle was one of the undergirding foundations of the Protestant Reformation in the sixteenth century. For hundreds of years, people had depended on the church to do the studying and interpreting of the Scriptures for them. There were no translations of the Bible in the language of the people. When attempts were made to produce such translations, the church strongly suppressed them.

Today there are a multitude of available translations and paraphrases, making access to the Bible easy for anyone who can read. Yet our generation seems to be producing biblically illiterate people. Even among conscientious Christians the Bible is little more than a devotional book in which to "meet" God. Digging for the great truths of the Bible is left for the theologians and other "experts." It is as though we were returning to the days before the Reformation.

The presence of the Holy Spirit and the ability of language to communicate truth combine to give you all you need to study and interpret the Bible for yourself. In the ministry of our Lord Jesus, He rebuked the Jews of His day for their inability to understand who He was. He attributed this failure directly to their ignorance of the Scriptures. "You diligently study the Scriptures because you think that by them you possess eternal life. These are the Scriptures that testify about me" (John 5:39).

Later Jesus said that a distinguishing mark of one who is His disciple is that he "continue in My Word" (John 8:31 KJV). All through the epistles this theme is picked up and emphasized. "Let the word of Christ dwell in you richly as you teach and counsel one another with all wisdom, and as you sing psalms, hymns and spiritual songs with gratitude in your hearts to God" (Colossians 3:16), Paul admonished the believers at Colosse. To his son in the faith he put it this way, "Do your best to present yourself to God as one approved, a workman who does not need to be ashamed and who correctly handles the word of truth" (2 Timothy 2:15).

In-depth study will not always give you the answers you seek. Frequently you will encounter a truth whose depths elude you. And your mind is so constituted that it can ask more questions than it can answer. Bible study will not answer all of your questions. Answers to some questions will come later, like finding the missing piece in a jigsaw puzzle. Some will never be answered this side of heaven. An appreciation for the mysteries in the Christian faith is in itself a sign of maturity.

When your private interpretation leads you to a conclusion different from the historic meaning men of God have given to the passage, an amber light of caution should flash in your mind. Any conclusion you come to that differs from the historic evangelical position should be considered suspect. More often than not, after further study, you will find that your interpretation was in error.

If you are blessed with a pastor and Sunday School that faithfully expound the Bible, you have a rich heritage indeed. This, however, could easily lull you into relying on others to feed you rather than disciplining yourself to feed your own soul. It should not be an either/or proposition, but a both/and. You should maintain a balance between being taught by others and feeding yourself. The more skilled you become in personal Bible study, the more you will rely on your pastor as a check on how you inter-preted the passage rather than as the primary source of your scriptural intake.

Even when you learn spiritual truth from the preaching of others, you are responsible for weighing this truth with what you find in your own Bible study and for forming your own convic-tions. This is what made the Berean Church noble in the eyes of Luke. Notice what he said about them. "Now the Bereans were of more noble character than the Thessalonians, for they received the message with great eagerness and examined the Scriptures every day to see if what Paul said was true" (Acts 17:11).

Underline the words *great eagerness*. The noble Bereans re-ceived Paul's teaching with openness and attentiveness. But they did not stop there. When Paul was through preaching, they exam-ined "the Scriptures every day to see if what Paul said was true." What a combination! Listen attentively to the Word and then study the Bible to form your own convictions.

When you accept an idea simply because someone else tells you it is so, you short-circuit the process, even if what you are told is accurate and worthy of belief. You have believed the right thing for the wrong reason. It has not yet become your conviction. This is why so many Christians fall prey to heretical groups such as the Jehovah's Witnesses and the Mormons.

A different illustration will make the same point. A Christian friend encourages you to memorize Scripture. You do it because he tells you to do it. You have no conviction of your own that you should do it, and it is hard work. After an enthusiastic beginning you let it slip. Unfaithful in your review, you soon forget the verses you have memorized, and in discouragement you quit. Only if you are *convinced* God wants you to memorize, will you jump the hurdles of discouragement and go on to victory.

As we have already seen, God commands us to spend time with Him in the Scriptures. Scripture memory, however, is a *method* of getting into the Word. You may not necessarily be convinced of the method that others use; in that case you must go before the Lord and ask Him *how* He wants you to go about investigating and interpreting the Bible.

Five methods of studying the Bible are presented later on in Section I of this book. Further suggestions for improving your investigation of the Word of God are given in Section IV.

A method is a vehicle for digging into the Word. The process of digging into Scripture and coming to your own conclusion is what changes mere beliefs into rock-ribbed convictions. Involvement in this process is not only your right as a child of God, but also your solemn responsibility.

RULE EIGHT

Church history is important but not decisive in the interpretation of Scripture.

In the introduction to this book, we compared the authority of *reason* and *tradition* to the authority of *Scripture*. Though all three authorities are important and have their proper place, reason and tradition must yield to Scripture. When there is disagreement among the three types of authority, Scripture must be the final court of appeal. It is the *final* authority.

There is a proper place for reason and tradition, and here we want to examine the place of tradition or church history. For the sake of simplicity we will equate the two.

Many doctrines considered essential by evangelicals are implied in the Scriptures. Because they are implied and not explicitly stated, there was a time when they were quite controversial. We are indebted to church history for the fact that such issues are settled.

One such doctrine is the deity of Jesus Christ, that is, that He is coeternal with the Father, that He is God. There never was a time when He was not. He is "very God of very God." This doctrine is biblical. It is taught in several places in the Bible. The prologue to the Gospel of John gives a clear example, "In the beginning was the Word, and the Word was with God, and the Word was God. . . . The Word became flesh and lived for a while among us" (John 1:1, 14). The correct interpretation of this and other related passages came with the maturing of the church. We are indebted to church history which records what the believers of past ages hammered out on the anvil of soul-searching, scriptural investigation and debate.

* * *

A corollary to this rule is:

The church does not determine what the Bible teaches; the Bible determines what the church teaches.

The interpretations of the church have authority only insofar as they are in harmony with the teachings of the Bible as a whole. History was not meant to be decisive in the interpretation of Scripture, for there have been times when the church has not been true to the Word of God. In early medieval times it taught the celibacy of the clergy, that priests could never marry. Later medieval times exalted Mary to a position equal with God. These were determinations of the church, not the Bible. The interpretations of the church must be carefully studied and evaluated in light of what the Bible teaches.

Having voiced this caution, however, we still must not overlook the importance of church history. It can provide a check and balance for you in your own study of the Bible. Charles H. Spurgeon, the famous English preacher, is reported to have said, "It seems odd that certain men who talk so much of what the Holy Spirit reveals to them should think so little of what He revealed to others." There is an important place for commentaries and the creeds in forming doctrine. God's saints of the past have a great deal to say to us today, if only we will listen.

Many evangelicals overreact by refusing to consider any source other than the Bible, and not without reason. The attack on the Word of God has been fierce these past decades. Many of the historic creeds of the church have been revised and watered down to include the philosophical biases of the day. You must be careful to maintain balance here. Learn from history and recognize its important contribution while remembering that the Bible is the final arbitrator in all matters pertaining to faith and practice.

RULE NINE

The promises of God throughout the Bible are available to the Holy Spirit for the believers of every generation.

The promises of God found in the Bible are a means by which God reveals His will to men. In saying this, we must acknowledge that claiming promises is a subjective thing. For that matter, so is using any method to determine God's will for one's life.

Many people become uneasy when biblical promises are used, partly because they are so often misused. A not-so-funny caricature of a person claiming a biblical promise shows him opening a Bible with eyes closed and placing his finger in the middle of the page. Where the finger rests is God's promise to him.

The problem is not in claiming a promise per se, but in determining the will of God. Use the same caution in claiming God's promises that you use when you determine the will of God. The Lord requires all of us to act on the basis of faith. The promises are given as a valuable tool in helping us respond properly.

Claiming the promises of God is a specific form of application. Note the emphasis that was given to application in Rule Six: *The primary purpose of the Bible is to change our lives, not increase our knowledge* (page 163). Just as it is essential that you interpret the passage properly before applying it, so also it is essential to interpret the promise properly before claiming it.

If you are not careful about what the passage says, all sorts of fanciful interpretations can follow. For example, you may desire leadership from the Lord for your life. After much prayer you claim Isaiah 30:21, "Whether you turn to the right or to the left, your ears will hear a voice behind you, saying, 'This is the way; walk in it.' " You are asking the Lord to tell you when to turn to the right and when to turn to the left. From now on you are going to get your directions straight from God, for is this not what He has promised?

As you study the context of Isaiah 30:21, you learn that the word spoken from behind you is from your teachers. From God, yes, but through your teachers. Failure to interpret the verse properly can lead you to misunderstand how God wants to lead you.

It is permissible to claim a promise outside of its historical context as long as you are true to what the passage says and means. For example, let us say you are surrounded by adverse circumstances and accused falsely. You pray, asking the Lord for guidance. He leads you to claim Exodus 14:14, "The Lord will fight for you; you need only to be still." This promise was originally given to Moses when Israel was surrounded by adverse circumstances. But with this promise God quiets your heart and you wait on Him to work things out.

The Bible gives numerous encouragements to claim the promises in this manner. Peter, exhorting his flock to a devout and holy life, said, "His divine power has given us everything we need for life and godliness through our knowledge of him who called us by his own glory and goodness. Through these he has given us his very great and precious promises, so that through them you may participate in the divine nature and escape the corruption in the world caused by evil desires" (2 Peter 1:3-4). The psalmist expressed it this way: "But the plans of the Lord stand firm forever, the purposes of his heart through all generations" (Psalm 33:11).

A proper attitude is important as you approach the promises. The Lord has given them to you to help you do His will. Yet so often people use them to try to get God to do their will. The Bible says, "Until now you have not asked for anything in my name. Ask and you will receive, and your joy will be complete" (John 16:24). Jesus Himself made that promise. You are in love with someone and want to marry that person. Or you and your spouse want a child. So you claim this promise, but don't get your wish. Why? Possibly because God did not give you that particular promise. You took it. But God is not your servant; you are His. You defeat the purpose of the promises when you make them self-serving.

A promise is God's commitment to do something, and requires your response of faith in the form of obedience. Sometimes that obedience means patiently waiting on the Lord to do what He promises. Another time it may mean launching out into the unknown or taking great risks. God's promises form the foundation for the expression of faith. Without the promise you have no basis for asking. With the promise you respond by faith. Faith is always active, never passive. As you, by faith, respond to God's promise, His will is performed and He is glorified.

Suppose you respond to the promise and it is not fulfilled? It appears that God did not do what He promised. To what conclusions can you then come? Three possibilities are:

1. *God let you down*. He failed to carry out His end of the bargain. If this is so, the Bible is not trustworthy; it is not worth following Christ; in short, the God of the Scriptures does not exist. For God Himself said, "God is not a man, that he should lie, nor a son of man, that he should change his mind. Does he speak and then not act? Does he promise and not fulfill?" (Numbers 23:19).

Though we list "God let you down" as a possible conclusion, it is in fact an impossibility. It is an impossibility because God promises He will *never* let us down. Paul was speaking to Timothy when he said, concerning the reliability of God, "He will remain faithful, for he cannot disown himself" (2 Timothy 2:13). We can rule out this possibility simply because God *always* does what He promises.

2. *You misclaimed the promise*. This is an unpleasant possibility, but a real one. If you have ever had the misfortune of claiming a promise God never intended for you to claim, don't think that you are alone. Many have done it. It usually happens when your motives become confused. Was the promise claimed with a sincere desire to do God's will and nothing else? Or was what you wanted interjected somewhere along the line?

If you felt you sought only to please God, then you should suspend judgment as to what happened. Even Paul wasn't always sure of his own motives. He said, "I care very little if I am judged by you or by any human court; indeed, I do not even judge myself. My conscience is clear, but that does not make me innocent. It is the Lord who judges me. Therefore, judge nothing before the appointed time; wait till the Lord comes. He will bring to light what is hidden in darkness and will expose the motives of men's hearts. At that time each will receive his praise from God" (1 Corinthians 4:3-5).

God knows your heart and will someday reveal what happened. You may have misappropriated the promise, but a third choice still remains.

3. *It will be fulfilled at a later time and/or in a way you don't expect*. God promised Abraham that his descendants would be as numerous as the stars in the heavens. He and Sarah were still waiting patiently for its fulfillment after she had passed through menopause and Abraham was about 100 years old. They had even tried to help God fulfill His promise, but all in vain. Abraham had a child by Sarah's handmaiden Hagar, but this wasn't what God had in mind. Old age had come to this family and still there were no children. The natural fulfillment of the promise was not to be. God wanted it fulfilled in a *supernatural* way.

Speaking of this, the writer of Hebrews said, "These were all commended for their faith, *yet none of them received what had been promised*" (Hebrews 11:39). Here were God's heroes of the faith who never lived to see God's promises fulfilled. God fulfilled them in another generation. They did not "abandon ship" and give up. They held tenaciously to the promises and trusted God to fulfill them in His own way.

God has not let you down, and you may not have misclaimed the promise. The Lord may fulfill it in a way and at a time you don't suspect. God's will according to God's timetable is what all of us should be trying to follow.

*　*　*

It may be helpful to consider the two types of promises found in the Bible:

1. *General Promises.* These are promises given by the Holy Spirit to every believer. When they were penned by the author no individual person or period of time was intended. Rather they are *general,* that is, intended for all people in all generations.

An example of this type of promise is: "If we confess our sins, he is faithful and just and will forgive us our sins and purify us from all unrighteousness" (1 John 1:9). This promise was true for the people to whom John was writing, and it is equally true for you today. There are many such promises throughout the Bible.

2. *Specific Promises.* These are promises given by the Holy Spirit to specific individuals on specific occasions. Like the general promises, specific promises are available to you as the Holy Spirit may lead. The difference is that specific promises must be given expressly to you by the Holy Spirit as they were given to the original recipients. In this sense they are much more subjective than general promises. You can *know* that *all* general promises are given to you, and to everyone else. Specific promises, however, are *available* to you, but don't become yours unless specially given to you by God. Specific promises are most often given for guidance and for blessing.

The Holy Spirit may choose to give you a specific promise to help you determine His will. That is, when He wants to guide you in a particular direction. For example, "Your gates will always stand open, they will never be shut, day or night, so that men may bring you the wealth of the nations—their kings led in triumphal procession'' (Isaiah 60:11).

As you pray over this verse and become increasingly convinced that the Lord wants you to claim it for your life, you may decide to open your home twenty-four hours a day for all whom the Lord sends you. The promise was originally given to the Messiah, but the Spirit of God can give it to you for your ministry.

On their first missionary journey, Paul and Barnabas were opposed by the Jews while they ministered the Word in Antioch of Pisidia. They felt God was calling them to the Gentiles, and to substantiate this leading Paul quoted from Isaiah, ''For this is what the Lord has commanded us: 'I have made you a light for the Gentiles, that you may bring salvation to the ends of the earth' '' (Acts 13:47; see Isaiah 42:6-7). Paul quoted a messianic verse which the Lord had given him for guidance.

Blessing is the other way specific promises are used. The Holy Spirit may not be seeking to guide you, but simply to reveal the blessing He plans for your life. To illustrate this, let us say your church is without a pastor. The last one you had was unsatisfactory, and the leaders of the congregation have been cautious in calling his successor. Months have gone by and you are concerned that the Lord give you the right pastor. As you pray over the situation, the Lord assures you of His promised blessing with the words, ''Then I will give you shepherds after my own heart, who will lead you with knowledge and understanding'' (Jeremiah 3:15).

Because specific promises are subjective, if you have been a Christian for only a short time, it is best to stay with the *general* promises found in the New Testament for the first couple of years. When you think you are ready to claim specific promises, then you should follow certain guidelines:

1. The Spirit of God gives them to individual Christians at particular times in their lives as He chooses.

2. Promises are often conditional and the condition is obedience. You can detect the condition by the presence of the little word *if* in the verse or context.

3. The Holy Spirit of God is sovereign. "But the plans of the Lord stand firm forever, the purposes of his heart through all generations" (Psalm 33:11). He can speak from any passage to any person at any time.

4. Do not prejudge the Lord as to when and how the promise will be fulfilled in your life.

5. God gives His promises to make you more dependent on Him, not independent. Claim them in a spirit of dependence and humility.

6. God's intent is to glorify Himself by giving you promises. Never fail to give Him the glory when the promise is fulfilled.

One further caution is in order before we draw this to a close. When you claim a promise from the Bible, you are determining the will of God in that particular matter. This in turn cuts you off from any further counsel, for who wishes to counsel against the will of God? For example, let us say you are praying and seeking counsel about changing jobs. You claim a promise from the Word that in effect tells you, "It is the will of God to make the change." At that point no further counsel is needed. Now you need to act on what God has said.

In doing this, however, you place full responsibility for the decision on your own shoulders. You have determined God's will by yourself. This is not bad, unless you have misclaimed the promise. The caution comes in making sure you allow for sufficient time and prayer to make the promise a conviction in your soul that this is truly what God wants.

15 Grammatical Principles of Interpretation

Grammatical principles deal with the very words of the text. How should you understand the words and sentences in the passages under study? What are the ground rules to remember when dealing with the text? These principles answer those questions.

* * *

RULE TEN

Scripture has only one meaning and should be taken literally.

In the everyday affairs of life, no serious, conscientious person intends what he says or writes to carry a diversity of meanings. Rather, he desires that the true and obvious sense be understood by his hearers or readers. If you were to say to an audience, "I crossed the ocean from the United States to Europe," you wouldn't want them to interpret your statement to mean that you crossed life's difficult waters into the haven of a new experience. Likewise, no journalist would like to write of the famine and suffering of a country such as India and have his words interpreted to mean that the people of India were experiencing a great intellectual hunger.

As ridiculous as this sounds, much of the ecumenical church does precisely that in their interpretation of the Bible. They call it the use of "connotative words." For example, they don't use *reconciliation* in the biblical sense of a man being reconciled to God. They draw the word from biblical passages, give it their meaning and talk about man's reconciliation with man. *Redemption* is not used in the scriptural sense of man being saved from sin and punishment. Rather, they take this word from a Bible text, give it a different "connotation," and suggest that it has to do with sociological and cultural improvements.

In order to communicate, you must assume (1) that the true intent of speech is to convey thought, and (2) that language is a reliable medium of communication.

The literal interpretation in context, therefore, is the only true interpretation. If you don't take a passage literally, all sorts of fanciful interpretations may result.

When you encounter a passage in which a literal interpretation is indicated from the context and you elect to give it an other-than-literal interpretation, evaluate your motives carefully. As honestly as you can, answer the following questions:

1. *Am I questioning this passage being literal because I do not want to obey it?* For example, Paul said, "Women should remain silent in the churches. They are not allowed to speak, but must be in submission, as the Law says" (1 Corinthians 14:34). Your response is that this was a cultural issue, relevant in its day but not in ours. What led you to that conclusion? A desire *not* to do what the Bible commands or a sincere desire to please God and keep His

commandments? If it is the former, then you are on shaky ground and need to deal with the issue of lordship in your life. If it is the latter, then you are free to pursue your study and see if the rules of interpretation warrant such a conclusion.

2. *Am I interpreting this passage figuratively because it does not fit my preconceived theological bias?* An Old Testament incident gives us an example: "From there Elisha went up to Bethel. As he was walking along the road, some youths came out of the town and jeered him. 'Go on up, you baldhead!' they said. 'Go on up, you baldhead!' He turned around, looked at them and called down a curse on them in the name of the Lord. Then two bears came out of the woods and mauled forty-two of the youths" (2 Kings 2:23-24). Your immediate reaction may be that God could never allow such an incident to occur. God is just not like that! Once again you must pause and analyze your motives. Is your response to this passage born out of an embarrassment over what God is reported to have done? If your conclusion is the result of your trying to get God to behave the way you think He should, then again your whole approach to interpretation is wrong. You are God's servant. Your task is to understand who He is and what He expects. The objective of your Bible study is not to confirm *your* ideas of what God is like.

The application of the rules of interpretation must always be founded on a correct motive.

So determine what is the usual and ordinary sense of the word or passage and consider it the correct meaning unless the context demands otherwise.

No statement may be considered to have more than one meaning. No word can mean more than one thing as it is used in a passage. The same word may change meaning within the same sentence as it is used more than once, however. An example of this is, "God is spirit, and his worshipers must worship in spirit and in

truth'' (John 4:24). *Spirit* is used twice in this verse. The first time
it refers to the Holy Spirit for it says, "God is spirit," and the Holy
Spirit is God. The second use of the word *spirit* can be seen from
the context to refer, not to God, but to the totality of the inner
person—his essential inner being, his very heart. The word *spirit*
changes meaning, but the word cannot mean more than one thing
at a time. That is, *spirit* as used the first time can *only* mean God. It
can never mean anything else.

When a passage or a word appears to have more than one
meaning, choose the clearest interpretation. The most obvious
meaning is usually the correct meaning.

This rule is frequently broken. For example, in Jesus' feeding of
the 5,000, most people reading the account would accept it as
meaning what it says. Yet some interpreters would have us believe
that the real meaning of the passage is that Jesus drew out of the
crowds a latent spirit of generosity. When they saw the boy share
his lunch, they followed his example by pulling their meals out
from under their robes.

Before we become overly harsh with those who would misuse
the Scripture in this way, we should examine our own practices.
The Book of Judges relates the story of Jephthah's vow to God. If
God would grant him victory, he would offer in sacrifice the first
thing he met when returning home. It was his beloved daughter
that he met. Jephthah had vowed, "I will sacrifice it as a burnt
offering" (Judges 11:31). Then the record states that he "did
to her as he had vowed" (11:39). You can easily become embarrassed by such stories and conclude that they didn't happen *exactly*
the way they were written.

The thought of a man offering his own daughter as a sacrifice to
the God of the Scriptures is, to say the least, repugnant. How easy
it would be to take the tools of interpretation and draw a different
conclusion. As you find yourself yielding to such an urge, remember this important rule of interpretation: *Scripture has only
one meaning and should be taken literally*.

RULE ELEVEN

Interpret words in harmony with their meaning in the times of the author.

In the closing days of Jesus' ministry He told several parables about the kingdom of heaven. One of these was the parable of the ten virgins (Matthew 25:1-13). Five were wise because they had sufficient oil for their lamps, and five were foolish because they did not. What was the lamp used for in the ancient wedding feast? What did it look like? These are some questions a student should ask when studying this passage. Here is an example of the need to understand the meaning and use of the word at the time of its writing.

Determining the correct meaning of words found in the Bible is not particularly difficult these days. Many excellent translations are available, and when the meaning of a word is not clear from these, a good Bible dictionary will usually be helpful.

Occasionally the biblical writer will give his own meaning to a particular word. For example, Jesus drove "the changers of money" (John 2:14 KJV) out of the temple. The Jews didn't like this and began arguing with Him. Jesus answered them by saying, "Destroy this temple, and I will raise it again in three days." The Jews then said, "It has taken forty-six years to build this temple, and you are going to raise it in three days?" Jesus, of course, was speaking of the "temple" of His body (John 2:19-21).

John tells us that the temple to which Jesus was referring was His body. Here he gives us the meaning of the word *temple*. Earlier John talked about "changers of money." He did not explain who they were and what they were doing, so you must research the answer to this yourself. By referring to a Bible dictionary or a commentary on the Gospel of John you should find your answer.

Paul interprets the meaning of *me* in his testimony about his own struggles, "I know that nothing good lives in me, that is, in my sinful nature. For I have the desire to do what is good, but I cannot carry it out" (Romans 7:18). *Me* can refer to the will, the intellect, the spiritual or the physical man. Or it can refer to the total person. Paul limits its use here and tells us its exact meaning.

As you study a passage, never skip over words you do not understand. An erroneous impression as to the meaning of a single word can easily obscure the meaning of the sentence and possibly the whole paragraph. Even words you think you understand should be investigated.

An example of this is in Proverbs 29:18. The *King James Version* reads, "Where there is no vision, the people perish." The word *vision* is a poor translation. The marginal reading of the *New American Standard Bible* is more accurate in translating it *revelation*. It refers to the need to be under the ministry of the Word for the purpose of moral restraint. An erroneous impression as to the meaning of the word *vision* obscures the meaning of the statement.

As you study a particular word you should determine four things:

1. *Its use by the writer*. Exciting word studies in English are possible if you care to do a little digging. If the word is central to the thought of the writer throughout the book, it can prove most helpful. For example, the word *sin* is important to the Apostle John. A study of this word as used by him in his first epistle will help you understand the whole letter.

2. *Its relation to its immediate context*. The context will almost always tell you a great deal about the word.

Paul and his companions were ministering in Philippi when he and Silas were arrested, beaten and cast into prison. At midnight while the men were praising God, an earthquake opened the prison doors and it seemed as though all the prisoners had escaped. The jailer was about to commit suicide, but Paul stopped him.

"The jailer called for lights, rushed in and fell trembling before Paul and Silas. He then brought them out and asked, 'Men, what must I do to be saved?' They replied, 'Believe in the Lord Jesus, and you will be saved—you and your household' " (Acts 16:29-31).

What did the jailer mean when he used the word *saved?* Was it the same as the meaning given it by Paul in verse 31? Since the task of this book is not the interpretation of certain biblical passages, but the presenting of *ground rules* for interpretation, you will have to study the context of the narrative to answer these questions yourself.

3. *Its current use at the time of writing.* This requires a more technical study. Generally a reliable translation gives you the best meaning of the word, since the best available scholarship in the church has been involved in these translations. If you desire to pursue it further, you can use a good commentary.

4. *Its root meaning.* This final way of studying the meaning of a word is generally for the more advanced student of the Bible. Reference works are available that give you the historical background of words. The most comprehensive work is the English translation of the *Theological Dictionary of the New Testament,* edited by Gerhard Kittel and Gerhard Friedrich (Wm. B. Eerdmans Publishing Co., Grand Rapids, Michigan). Other good reference works are *Word Studies in the New Testament* by Marvin R. Vincent (Eerdmans) and *The New International Dictionary of New Testament Theology* edited by Colin Brown (Zondervan). A smaller, one-volume work that is excellent is *An Expository Dictionary of Bible Words* by Lawrence O. Richards (Zondervan). Determining the root meaning of a word, however, is not the most important consideration, and you should not be discouraged if you feel it is beyond you.

We have mentioned the existence and blessing of modern translations. Many of them, however, are more paraphrases than accurate translations, and therefore the personal interpretation and bias of the translator is often apparent. As long as the translator or committee are committed to the authority and inspiration of the Scriptures, the danger is not too severe. However, any time the original text is changed for the sake of clarity, a dangerous precedent is being established. An illustration of this is in the *New English Bible's* translation of Genesis 11:1 which begins, "Once upon a time." The Hebrew word is simply *and*. The phrase "once upon a time" is used in fairy tales and suggests to the reader that the story of the building of the Tower of Babel is simply fiction. Whether such a phrase reflects the bias of the translators is a matter of guesswork. Its presence in the Word of God is unfortunate.

The use of modern translations is helpful, but when doing serious study it is best that you stay with one of the reliable translations. These are: The *King James Version* (KJV), the *American Standard Version* (ASV), the *New American Standard Bible* (NASB), the *Revised Standard Version* (RSV), and the *New International Version* (NIV).

When interpreting a word or a passage, your goal is to determine the author's meaning when he wrote it. Try to free yourself of any personal bias when studying a passage. Your objective is to understand the thought of the writer, not what you think he ought to have said.

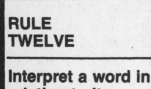

RULE TWELVE

Interpret a word in relation to its sentence and context.

We have already noted that it is important to study a word in relation to its immediate context (Rule 11). This is so basic and essential in interpreting the Bible that we list it as a separate rule. The best way to explain it will be to have a series of examples from the Bible when this is necessary.

We begin with the word *faith*. It is an important word in the Bible, especially in the New Testament. Yet we find that it has different meanings in different passages. In one letter Paul said, "They only heard the report: 'The man who formerly persecuted us is now preaching the faith he once tried to destroy' " (Galatians 1:23). As you study the context you find that *faith* here means, "the doctrine of the gospel."

When Paul wrote to the Romans he said, "But the man who has doubts is condemned if he eats, because his eating is not from faith; and everything that does not come from faith is sin" (Romans 14:23). Here the context leads you to conclude that *faith* means, "conviction that this is what God wants you to do."

In giving advice to his co-laborer Timothy, Paul said, "But the younger widows refuse, for when they have begun to wax wanton against Christ, they will marry; having damnation, because they have cast off their first faith" (1 Timothy 5:11-12 KJV). Here *faith* means, "a pledge or promise made to the Lord." There is, of course, a relationship between the uses of *faith* in these three passages, but the differences are significant enough to note in order to understand what Paul is saying.

A second example is the use of the word *blood*. Luke recorded the message Paul gave to the Athenians on Mars Hill. In it Paul said, "God that made the world and all things therein, seeing that he is Lord of heaven and earth, dwelleth not in temples made with hands; neither is worshiped with men's hands, as though he needed any thing, seeing he giveth to all life, and breath, and all things; and hath made of one blood all nations of men for to dwell on all the face of the earth, and hath determined the times before appointed, and the bounds of their habitation" (Acts 17:24-26 KJV). Paul has said, "And hath made of one blood all nations." As you study the context it becomes obvious that *blood* means a group of people.

Paul wrote of the salvation we have through Christ: "In him we have redemption through his blood, the forgiveness of sins, in accordance with the riches of God's grace" (Ephesians 1:7). The word *blood* here refers to the atoning death of Christ.

In another Scripture we read, "When everything had been arranged like this, the priests entered regularly into the outer room to carry on their ministry. But only the high priest entered the inner room, and that only once a year, and never without blood, which he offered for himself and for the sins the people committed in ignorance" (Hebrews 9:6-7). *Blood* here refers to that fluid which circulates in the veins and arteries of animals that carries nourishment to the body.

Using a different kind of illustration, we look at Paul's exhortation to the church at Corinth, "Now concerning the things about which you wrote, it is good for a man not to touch a woman" (1 Corinthians 7:1).

Some use this verse to support the idea that a man ought never even to touch a woman in any kind of bodily contact. The context, however, talks about the need to abstain from sexual immorality. In this sense you should not "touch" a woman. It would be erroneous to conclude that a man ought never to touch a woman, like shaking hands with her. In your own study of this passage, you might conclude that in order to maintain sexual purity the Lord would have you avoid physical contact with a member of the opposite sex. It would be wrong, however, to make this application normative for all people.

The ancient manuscripts, from which we make our translations of the Bible, have no punctuation marks. There are no periods, commas, paragraphs, verses, or chapters. These have since been introduced by the translators for clarity and ease of study. When you do your study it is well to remember this. The context will not always be found within the limits of the verse or chapter. You may have to include verses from the chapter before or after.

This study of the context to determine the proper meaning of a word is one of the most basic and important rules of interpretation. You will find yourself referring to it again and again in your study of the Bible.

RULE THIRTEEN

Interpret a passage in harmony with its context.

Each of the writers of the Bible had a particular reason for writing his book(s). As the writer's argument unfolds, there is a logical connection from one section to the next. You must try to find the overall purpose of the book in order to determine the meaning of particular words or passages in the book. These four questions will help:

1. How does the passage relate to the material surrounding it?
2. How does it relate to the rest of the book?
3. How does it relate to the Bible as a whole?
4. How does it relate to the culture and background in which it was written? This fourth question will be handled in a more comprehensive way under *Historical Principles of Interpretation* (Chapter 16), but is important to consider here also.

Answering these four questions becomes especially important when you are trying to interpret a difficult passage. This passage is an example: "No one who lives in him [Christ] keeps on sinning. No one who continues to sin has either seen him or known him. Dear children, do not let anyone lead you astray. He who does what is right is righteous, just as he is righteous. He who does what is sinful is of the devil, because the devil has been sinning from the beginning. The reason the Son of God appeared was to destroy the devil's work. No one who is born of God will continue to sin, because God's seed remains in him; he cannot sin, because he has been born of God. This is how we know who the children of God are and who the children of the devil are: Anyone who does not do what is right is not a child of God; neither is anyone who does not love his brother" (1 John 3:6-10).

When you read this passage by itself, you might conclude that the Christian never sins. Or if he does sin, he cannot be a believer, for "no one who continues to sin has either seen him [Christ] or known him'' (verse 6). If this is the correct interpretation, then only Jesus can ever go to heaven, for He is the only sinless person ever to walk the earth—Christian or non-Christian.

What does this passage mean? How should you interpret it? You must interpret it in the light of its context, and answering these four questions will help you do that.

You will see another example of this in the four Gospels. They have many things in common, not the least of which is that they all give an account of the life, ministry, crucifixion, and resurrection of Jesus Christ. The emphasis of each, however, is different. An understanding of this difference will help you in your study of the parts.

In Matthew we see Jesus as King. He is the fulfillment of all the Old Testament messianic prophecies. Thus you find numerous Old Testament quotations in Matthew.

In Mark Jesus is portrayed as the Servant. The emphasis in this Gospel is on the deeds of Christ. No genealogy is given, for who is interested in the genealogy of a servant?

In Luke Jesus is the Son of Man. Here we note the emphasis given to His humanity. His genealogy is traced back to Adam, the first man.

In John we see Jesus as the Son of God. The Gospel opens by revealing Him as the eternal Word, ''He was with God in the beginning'' (John 1:2).

This is not to suggest that the teachings of one Gospel cannot be seen in the other three. Quite the contrary. The emphasis of each is different. You need to study each Gospel as a whole to catch the panoramic view painted in it. In this way you will see the uniqueness of each, and will be better able to interpret the events and teachings recorded in it.

The importance of this principle cannot be overstated. It is one of the essential rules of interpretation.

RULE FOURTEEN
When an inanimate object is used to describe a living being, the statement may be considered figurative.

The great "I am" passages in John's Gospel illustrate this rule. Jesus said:

"I am the *bread* of life" (John 6:35).

"I am the *light* of the world" (8:12).

"I am the *door* of the sheep" (10:7 KJV).

Jesus is neither *bread* nor a *door* in the literal sense. Because an inanimate object such as *bread* is used to describe the Savior, you can conclude that *bread* must be taken figuratively rather than literally.

Many such examples are found throughout the Bible. The psalmist writes, "The righteous will flourish like a palm tree, they will grow like a cedar of Lebanon" (Psalm 92:12). The righteous person is likened to a palm or cedar tree. Obviously this is figurative language; an inanimate object is used to describe a living being. It is important to have a clear understanding of the thing on which the figure is based or from which it is borrowed. In this example, your study will be enriched by understanding the characteristics of palm and cedar trees and how they grow.

Another example may be drawn from the great prayer of David in which he asks for forgiveness. "Cleanse me with hyssop, and I will be clean; wash me, and I will be whiter than snow" (Psalm 51:7). What is hyssop and how was it used in those days? A study of the ceremonial purification used in Israel will help you have a fuller appreciation for what David was praying.

Periodically you will come across a passage about which there is disagreement in the church as to its figurative or literal interpretation. For an illustration of this, note Jesus' words regarding the Lord's Supper. "While they were eating, Jesus took bread, gave thanks and broke it, and gave it to his disciples, saying, 'Take and eat; this is my body.' Then he took the cup, gave thanks and offered it to them, saying, 'Drink from it, all of you. This is my blood of the covenant, which is poured out for many for the forgiveness of sins' " (Matthew 26:26-28).

The Apostle Paul, explaining the meaning of the Lord's Table to the Corinthians, virtually uses the same words. "For I received from the Lord what I also passed on to you: The Lord Jesus, on the night he was betrayed, took bread, and when he had given thanks, he broke it and said, 'This is my body, which is for you; do this in remembrance of me.' In the same way, after supper he took the cup, saying, 'This cup is the new covenant in my blood; do this, whenever you drink it, in remembrance of me.' For whenever you eat this bread and drink this cup, you proclaim the Lord's death until he comes" (1 Corinthians 11:23-26).

Are the bread and wine in reference to the body and blood of Jesus to be taken figuratively or literally? The church has been and continues to be divided by various interpretations on how the bread and wine are to be understood. You should study the related passages, read what others believe regarding its meaning and why, then form your own convictions. You should, however, allow room for tolerance of the conviction of others regarding their views of the meaning of communion.

* * *

A corollary to this rule is:

When life and action are attributed to inanimate objects, the statement may be considered figurative.

Since this is the same principle viewed another way, one example will bring it into focus.

Micah said, "Hear, O mountains, the Lord's accusation; listen, you everlasting foundations of the earth. For the Lord has a case against his people; he is lodging a charge against Israel" (Micah 6:2). When the writer suggests that the mountains "hear," this should be taken figuratively. He is not suggesting that mountains hear and respond as humans do.

The application of this rule and its corollary in your Bible study should come quite naturally. The context more often than not will tell you immediately whether an inanimate object is used to describe an animate being or is ascribed life and action.

RULE FIFTEEN

When an expression is out of character with the thing described, the statement may be considered figurative.

A group of Jews followed Paul throughout Galatia teaching that Gentile Christians had to be circumcised in order to be saved. They became the object of Paul's wrath in his letter to the Philippians. "Watch out for those dogs, those men who do evil, those mutilators of the flesh. For it is we who are the circumcision, we who worship by the Spirit of God, who glory in Christ Jesus, and who put no confidence in the flesh" (Philippians 3:2-3). When Paul warns his readers to beware of the dogs, the context does not warrant concluding that he is talking about those four-legged furry animals used as house pets in the western world. He is referring to those who insisted on imposing on Gentile Christians all the ordinances of the Old Testament. Therefore, *dogs* should be interpreted figuratively.

Jesus was en route to Jerusalem, teaching on the way, when some Pharisees warned Him that King Herod was out to kill Him. To this warning Jesus responded, "Go tell that fox, 'I will drive out demons and heal people today and tomorrow, and on the third day I will reach my goal'" (Luke 13:32). *Fox* refers to Herod; we know from the rest of the Gospels that Herod isn't the name of a fox, but of an evil king, the one who beheaded John the Baptist.

Therefore we can conclude that *fox* must be interpreted in a figurative rather than in a literal way.

Usually the context will tell you whether the statement is figurative or literal, as well as to whom it refers. If you study parallel passages on the subject, they often will help you find the proper interpretation. For example, John the Baptist said concerning Jesus, "Look, the Lamb of God" (John 1:36). This same phrase is used by Isaiah in his great messianic passage: "He was oppressed and afflicted, yet he did not open his mouth; he was led like a lamb to the slaughter, and as a sheep before her shearers is silent, so he did not open his mouth" (Isaiah 53:7). Here the Messiah is referred to as a lamb brought to the slaughter. This and other related passages throughout the Scriptures substantiate the idea that *lamb* is a figurative expression referring to Christ.

At times the same word may be used figuratively, but with different meanings in different places in the Bible. For example, Peter said, "Be self-controlled and alert. Your enemy the devil prowls around like a roaring lion looking for someone to devour" (1 Peter 5:8). Here the context tells you that *lion* refers to Satan.

The Apostle John said, "Then one of the elders said to me, 'Do not weep! See, the Lion of the tribe of Judah, the Root of David, has triumphed. He is able to open the scroll and its seven seals'" (Revelation 5:5). Here, too, *lion* is used, but the context suggests that it refers to Christ. Generally, you can arrive at the correct interpretation from the context.

Quite often figurative language is used to describe God. In His endeavor to communicate with man, He describes Himself with human qualities. The chronicler said, "The eyes of the Lord range throughout the earth to strengthen those whose hearts are fully committed to him. You have done a foolish thing, and from now on you will be at war" (2 Chronicles 16:9). The *eyes of the Lord* is a figurative phrase.

Again, God said to His servant Moses, "Then I will remove my hand and you will see my back; but my face must not be seen"

(Exodus 33:23). The words *hand, back,* and *face* are all to be interpreted figuratively.

> In order for God to speak to us, He must use human figures and imageries in order to convey the divine truth. Nowhere is this so evident as in the Tabernacle in the Old Testament and the parables of the New Testament. In both situations there is a vehicle (the earthly, human) that bears the spiritual truth. Our understanding of the spiritual world is *analogical*. The fact of God's almightiness is spoken in terms of a right arm because among men the right arm is the stronger of the two and with it the most telling blows are delivered. The fact of pre-eminence is spoken of in terms of sitting at God's right hand because in earthly social situations that is the place of honor. Judgment is spoken of in terms of fire because pain from burning is the most intense known in our more general experience, and the gnawing worm is a symbol of that which is slow, steady, remorseless, and painful. Similarly the glories of heaven are in terms of human experience—costly structures of gold, silver, and jewels, no tears, no death, the tree of life, etc. The question as to whether descriptions of hell and heaven are not literal or symbolic is not the point. In either case they are real, e.g., whether it be literal fire, or that spiritual suffering of which fire is the closest symbol.*

In conclusion, note two important things:

1. *A word cannot mean more than one thing at a time.* It cannot have a figurative and literal meaning at the same time. When a word is given a figurative meaning, as has been the case in the illustrations used in this rule, the literal meaning of the word is replaced.

2. *When at all possible a passage should be interpreted literally.* Only if the literal meaning of the word does not fit should it be interpreted figuratively. The literal meaning of a word is always preferred, unless the context makes it impossible.

---

*From *Protestant Biblical Interpretation* by Bernard Ramm. Baker Book House, Grand Rapids, Michigan.

RULE SIXTEEN

The principal parts and figures of a parable represent certain realities. Consider only these principal parts and figures when drawing conclusions.

The ministry of our Lord Jesus was especially rich with parables. He used them to give dynamic and colorful emphasis to spiritual truths. This rule suggests that you should not exceed the intended limits of the parable; don't try to make it say more than it was intended to say. A look at a couple of parables helps us define their limits.

The first is the parable of the sower.

"While a large crowd was gathering and people were coming to Jesus from town after town, he told this parable:

'A farmer went out to sow his seed. As he was scattering the seed, some fell along the path; it was trampled on, and the birds of the air ate it up. Some fell on rock, and when it came up, the plants withered because they had no moisture. Other seed fell among thorns, which grew up with it and choked the plants. Still other seed fell on good soil. It came up and yielded a crop, a hundred times more than was sown.'

"When he said this, he called out, 'He who has ears to hear, let him hear.'

"His disciples asked him what this parable meant. He said, 'The knowledge of the secrets of the kingdom of God has been given to you, but to others I speak in parables, so that, "though seeing, they may not see; though hearing, they may not understand."

" 'This is the meaning of the parable: The seed is the word of God. Those along the path are the ones who hear, and then the devil comes and takes away the word from their hearts, so that they cannot believe and be saved. Those on the rock are the ones who receive the word with joy when they hear it, but they have no root.

They believe for a while, but in the time of testing they fall away.

The seed that fell among thorns stands for those who hear, but as they go on their way they are choked by life's worries, riches and pleasures, and they do not mature. But the seed on good soil stands for those with a noble and good heart, who hear the word, retain it, and by persevering produce a crop' " (Luke 8:4-15).

This is a good parable to study because Jesus gives us the intended interpretation. These verses can be divided into two paragraphs, the parable itself (verses 4-9) and Jesus' interpretation of it (verses 10-15). The principal parts of the parable, as Jesus makes clear in His explanation, are the *seed* and the *types of soil* in which the seed was sown. Though it is often called the parable of the sower, the sower is not the main character. He is incidental to the story.

The purpose of the parable is to illustrate the different types of responses the Word receives when it is proclaimed. As you study the parable, don't extend its purpose beyond the author's intent.

The second parable is Jesus' story of the Good Samaritan.
"A man was going down from Jerusalem to Jericho, when he fell into the hands of robbers. They stripped him of his clothes, beat him and went away, leaving him half dead. A priest happened to be going down the same road, and when he saw the man, he passed by on the other side. So too, a Levite, when he came to the place and saw him, passed by on the other side. But a Samaritan, as he traveled, came where the man was; and when he saw him, he took pity on him. He went to him and bandaged his wounds, pouring on oil and wine. Then he put the man on his own donkey, took him to an inn and took care of him.

"The next day he took out two silver coins and gave them to the innkeeper. 'Look after him,' he said, 'and when I return, I will reimburse you for any extra expense you may have'" (Luke 10:30-35).

As you interpret this or any other parable, follow this procedure:

1. *Determine the purpose of the parable.* In this example the clue is in the opening question. "But he wanted to justify himself, so he asked Jesus, 'And who is my neighbor?'" (verse 29).

2. *Make sure you explain the different parts of the parable in accordance with the main design.* In this parable there was the need, there were those who should have met the need but didn't and there was the meeting of the need from an unexpected source. These parts illustrate the duty of universal kindness and doing good.

3. *Use only the principal parts of the parable in explaining the lesson.* It is when people try to interpret the details that error can easily creep in. Do not make the parable say too much. For example, you may be tempted to suggest that the oil and wine symbolize the Holy Spirit and the blood of Christ (verse 34), the two ingredients necessary for salvation. To do this is to go beyond the intended purpose of the parable.

Determine the main intent of the parable and stay with that. With some parables you will find this easy to do. For example, Jesus asked, "What shall I compare the kingdom of God to? It is like yeast that a woman took and mixed into a large amount of flour until it worked all through the dough" (Luke 13:20-21). *Yeast* is a figure which designates a reality, *the kingdom of heaven*. With other parables, you will need to study further before drawing your conclusions.

Each parable has one chief point of comparison. Try to relate this one main point to what the speaker was teaching.

RULE SEVENTEEN

Interpret the words of the prophets in their usual, literal and historical sense, unless the context or manner in which they are fulfilled clearly indicates they have a symbolic meaning. Their fulfillment may be in installments, each fulfillment being a pledge of that which is to follow.

In some ways prophecy is to the Christian what politics is to the secular man, a source of much controversy, heat, and emotion. This rule of interpretation is not meant to bias your conviction on prophecy, but simply to establish a guideline for the formation of your convictions. One of the rules already studied states that "Scripture has only one meaning and should be taken literally" (Rule 10, page 179).

Prophecy should be interpreted literally unless the context or some later reference in Scripture indicates otherwise. An example of where a later reference in Scripture indicates that it cannot be taken literally is the prophecy of Malachi regarding the forerunner of Christ. "See, I will send you the prophet Elijah before that great and dreadful day of the Lord comes. He will turn the hearts of the fathers to their children, and the hearts of the children to their fathers; or else I will come and strike the land with a curse" (Malachi 4:5-6).

Malachi says that God will send "Elijah the prophet." When John the Baptist showed up as the forerunner to Jesus Christ, much confusion was generated, which indicates that the people of that day expected prophecy to be fulfilled literally. Jesus, however, said that this prophecy was to have a figurative rather than a literal fulfillment.

On one occasion Jesus stated, "All the prophets and the Law prophesied until John. And if you are willing to accept it, he is the Elijah who was to come" (Matthew 11:13-14). On another occa-

sion, when His disciples asked Him, "Why then do the teachers of
the law say that Elijah must come first?" He answered, "Elijah
comes and will restore all things. But I tell you, Elijah has already
come, and they did not recognize him, but have done to him
everything they wished. In the same way the Son of Man is going
to suffer at their hands." Finally the disciples understood that
Jesus called John the Baptist Elijah (Matthew 17:10-13). John the
Baptist was the fulfillment of Malachi's prophecy.

Such illustrations are the exception rather than the rule in interpreting prophecy. Most prophecies can and should be interpreted
literally. There may be times when you can derive two apparent
meanings from a prophecy. Give preference to the one that would
have been most obvious to the understanding of the original
hearers.

There will also be times when a New Testament writer will
ascribe to an Old Testament passage a prophetic interpretation
when the Old Testament passage does not appear to be prophetic.
You will find an example of this in Hosea. Israel had gone away
from God and was referred to as the Lord's adulterous wife. God
was speaking to Israel when He said, "When Israel was a child, I
loved him; and out of Egypt I called my son" (Hosea 11:1). The
original hearers could conclude, and rightly so, that this referred to
Israel's deliverance from Egypt under Moses. But Matthew quotes
this passage and says it is prophetic of Jesus Christ when Mary and
Joseph returned with Him to Nazareth. "[He was there in Egypt]
until the death of Herod. And so was fulfilled what the Lord had
said through the prophet: 'I called my son out of Egypt'"
(Matthew 2:15).

We note that the Hosea passage is prophetic because Matthew,
writing by inspiration of the Holy Spirit, says it is. In your Bible
study you may not take such liberties. Matthew could because he
wrote by inspiration of the Spirit, and the Spirit knew the correct
interpretation of Hosea since He inspired that also. Matthew,
however, does not tell you why he uses the prophecy from Hosea
in that way.

Often a prophecy is partially fulfilled in one generation with the remainder fulfilled at another time. At the time when the prophecy is given this is not apparent. It becomes clear when a part is fulfilled and the other is not. It would be much like your looking toward the mountains and seeing but one range. As the prophets looked toward the coming Messiah they saw His two advents as one. As you climb the mountain and descend into the valley on the other side, you see a second range of mountains. You look behind you and see a range; you look in front of you and see another. Christians today are like this in that they stand between the two advents of Christ. Behind us was His first coming; in front of us is His second coming.

We can see in a couple of prophecies that this is what happened. God prophesied through Joel, "And afterward, I will pour out my Spirit on all people. Your sons and daughters will prophesy, your old men will dream dreams, your young men will see visions. Even on my servants, both men and women, I will pour out my Spirit in those days. I will show wonders in the heavens and on the earth, blood and fire and billows of smoke. The sun will be turned to darkness and the moon to blood before the coming of the great and dreadful day of the Lord" (Joel 2:28-32).

Peter quotes these exact words on the day of Pentecost (Acts 2:15-21). When the Spirit descended on the church Peter said, "This is what was spoken by the prophet Joel" (Acts 2:16). Indeed the Spirit was poured out upon them. But when did the sun turn into darkness and the moon into blood, "before the coming of the great and dreadful day of the Lord"? This portion of Joel's prophecy refers to the Second Advent and will be fulfilled in the future. From Joel's perspective the two advents appeared as one.

We can observe the same thing in Isaiah's prophecy concerning the Messiah. "The Spirit of the Sovereign Lord is on me, because the Lord has anointed me to preach good news to the poor. He has sent me to bind up the broken-hearted, to proclaim freedom for the captives and release for the prisoners, to proclaim the year of the

Lord's favor and the day of vengeance of our God, to comfort all who mourn'' (Isaiah 61:1-2).

Jesus was in His hometown of Nazareth when He went into the synagogue to worship on the Sabbath. "The scroll of the prophet Isaiah was handed to him. Unrolling it, he found the place where it is written: 'The Spirit of the Lord is on me; therefore he has anointed me to preach good news to the poor. He has sent me to proclaim freedom for the prisoners and recovery of sight for the blind, to release the oppressed, to proclaim the year of the Lord's favor.' Then he rolled up the scroll, gave it back to the attendant and sat down. The eyes of everyone in the synagogue were fastened on him, and he said to them, 'Today this scripture is fulfilled in your hearing' " (Luke 4:17-21).

As you compare the Nazareth declaration with the prophecy in Isaiah, you note that Jesus stopped reading in the middle of the sentence (Isaiah 61:2). He left out the words, "and the day of vengeance of our God, to comfort all who mourn." This part of the prophecy refers to Christ's second coming. Isaiah combined the prophecy regarding the two advents. From his vantage point they appeared as one.

Recognizing this will help you in your Bible study as well as encourage your heart. For the fulfillment of the first installment is a guarantee of its total fulfillment; just as the Holy Spirit is a down payment or guarantee of your inheritance in Christ. Be encouraged. He came the first time as promised. He will come the second time also, as prophesied!

16 Historical Principles of Interpretation

The historical principles deal with the historical setting of the text. To whom and by whom was the book written? Why was it written and what role did the historical setting play in shaping the message of the book? What are the customs and surroundings of the people? These are the kinds of questions you try to answer when considering the historical aspect of your study.

* * *

RULE EIGHTEEN

Since Scripture originated in a historical context, it can be understood only in the light of biblical history.

As you begin your study of a passage, imagine yourself to be a reporter searching for all the facts. Bombard the text with questions such as:

• To whom was the letter (book) written?

• What was the background of the writer?

• What was the experience or occasion that gave rise to the message?

• Who are the main characters in the book?

203

Your objective is to place yourself into the setting at the time the book was written and feel with the people involved. What were their concerns? How did God view their situation? Feel the pulse, if you can, of the author as he expresses himself.

A brief background on the Book of Galatians may help bring the importance of this rule into focus.

The New Testament church as God gave it birth was Jewish. The chosen people of the Old Testament were Hebrews and it was from among the Jews that Jesus chose His disciples. On the day of Pentecost (Acts 2) the non-Jews or Gentiles who were converted were all proselytes of or converts to Judaism. These early followers of Jesus *assumed* that the way to Christ was through the Jewish religion. This was *not* so much a matter of conviction; it was simply the way it happened.

Then Cornelius came to Christ without being circumcised into Judaism (Acts 10), and this caused no small stir among the believers. But this soon quieted down and the subject did not present itself again till the ministry of Paul got under way. Paul, the great scholar of Judaism who was tutored by the famous Rabbi Gamaliel, was God's chosen instrument to refine the doctrine of how Gentiles could become Christians.

While on his first missionary journey, Paul began including Gentile converts in the fellowship of the church without first bringing them through the laws of Judaism. To many Jewish Christians this was unacceptable. The more legalistic of them began to follow Paul's ministry through the Roman province of Galatia (modern-day Turkey), preaching that these Gentile Christians had to be circumcised into the Jewish religion.

Paul was furious. But what could he do? The only Scriptures the church had at that time were the books of the Old Testament, and the Old Testament was what these Judaizers were preaching to the Galatians. When he returned to Jerusalem, Paul attended a council of the church leaders and posed the question to them (Acts 15). Does a Gentile need to become a Jew first before becoming a

Christian? How is a man justified before God? "By faith apart from the works of the law" was Paul's contention.

The leadership at the Jerusalem council agreed with Paul. This marked a major change in the direction of the church. Before this Christianity was not considered to be a separate religion. It was viewed as the natural evolution of Judaism—its fulfillment. From this point on Christianity began to be seen as distinct from the Jewish religion.

How was Paul going to share this news with the Galatians? How could he undo the damage caused by the Judaizers? Paul turned to Old Testament law and proved from the law that the law cannot save. Throughout the letter to the Galatians numerous quotes come from the Old Testament law. The Old Testament law, not Paul, preaches that a man is justified by faith apart from the law.

Understanding the historical background helps in understanding and interpreting the Book of Galatians. This type of study will pay rich dividends and you will find it indispensable in the interpretation of any passage you study.

RULE NINETEEN

Though God's revelation in the Scriptures is progressive, both Old and New Testaments are essential parts of this revelation and form a unit.

It is not uncommon to hear a person say, "The God of the Old Testament is different from the God of the New Testament. In the Old Testament He seems so harsh and judgmental, while in the New Testament He is more loving and gracious." Though this is a commonly held belief, it is not based on fact and, if held, will lead you astray in your interpretation of the Bible. For example, Jesus talked more about hell and the judgment of God than did anyone else in the Bible.

The Old Testament sets the stage for the correct interpretation of the New

Testament. You would have difficulty understanding what the New Testament is talking about if you were unfamiliar with the Old Testament account of such events as the creation and the fall of man. Jesus assumes that His listeners are familiar with the account of how the Israelites were bitten by serpents for their murmurings and delivered by looking to a serpent of brass placed on a pole (Numbers 21). Referring to this event Jesus said, "As Moses lifted up the snake in the desert, so the Son of Man must be lifted up" (John 3:14).

In another sense, the New Testament is a commentary on the Old Testament—how God revealed Himself and how His plan is progressive. The further you read, the more you know about Him and what He plans to do. The New Testament explains the purpose of much that happened in the Old Testament.

The whole Book of Hebrews is an example of this. Unless you are familiar with the Old Testament tabernacle, priesthood, and sacrificial systems, you will have difficulty following the argument in the book. This letter explains the purpose and significance of the Old Testament forms of worship.

People were saved in Old Testament times the same way they are saved in the New. Justification before God has always been by faith. In the Old Testament people were saved by faith in Christ (the Messiah) who *was* to come. In the New Testament we are saved by faith in Christ who *has* come. Jesus said, "I am the way—and the truth and the life. No one comes to the Father except through me" (John 14:6). This is as true for the Old Testament as for the New Testament.

The means and content of this salvation become progressively clearer as Old Testament history unfolds. The prophet Isaiah understood more than Adam, but not as much as we do today. But it is clear that there is a unity between the Old and New Testaments on how people are saved.

The unity of the Scriptures can also be seen in the frequent quotations of the Old Testament in the New. Matthew, showing that Jesus is the fulfillment of the Old Testament prophecies, quotes about 70 times from the Old Testament.

From the fall of Adam to the consummation of history all people need Christ as their Redeemer. All believers are born anew by the Holy Spirit. All receive the same inheritance of heaven. God used different methods to communicate these truths. For example, in the Old Testament one of the signs and seals of the covenant relationship was the observance of the Passover and the eating of the paschal lamb; in the New Testament it is the celebration of the Lord's Supper. But the truths themselves are applicable in both testaments.

God does progressively reveal Himself as history unfolds. But this does not mean that God's standards become progressively higher or that God changes along the way. Rather, it is our understanding of God and His revelation that is progressive. God never changes.

Certain practices in the Old Testament were cancelled by the New Testament, but that is only because they found their fulfillment in Christ. An example of this is the offering of animal sacrifices. When Christ, the perfect sacrifice, offered Himself, there was no longer a need to offer animals. These animal sacrifices were a preview of what God planned to do through Jesus Christ. But the Scriptures make it quite clear that animal sacrifices could not save, "for it is impossible for the blood of bulls and goats to take away sins" (Hebrews 10:4).

God's character in the Old Testament did not change by some process of moral evolution. His perfect holiness is an unchanging, uncompromising part of His nature. For example, Jesus was interrogated on the subject of divorce (Matthew 19). Some argued in its favor on the basis of the law of divorce in the Mosaic code. "Why then," they asked, "did Moses command that a man give his wife a certificate of divorce and send her away?" (verse 7; see Deuteronomy 24:1-4).

Jesus replied, "Because of your hardness of heart, Moses permitted you to divorce your wives; but from the beginning it has not been this way" (verse 8). Jesus said that the laws against divorce were temporarily set aside in the Old Testament because of the moral callousness of the people, not because of any change in the character of God or His moral requirements.

God's revelation of Himself is progressive as you read through the Bible, but His character is unchanging. God's great plan of redemption is the same in both testaments. As you study the Bible you can consider them two parts of the same book, not two separate books.

RULE TWENTY
Historical facts or events become symbols of spiritual truths only if the Scriptures so designate them.

Webster defines *symbol* as "something that stands for or suggests something else by reason or relationship, association, convention, or accidental resemblance; especially a visible sign of something invisible." Though there are differences between the words *symbol, type, allegory, simile,* and *metaphor,* they are closely enough related to combine them here. This rule applies to all of them since they are often used as visible signs of something invisible.

An example of the Bible's use of a historical event as a symbol of a spiritual truth is Paul's statement:

"For I do not want you to be ignorant of the fact, brothers, that our forefathers were all under the cloud and that they all passed through the sea. They were all baptized into Moses in the cloud and in the sea. They all ate the same spiritual food and drank the same spiritual drink; for they drank from the spiritual rock that accompanied them, and that rock was Christ" (1 Corinthians 10:1-4).

Israel's passing through the Red Sea (Exodus 14:22) symbolized their baptism. The rock from which Israel drank (Numbers 20:11) was a type of Christ. In a number of places the writer borrows from a historical event to represent a spiritual truth.

To carry this further than Paul does would be to detract from the literal meaning of the passage. To say that the Red Sea symbolizes the atoning blood of Christ, which offers a safe way to the heavenly Canaan, is an improper interpretation of the Corinthian passage.

This same rule is also applied to allegorizing. As Paul develops his theme in the Book of Galatians, that justification is through faith in Jesus Christ apart from the law, he uses an allegory to drive home his point. Not only does he allegorize Sarah and Hagar (who both bore Abraham children), he tells us he is doing so. "For it is written that Abraham had two sons, one by the slave woman and the other by the free woman. His son by the slave woman was born in the ordinary way; but his son by the free woman was born as the result of a promise. These things may be taken figuratively, for the women represent two covenants. One covenant is from Mount Sinai and bears children who are to be slaves: This is Hagar" (Galatians 4:22-24).

Paul made these interpretations of the Old Testament under the inspiration of the Holy Spirit. He did so occasionally and for specific reasons. But for you to make a habit of allegorizing historical facts is to detract from the literal interpretation of the Bible and to change its intended meaning. The objective of Bible study is to understand the intended meaning of the author, not to pour into his words your own content.

A negative example often helps, especially when a passage has been used to symbolize something that it should not have.

A common Scripture so used is the Book of Philemon. Paul is writing to his good friend Philemon on behalf of a runaway slave, Onesimus. Onesimus, the slave of Philemon, had robbed his master and fled to Rome. There, through Paul, he became a Christian and Paul was sending him back to his master in Colosse with this letter. Paul's plea to his friend is that he forgive Onesimus and restore him as "a dear brother." "If he has done you any wrong or owes you anything, charge it to me," was Paul's request (verses 16, 18). It is a beautiful example of Christian love, forgiveness, and brotherhood.

For no apparent reason many allegorize this book, equating Philemon with God, Onesimus with mankind and Paul with Christ. Christ (Paul) intercedes with the Father (Philemon) on behalf of the converted runaway (Onesimus). Paul does not make this analogy here or in any other passage. Neither should you.

This kind of allegorizing is different from making application. For example, we can say that what Paul was asking of Philemon on behalf of Onesimus is what Christ did for us. We should in the same way forgive those who have wronged us. Our application is drawn from the historical event or fact without changing the intended meaning of the fact.

17 Theological Principles of Interpretation

Theology is the study of God and His relation to the world. The source book for this study is the Bible. Theology seeks to draw conclusions on various broad and important topics in the Bible. What is God like? What is the nature of man? What is a proper doctrine of salvation? These are the kinds of subjects with which theology deals. Theological principles are those broad rules that deal with the formation of doctrine. For example, how can we tell if a doctrine is truly biblical? One of our theological principles will seek to answer this.

* * *

RULE TWENTY-ONE

You must understand the Bible grammatically before you can understand it theologically.

Another way to state this rule is to say, "You must understand what the passage says before you can expect to understand what it means." An example of this may be seen in this Pauline statement:

"But the gift is not like the trespass. For if the many died by the trespass of the one man, how much more did God's grace and the gift that came by the grace of the one man, Jesus Christ, overflow to the many! Again, the gift of God is not like the result of the one man's sin: The judgment followed one sin and brought condemnation, but the gift followed many trespasses and brought justification. For if, by the trespass of the one man, death reigned through that one man, how much more will those who receive God's abundant provision of grace and of the gift of righteousness reign in life through the one man, Jesus Christ.

"Consequently, just as the result of one trespass was condemnation for all men, so also the result of one act of righteousness was justification that brings life for all men. For just as through the disobedience of the one man the many were made sinners, so also through the obedience of the one man the many will be made righteous.

"The law was added so that the trespass might increase. But where sin increased, grace increased all the more, so that, just as sin reigned in death, so also grace might reign through righteousness to bring eternal life through Jesus Christ our Lord" (Romans 5:15-21).

You must study this passage carefully to understand what Paul is saying. He is comparing Christ with Adam. Just as you are considered to be unrighteous because of the sin of Adam, so you are considered to be righteous because of what Jesus Christ did. The sin of Adam was imputed to you, even though you did nothing to deserve it; so also the righteousness of Christ was imputed to you, even though you did nothing to deserve it. This, in part, is what the passage says.

From this we can draw certain conclusions. For example, we see that imputation does not affect your moral character, but your legal standing. When you were considered righteous because of the work of Christ your moral character was not changed; you did not become morally righteous and perfect, only legally righteous and perfect in the sight of God. This is why some non-Christians are more righteous in their behavior than Christians.

Another example is this statement: "If we deliberately keep on sinning after we have received the knowledge of the truth, no sacrifice for sins is left" (Hebrews 10:26). Many use this verse to teach that it is possible for a Christian to lose his salvation. A study of this verse in its context leads you to an entirely different conclusion. This passage speaks specifically to Jews who believed in animal sacrifices in anticipation of the coming Messiah, not realizing that He had already come.

The writer to the Hebrews sets forth the fact of Jesus' sacrifice. This statement says that once these Jews understood the reason for Jesus' death and deliberately ignored it, if they returned to their sacrifices there would be no future sacrifice provided by God.

You can see how such a problem can be alleviated by using sound grammatical principles (Rules 10-17). You must understand what a passage says before you draw any doctrinal conclusions from it.

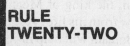

**RULE
TWENTY-TWO**

**A doctrine cannot
be considered
biblical unless it
sums up and
includes all that the
Scriptures say
about it.**

It is immediately apparent that this is an important procedure in Bible study, just as it is in all of life. Solomon warned, "He who answers before listening—that is his folly and his shame" (Proverbs 18:13). It is foolish to come to a conclusion before hearing all of the arguments. So also, it is a mistake to come to conclusions regarding a certain doctrine before studying all the Bible says on the subject.

For example, there are numerous passages in the New Testament which tell you that you are not under the law. "For we maintain that a man is justified by faith apart from observing the law" (Romans 3:28). "But if you are led by the Spirit, you are not under law" (Galatians 5:18). When reading such statements, can you conclude that the grace of God frees you from any obligation to live a disciplined, holy life?

Not at all. Such a conclusion would be countered by statements such as: "What shall we say, then? Shall we go on sinning so that grace may increase? By no means! We died to sin; how can we live in it any longer? Or don't you know that all of us who were baptized into Christ Jesus were baptized into his death? We were therefore buried with him through baptism into death in order that, just as Christ was raised from the dead through the glory of the Father, we too may live a new life" (Romans 6:1-4).

This is where a topical type of Bible study proves useful. You take a theme, idea, or teaching and study all the passages on the subject. Three kinds of parallel studies are:

1. *Word Parallels*. You may, for example, decide to study the life of Balaam. The main passage regarding him is found in Numbers 22–24. He was one of God's prophets who allowed

himself to be enticed by an invitation from the king of Moab to curse Israel. What conclusions can you draw from his life? A study of what the New Testament writers say of Balaam will help in your evaluation. Peter tells us that he "loved the wages of wickedness" (2 Peter 2:15). Jude tells us that he was greedy for profit (Jude 11). John further informs us that he counseled the king of Moab to "entice the Israelites to sin by eating food sacrificed to idols and by committing sexual immorality" (Revelation 2:14).

2. *Idea Parallels*. An idea parallel differs from a word parallel in that you can't cross-reference the word, as you can with Balaam. The idea is more encompassing than any one word. An example might be the whole question of authority. The chief priests and elders asked Jesus, "By what authority are you doing these things? . . . And who gave you this authority?" (Matthew 21:23). You would want to study not only this passage in Matthew 21, but many other passages in the Scriptures on the subject. Moses records man's first rebellion against authority (Genesis 3); Scripture also shows God dealing severely with those who rejected the authority of one of His servants (Numbers 16).

3. *Doctrinal Parallels*. This would include topical studies on the great doctrines of the Bible such as the attributes of God, the nature of man, redemption, justification, and sanctification.

In this type of study you gather all the pieces of information together and draw a conclusion. It is much like putting the pieces of a puzzle together. This is called *inductive reasoning*, that process of reasoning from all the parts to the whole. If you were going to study the doctrine of the church inductively, for instance, you would find all the passages on the subject, study each one, and then put them all together to form your conclusions.

In Rule 24 we will consider a principle dealing with *deductive reasoning*, but we need to look briefly at deductive reasoning here. This is the method that approaches the study by looking at the whole and coming to conclusions regarding the smaller pieces, again, like a jigsaw puzzle. From the whole puzzle you can conclude certain things about the individual pieces. Deductive reasoning is that process of reasoning from the general to the particular. An example of deductive reasoning is:

● *First Premise*—If we ask according to His will, God hears us (1 John 5:14-15).

● *Second Premise*—Sanctification is according to God's will (1 Thessalonians 4:3).

● *Conclusion*—When we pray for our sanctification, God hears us.

The reason we are discussing deductive reasoning here is the need to relate it to your inductive study. As a general rule, the first premise in your *deductive* study can be made only after *inductive* study has brought you to the understanding of what the premise is and means. Other examples of *deductive* study may be seen in Rule 24.

Inductive Bible study is extremely important in developing your convictions. As you study the parts you are able to get an increasingly clearer picture of the whole. If you are not involved in an inductive study, you should be. For if your convictions regarding the doctrines of the Bible have been formed by what others have told you, rather than by your own personal investigation of the Scriptures, will they stand during times of testing? You cannot count on remaining faithful during times of adversity on the basis of hearsay. You must dig into the Scriptures for yourself and get your own convictions.

Unfortunately, as is so often the case, what is important requires hard work. This is true in the formation of vital convictions. Careful and thorough Bible study is required. No shortcut exists. Your doctrinal studies form the backbone of your spiritual convictions, and these in turn can be arrived at only by studying all that the Bible says on a given subject.

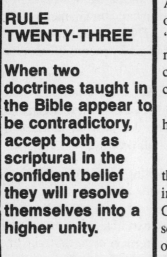

RULE TWENTY-THREE

When two doctrines taught in the Bible appear to be contradictory, accept both as scriptural in the confident belief they will resolve themselves into a higher unity.

A number of seeming contradictions or paradoxes exist in the Scriptures. "Seeming" because they really are not. They appear contradictory because the finite mind of man cannot comprehend the infinite mind of God.

Some familiar paradoxes to the human mind are:

1. *The Trinity*. We do not serve three Gods, but one, yet *each* Person in the Godhead is fully and completely God, not just one-third God. In essence we must conclude that one plus one plus one equals one. No human illustration can adequately explain this theological mystery. It is utterly beyond our comprehension.

2. *The dual nature of Christ*. Jesus Christ is all God and all Man. He is not half God and half man; yet He is not two persons but one. Again one plus one equals one.

3. *The origin and existence of evil*. Logically the human mind deduces that one of two things must be true. Either God created evil, or it is coeternal with Him. The Bible leads us to believe that neither is true. It is a mystery.

4. *The sovereign election of God and the responsibility of man*. Paul states that God has chosen the believer in His sovereign counsel before the foundation of the world (Ephesians 1:4). Yet Peter says, "The Lord is not slow in keeping his promise, as some understand slowness. He is patient with you, not wanting anyone to perish, but everyone to come to repentance" (2 Peter 3:9). All through the Scriptures there is a well-meant offer of the gospel to

all men. Man is viewed as a responsible moral agent who is held accountable by God, and "everyone who calls on the name of the Lord will be saved" (Romans 10:13). There is no way that our minds can reconcile these two difficult and seemingly opposite truths.

Of all the difficulties none causes as much emotional controversy as the last one. Possibly this is because the first three strike us as rather academic, while the fourth touches our moral sensibilities. It has to do with man's eternal destiny.

When the Bible leaves two "conflicting" doctrines unreconciled, so must you. Living in tension is not pleasant, but you must take care not to lose biblical balance in seeking to relieve the tension. Do not wrench the Scriptures apart in an attempt to force two "conflicting" doctrines into compromise.

You can make application of such "conflicting" doctrines by preaching the right doctrine to the right person. For example, as a Christian you preach to yourself that God chose you; you did not choose Him. If the choice had been yours, you would have voted *against* Him. All you are and have is a gift of God's grace. This should fill you with humility and meekness.

But you can boldly proclaim to the non-Christian that God loves him. For Jesus Himself said, "God so loved the *world* that he gave his one and only Son" (John 3:16).

Our allegiance is not first and primarily to a system of theology, but to the Scripture. When you interpret the Bible, don't allow human logic to make it say any more or less than it in fact says. To the degree that the Scriptures speak with clarity, you may speak with clarity. When the Scriptures are silent, you must remain silent. Where the Bible teaches two "conflicting" doctrines, you must follow its example and hold to both, keeping each in perfect balance with the other.

RULE TWENTY-FOUR

A teaching merely implied in Scripture may be considered biblical when a comparison of related passages supports it.

The Jewish religious community in Jesus' time was split into various groups: Herodians, Essenes, Zealots, Sadducees, and Pharisees. These last two groups were divided over certain doctrinal issues, notably the resurrection of the dead. The Pharisees believed it; the Sadducees denied it.

On one occasion Jesus found Himself in an argument with the Sadducees on this question of the afterlife. Did the Old Testament really teach it? Listen to Jesus' line of reasoning, "Now about the dead rising—have you not read in the book of Moses, in the account of the bush, how God said to him, 'I am the God of Abraham, the God of Isaac, and the God of Jacob'? He is not the God of the dead, but of the living. You are badly mistaken!" (Mark 12:26-27).

The Lord said that the resurrection could be proved from the Old Testament (Exodus 3:15), where God identified Himself as the God of Abraham, Isaac, and Jacob. Since God is the God of the living, these three men must be alive or resurrected. This is deductive reasoning, and could be charted in the following form:

• *First Premise*—God is the God of the living.
• *Second Premise*—God is the God of Abraham, Isaac, and Jacob.
• *Conclusion*—Abraham, Isaac, and Jacob are among the living.

The doctrine of the resurrection is *implied* in the Old Testament, reasoned Christ. It is not expressly stated in the Old Testament that there is a resurrection of the dead, but when you compare related passages on the subject you deduce that such is true.

Another example is the question of admitting women to the Lord's Table. We conclude that they should be admitted to com-

munion, but not on the basis of any specific command or example
in the Bible, since none is given. We assume that they should be
admitted on the basis of the *implied* teachings of the New Testament. In this example, the deductive process is as follows:

When Paul wrote to the Corinthian church, it is obvious that
women were members of the church. ''My brothers, some from
Chloe's household have informed me that there are quarrels among
you'' (1 Corinthians 1:11). ''The churches in the province of Asia
send you greetings. Aquila and Priscilla greet you warmly in the
Lord, and so does the church that meets at their house'' (1 Corinthians 16:19). Both Chloe and Priscilla were women. Paul also
instructed the church on how to conduct itself at the Lord's Supper
(1 Corinthians 11). Therefore we infer from these passages of
Scripture that women partook of communion.

• *First Premise*—The Corinthian church received instruction
on communion.

• *Second Premise*—Women were part of the church at
Corinth.

• *Conclusion*—Women may partake in communion.

You must be certain the deductions you make are truly implied
in the Scriptures from which you derive them, and that you have
investigated and compared related passages on the subject. It is
easy to misuse the principle and arrive at unbiblical conclusions.
This is frequently done with passages that give us examples from
the life of Christ.

Mark says of Jesus, ''Very early in the morning, while it was
dark, Jesus got up, left the house and went off to a solitary place,
where he prayed'' (Mark 1:35). From this we are likely to deduce
that a faithful Christian should have his quiet time in the early
morning.

• *First Premise*—The believer is to be Christlike.

• *Second Premise*—Christ had early morning devotions.

• *Conclusion*—The believer should have early morning devotions.

Yet, you will remember that under Rule 5, *Biblical examples are authoritative only when supported by a command,* we discussed this, using this very example. Using the reasoning spelled out here you can properly conclude that you *may* have early morning devotions, but not that you *must* have them. This passage supports the validity of the quiet time in the morning, but not its necessity.

You cannot violate one principle of interpretation in order to substantiate another. Your Bible study must take all the principles into account if you are to make a proper interpretation.

Believing something to be true because of an implied teaching in the Bible is not only valid, but also necessary (Jesus' argument for the resurrection from the Old Testament, for example). Like Rule 23, however, such reasoning requires careful study, and this is hard work; but the fruit of such labor is rewarding and well worth the effort.

Do not be afraid to use deductive reasoning in your Bible study. In everyday life, you do it all the time. Suppose you are working for a data processing firm and you have been on this job for some time. Today, as you are going to work, you find yourself returning to that job even though your employer did not specifically ask you to come in this day. You are doing it because you reason:

- *First Premise*—Your employer wants you as an employee.
- *Second Premise*—Your employer has had you on this particular job for some time.
- *Conclusion*—Your employer wants you on that job today.

Think back on the number of times you have *deduced* something to be true on the basis of certain facts; or how someone *implied* something to be true even though he did not specifically say so.

This process is valid in your Bible study as well, providing you abide carefully by Rule 24.

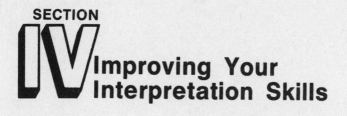

SECTION

IV Improving Your Interpretation Skills

18 Practicing Your Skills

I have stated the rules of biblical interpretation so that they can be easily understood by the average layperson: the questions in this chapter are designed the same way. I have sought to make them sufficiently challenging and easily understandable.

The questions that accompany each of the interpretation rules vary in difficulty. Depending on your level of proficiency in interpreting the Bible, you will find some to be too easy, others to be quite difficult, and still others impossible. The questions should, however, help you come to grips with the application of the principle. If you encounter a question that is beyond your ability, don't be discouraged. Simply pass over it and go on to the next question.

This chapter is best used in a group study. Each person should answer the questions before discussing the answers with the group. Through this process of personal investigation and group sharing, learning can best take place.

At the end of the chapter you will find a series of case studies designed to incorporate as many of the principles as possible. They represent typical situations encountered in daily Christian experience. Like the questions and answers, they are best studied individually and then discussed in a group.

As you begin, do a section at a time, rewording the principles. Don't merely answer the questions, but take time to think through the implications of each rule. Use your Bible, concordance, Bible dictionary, and any other useful tools you may have. After working through a section, seek to apply the rules in your Bible study. Don't be in a hurry to fill in the blanks. Take time to work through the principles carefully so that they become yours. With practice and use, they should appreciably enhance your Bible study.

INTRODUCTION

An assumption is an unprovable basis for action.

In the blanks below list the references to as many verses as you can that support these assumptions.

1. The rules of interpretation covered in this study assume the following to be true:

a. The Bible is authoritative. _____

b. The Bible contains its own laws of interpretation, which, when properly understood and applied, will yield the correct meaning to a given passage. _____

c. The primary aim of interpretation is to discover the author's meaning. _____

d. Language can communicate spiritual truth. _____

Do you agree or disagree with these assumptions? Why? _____

_____

_____

_____

_____

2. List any other assumptions under which you operate as you study the Bible. _____

_____

_____

_____

3. Relate, with references, any incidents in Jesus' ministry that would seem to indicate that He believed these assumptions to be true.

a. _____

_____

b. _____

_____

c. _____

_____

d. _____

_____

General Principles of Interpretation

RULE ONE ⎯⎯⎯⎯ **Work from the assumption that the Bible is authoritative.**	1. List as many religious beliefs as you can that you or other Christians hold that are not based on Scripture but tradition. ⎯⎯⎯⎯⎯⎯⎯ ⎯⎯⎯⎯⎯⎯⎯⎯⎯⎯⎯⎯ ⎯⎯⎯⎯⎯⎯⎯⎯⎯⎯⎯⎯

2. What are some spiritual truths that you embrace that come not from the Bible but from reason? (Examples may include polygamy, gambling, use of narcotics, etc.) ⎯⎯⎯⎯⎯⎯⎯⎯⎯⎯⎯⎯

⎯⎯⎯⎯⎯⎯⎯⎯⎯⎯⎯⎯⎯⎯⎯⎯⎯⎯⎯⎯⎯⎯⎯⎯⎯⎯⎯⎯⎯⎯⎯

⎯⎯⎯⎯⎯⎯⎯⎯⎯⎯⎯⎯⎯⎯⎯⎯⎯⎯⎯⎯⎯⎯⎯⎯⎯⎯⎯⎯⎯⎯⎯

3. To put into practice the statement "The Bible is authoritative," a response of faith is necessary. *Faith,* or *risk taking,* is commitment before knowledge (Hebrews 11:1). Name several experiences in everyday life in which you "know" *only* after you commit yourself. ⎯⎯⎯⎯⎯⎯⎯⎯⎯⎯⎯⎯⎯⎯⎯⎯⎯⎯⎯

⎯⎯⎯⎯⎯⎯⎯⎯⎯⎯⎯⎯⎯⎯⎯⎯⎯⎯⎯⎯⎯⎯⎯⎯⎯⎯⎯⎯⎯⎯⎯

⎯⎯⎯⎯⎯⎯⎯⎯⎯⎯⎯⎯⎯⎯⎯⎯⎯⎯⎯⎯⎯⎯⎯⎯⎯⎯⎯⎯⎯⎯⎯

4. Give an example of one area of your life in which God through the Bible is asking you to obey Him before you know the outcome (see Ecclesiastes 11:1; Matthew 11:28–30). _____

_____

_____

5. Study each of the following passages and state how God would have you respond in light of the fact that the Bible is authoritative:

Leviticus 19:11 _____

_____

Matthew 19:21 _____

_____

Acts 15:36–41 _____

_____

RULE TWO

The Bible interprets itself; Scripture best explains Scripture.

1. Interpret Matthew 3:9 in light of Romans 9:6–7. _____

_____

_____

_____

2. Pick two cross references that best explain 2 Corinthians 5:10. _____

_____

3. Using Matthew 27:33–50, Mark 15:22–41, Luke 23:33–44, and John 19:17–37, list the order of events at the crucifixion. (Do not use any commentaries or Bible study aids.) _____

_____

_____

4. Cross reference the Beatitudes for clarification and support (Matthew 5:3–11).

a. Poor in spirit _____

b. Meek _____

c. Mourn _____

d. Merciful _____

e. Pure in heart _____

f. Peacemakers _____

5. Give one illustration of Jesus' use of the Old Testament to explain His teaching. _____

RULE THREE

_____

Saving faith and the Holy Spirit are necessary for us to understand and properly interpret the Scriptures.

1. Meditate on 1 Corinthians 2:6–14.

a. What is the secret to understanding God's wisdom? _____

_____

b. According to verse 11, what is the correlation between the thoughts of man and the thoughts of God? _____

_____

c. How does the unenlightened person respond to the truth of God? (verse 14) _____

_____

2. List at least three illustrations of spiritual blindness in the Bible. _____

_____

3. If one cannot properly understand the Scriptures without the aid of the Holy Spirit, is there any advantage in encouraging non-Christians to study the Bible? _____ Explain. _____

_____

_____

4. What was Jesus' promise concerning the Holy Spirit and enlightenment in John 16:13? _____

_____

RULE FOUR
_____
Interpret person-al experience in the light of Scripture and not Scripture in light of personal experience.

1. Meditate on Matthew 5:27–48.

a. What three issues of the day was Jesus here addressing?
(1) _____
(2) _____
(3) _____

b. What did Jesus say were the positions of the people on these issues?
(1) _____
(2) _____
(3) _____

c. What did Jesus say were God's positions?
(1) _____

(2) _____

(3) _____

d. In light of Rule Four why do you think there were differences between how Jesus saw the issues and how the people saw them? _____

_____

_____

_____

2. In the book, speaking in tongues and deficit spending are two illustrations of how people interpret the Bible in light of their own experience.

a. Give a different example of your doing the same thing. _____

_____

b. Give two additional examples of your observing it happening in the life of the church. _____

_____

_____

_____

_____

3. Personal experience is an important part of the Christian life. Name three areas in which you feel it has validity.

a. _____

b. _____

c. _____

RULE FIVE

Biblical examples are authoritative only when supported by a command.

1. In light of Jesus's example, what is our obligation toward Mark 1:35? ___

_____

_____

_____

_____

2. What practical value can Mark 1:35 be for the believer? _____

_____

_____

_____

Corollary: The believer is free to do anything that the Bible does not prohibit.

3. Your spiritual leadership comes to you with the command to not marry, thus following the example of Jesus and Paul.

a. What should your response be? _____

_____

_____

b. What are the limits of authority your spiritual leadership has over you? _____

_____

_____

_____

c. How do we guard against misusing our freedom and liberty in Christ? _____

_____

_____

d. Give an illustration of someone you feel has misused their Christian liberty and state why. _____

_____

_____

_____

RULE SIX

The primary purpose of the Bible is to change our lives, not increase our knowledge.

1. Meditate on Matthew 13:10–18 and write out in your own words why Jesus is speaking in parables. _____

_____

_____

_____

_____

_____

2. How does what He is saying affect our obedience and our personal application of the Bible? _____

_____

_____

3. Meditate on 2 Timothy 3:16. Define the following words and explain how the Word affects your life in each of these areas:

a. *Teaching* _____

_____

Its effect _____

_____

b. *Reproof* _____

_____

Its effect _____

_____

c. *Correction* _____

_____

Its effect _____

_____

d. *Training* _____

_____

Its effect _____

_____

Corollary: Some passages are not to be applied in the same way they were applied at the time they were written.

4. Interpret Matthew 5:23–24 and write out a possible application of Jesus' statement for today. _____

_____

_____

Corollary: When you apply a passage, it must be in keeping with a correct interpretation.

5. Interpret Isaiah 43:4 in the light of its context and evaluate the following application: "Jesus gave His life in exchange for people. Here in Isaiah 43:4 He promises that I can do the same. On the basis of this promise I will trust Him to give me people in exchange for my life." _____

_____

_____

6. Meditate on John 9:4. Interpret the verse in light of its context and write a correct application. _____

_____

_____

**RULE
SEVEN**
———————
**Each Christian
has the right
and responsibil-
ity to investigate
and interpret
the Word of
God for himself.**

1. In John 8:31 we find Jesus laying down one of the conditions for being His disciple. Write out what you understand to be the meaning of His condition and its implications. _____

_____

_____

_____

_____

_____

2. Meditate on 2 Timothy 2:15.

a. According to the context of this verse, with what is the "Word of Truth" contrasted? _____

_____

_____

_____

b. According to 2 Timothy 2:15 when is the Lord "well pleased"? _____

_____

_____

_____

c. How can the believer insure that he or she is correctly handling the Scriptures? _____

_____

_____

3. Write out a modern-day application of Acts 17:11. _____

_____

_____

_____

4. Evaluate your application of Rule Seven in light of the following ways in which one can assimilate the Word of God.

   a. Hear _____

_____

   b. Read _____

_____

   c. Study _____

_____

   d. Memorize _____

_____

   e. Meditate _____

_____

RULE EIGHT

Church history is important but not decisive in the interpretation of Scripture.

1. Name several doctrines or truths that you embrace that are implied in the Bible but clarified in the course of church history. _____
_____
_____

2. Name several doctrines or truths that other Christian groups believe but which you reject because you do not find them in the Scriptures. (Avoid cults and sects in your examples.) _____
_____
_____

Corollary: The church does not determine what the Bible teaches; the Bible determines what the church teaches.

3. Give a current illustration of evangelical Christianity wrestling with this corollary. _____
_____
_____

4. Select from the life of Christ in the Gospels two examples in which this corollary was tested. _____
_____
_____
_____

5. What was Jesus' view of the traditions of Israel's religious leaders as seen in Matthew 23:13–23? _____

_____

_____

_____

RULE NINE

The promises of God throughout the Bible are available to the Holy Spirit for the believers of every generation.

1. Meditate on 2 Peter 1:3–4 and answer the following questions:

a. What is the source of the promises to which Peter refers? _____

_____

b. What is (are) the purpose(s) of the promises? _____

_____

2. Give several examples of *general promises* from the Bible on which you daily rely, for example, 1 John 1:9. _____

_____

_____

3. Give at least one example of a *specific promise* from God's Word that you have claimed for your own life. _____

_____

a. To whom was this promise first given? _____

_____

b. What were the circumstances surrounding its being given? _

_____

c. What led you to believe it was a promise God was giving you to claim? _____

_____

_____

4. Find two conditional and two unconditional promises from the Scriptures.

a. Conditional _____

_____

b. Unconditional _____

_____

5. God's promises do not eliminate risk in the Christian life because God requires that we walk by faith (Hebrews 11:6). What function have the promises played in your spiritual development? _____

_____

_____

_____

6. Give an example of how one could improperly claim a promise of God. _____

_____

_____

Grammatical Principles of Interpretation

1. Interpreters disagree about the interpretation of Luke 16:19–31—whether it should be taken literally or as a parable. Read the passage carefully. Do you think it is a parable or something that actually happened? State the reasons for your conclusion. _____ _____ _____ _____ _____

2. Give an illustration of a biblical statement or command that some people have a hard time taking literally (for instance, Jesus' comment on hell as in Matthew 25:41). _____ _____

3. In Matthew 6:19–34 Jesus is discussing a proper value system with His disciples.

a. How do you interpret verse 25? _____

_____

b. In light of Rule Ten write out an application of this verse for your life. _____

_____

4. Meditate on Mark 7:1–23. In what ways was this principle violated by the religious leaders of Jesus' day? _____

_____

| **RULE ELEVEN**

 Interpret words in harmony with their meaning in the times of the author. | 1. In James's epistle he constantly refers to his "brothers" (James 1:16; 2:1; 3:1, and others). Who are these brothers? How is James using this word? _____ |

_____

2. According to the context, the "lion" is likened to whom?

a. Deuteronomy 33:20 _____

b. 1 Kings 13:24 _____

c. Proverbs 19:12 _____

d. Proverbs 28:1 _____

e. Ezekiel 22:25 _____

f. 1 Peter 5:8 _____

g. Revelation 5:5 _____

3. Look up "atonement." What is its root meaning in the Old Testament? (Use a concordance, Bible dictionary, or commentary.) _____

4. Using a Bible dictionary or Bible encyclopedia determine the meaning of the following words:

a. Argob (2 Kings 15:25) _____

b. Carnelian (RSV) or Sardius (KJV) (Revelation 21:20) _____

_____

c. Bishopric (KJV) or office (RSV) or Episkopen (Greek) (Acts 1:20) _____

d. Phylacteries (Matthew 23:5) _____

_____

e. Feast of Booths (Leviticus 23:33–44) _____

_____

f. Emerods (KJV)/tumors (RSV) (1 Samuel 5:6) _____

_____

g. Corban (Mark 7:11) _____

RULE TWELVE

Interpret a word in relation to its sentence and context.

1. The following all use the same word for house. Look up each reference and give the meaning of "house" from its context.

a. Luke 1:27 _____

b. Luke 11:17 _____

c. Acts 2:36 _____

d. Acts 10:2 _____

e. Acts 19:16 _____

2. The same word for body is used in the following verses. After studying the context, record the way the word is used.

   a. Matthew 5:29 _____

   b. Romans 7:4 _____

   c. Ephesians 2:16 _____

   d. Hebrews 13:3 _____

3. Study Romans 7:1–8:4 and note Paul's use of the word "law." How many different kinds of law can you find? Note them. _____

_____

_____

4. The Greek word for "fruit" is *karpos*. In the New Testament it is used in various ways.

   a. Study the following passages and determine the meaning of "fruit" in light of its context.

      (1) Matthew 3:8 _____

      (2) Matthew 21:19 _____

      (3) Luke 1:42 _____

      (4) John 15:2 _____

      (5) Romans 1:13 _____

      (6) Galatians 5:22 _____

   b. How does the meaning of "fruit" differ in John 15:2, Romans 1:13, and Galatians 5:22? _____

_____

   c. What practical differences or consequences will your answer to "b" make? _____

_____

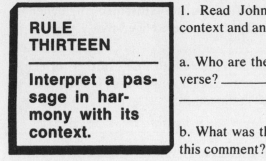

RULE THIRTEEN

Interpret a passage in harmony with its context.

1. Read John 3:30 along with its context and answer the following:

a. Who are the "he" and "I" in this verse? _____
_____

b. What was the issue that prompted this comment? _____

c. In the illustration of the bridal party, who is John? _____
_____

2. Read 1 Thessalonians 4:16–17 and note its context.

a. Why does Paul mention the resurrection of God's people?
_____

b. What concern did the Thessalonians have that prompted Paul to give this assurance? _____

3. Interpret Luke 16:9 in light of its context. _____
_____

RULE FOURTEEN

When an inanimate object is used to describe a living being, the statement may be considered figurative.

1. The great "I am" passages in John regarding Jesus are an example of this rule. Find three more examples of this rule in the New Testament and three in the Old Testament.

a. New Testament _____
_____

b. Old Testament _____
_____

Corollary: When life and action are attributed to inanimate objects, the statement may be considered figurative.

2. Psalm 24:9 and Isaiah 55:12 are illustrations of this corollary. Using a concordance, find two other illustrations in each the Old Testament and the New Testament.

a. Old Testament _____

_____

b. New Testament _____

_____

RULE FIFTEEN

When an expression is out of character with the thing described, the statement may be considered figurative.

1. Read the following passages and interpret which part should be taken literally and which part figuratively.

a. Malachi 3:1–3 _____

_____

_____

b. Isaiah 59:1–2 _____

_____

_____

c. Revelation 5:5–7 _____

_____

_____

d. Exodus 19:16–20 _____

_____

_____

RULE SIXTEEN

The principal parts and figures of a parable represent certain realities. Consider only these principal parts and figures when drawing conclusions.

1. Consider Judges 9:8–15.

a. What is the purpose of this parable? _____
_____
_____

b. What are the principal parts and the realities they represent? _____
_____
_____
_____

2. Meditate on Luke 18:1–8.

a. What is the purpose of this parable? _____
_____

_____

b. What are the principal parts and the realities they represent?

_____

_____

_____

_____

c. What are some possible ways of making the parable say more than Jesus intended it to say? _____

_____

_____

_____

**RULE
SEVENTEEN**

Interpret the
words of the
prophets in their
usual, literal
and historical
sense, unless
the context or
manner in which
they are fulfilled
clearly indicates
they have a
symbolic mean-
ing. Their
fulfillment may
be in install-
ments, each
fulfillment being
a pledge of that
which is to fol-
low.

1. Try to put yourself in the place of
one who lived before the first advent
of Christ. You have just read Isaiah
9:6–7. Applying Rule Seventeen to
these verses, what conclusions regarding the future could you draw?

_____
_____
_____

2. Zechariah is divided between Israel present (chapters 1–8) and Israel
future (chapters 9–12). In the prophetic portion (9–12) the prophet
predicts both advents of Christ, but
views them as one. Read through
Zechariah 9–12 and from your vantage of living between the two advents write out which passages refer
to which._____

_____
_____
_____
_____
_____

Historical Principles of Interpretation

RULE EIGHTEEN

Since Scripture originated in a historical context, it can be understood only in light of Biblical history.

1. Using a Bible dictionary, Bible encyclopedia, or commentary, determine the historical setting for the following:

a. Isaiah 39:1–8 _____

_____

_____

_____

b. Who are the Philistines? From where did they come and what ultimately happened to them? _____

_____

_____

_____

_____

c. Jeremiah 52:31–34 _____

_____

_____

_____

d. Philippians 1:12–14 _____

_____

_____

_____

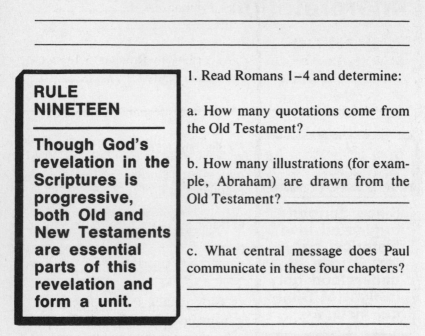

RULE NINETEEN

Though God's revelation in the Scriptures is progressive, both Old and New Testaments are essential parts of this revelation and form a unit.

1. Read Romans 1–4 and determine:

a. How many quotations come from the Old Testament? _____

b. How many illustrations (for example, Abraham) are drawn from the Old Testament? _____
_____

c. What central message does Paul communicate in these four chapters?
_____
_____
_____

d. Why does he so frequently refer to the Old Testament in communicating this message? _____

_____

_____

2. Find an illustration of God's wrath in the New Testament.

_____

3. Find an illustration of God's grace and mercy in the Old Testament. _____

_____

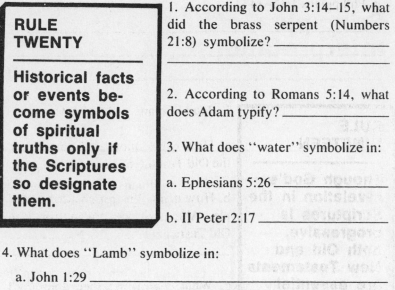

RULE TWENTY

Historical facts or events become symbols of spiritual truths only if the Scriptures so designate them.

1. According to John 3:14-15, what did the brass serpent (Numbers 21:8) symbolize? _____

_____

2. According to Romans 5:14, what does Adam typify? _____

3. What does "water" symbolize in:

a. Ephesians 5:26 _____

b. II Peter 2:17 _____

4. What does "Lamb" symbolize in:

   a. John 1:29 _____

   b. Luke 15:6 _____

5. Clement of Alexandria, an early church father, interpreted Exodus 15:1 as follows: "The many-limbed and brutal affection, lust, with the rider mounted, who gives the reins to pleasures, he casts them into the sea—throwing them away to the disorders of the world." Evaluate this interpretation in light of Rule Twenty.

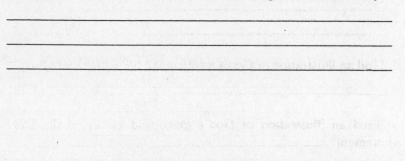

Theological Principles of Interpretation

<table>
<tr><td>

RULE TWENTY-ONE

You must understand the Bible grammatically before you can understand it theologically.

</td><td>

1. 1 Corinthians 7:14, 15:29, and 1 Peter 3:18–22 are three passages that are difficult to understand and interpret.

a. Can you list other passages in the Bible that are difficult for you? _____
_____

b. How should you handle such passages? _____

</td></tr>
</table>

_____
_____

2. Read 1 John 5:6–12.

a. Write out in your own words what this paragraph says. _____
_____
_____
_____
_____

b. Interpret the paragraph—that is, what does it mean?_____

_____

_____

_____

c. What parts do you find difficult to interpret? _____

_____

d. Is there any correlation between your difficulty in interpreting this passage and your understanding of what it says? _____ Explain. _____

_____

_____

_____

RULE TWENTY-TWO

A doctrine cannot be considered biblical unless it sums up and includes all that the Scriptures say about it.

1. Using a concordance, look up all the references to Lot in the Bible. On the basis of these verses, write out an evaluation of the man. _____

_____

_____

_____

_____

2. Most, if not all, Christians fail to apply this rule in some area of their lives. For example, one may believe that "God helps those who help themselves" without doing an in-depth study of the Word to determine if the principle is true. What is a biblical conviction that you hold that you suspect might be altered if you applied Rule Twenty-Two? _____

_____

3. Write out a plan to rectify your deficiency in this area. _____

_____

_____

_____

4. Give an illustration of how Jesus used this principle to correct
the religious leaders of His day. _____

_____

_____

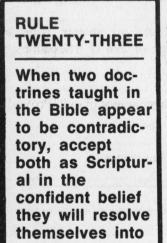

**RULE
TWENTY-THREE**
_____
When two doc-
trines taught in
the Bible appear
to be contradic-
tory, accept
both as Scriptur-
al in the
confident belief
they will resolve
themselves into
a higher unity.

1. Give an illustration of when someone within your acquaintance has
forced the Bible to say more than it
does to resolve a theological or intellectual problem. _____

_____

_____

2. List some passages that teach that
Jesus is:

a. God _____

b. Man _____

3. What are some possible errors you
could fall into in emphasizing Jesus' manhood over His divinity
or vice versa? _____

_____

_____

_____

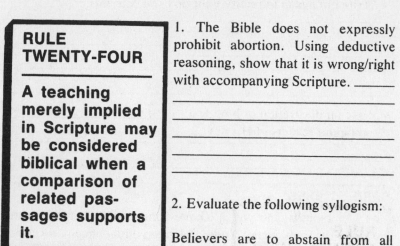

RULE TWENTY-FOUR

A teaching merely implied in Scripture may be considered biblical when a comparison of related passages supports it.

1. The Bible does not expressly prohibit abortion. Using deductive reasoning, show that it is wrong/right with accompanying Scripture. _____

_____

_____

_____

_____

_____

2. Evaluate the following syllogism:

Believers are to abstain from all appearance of evil (1 Thessalonians 5:22).

Drinking alcoholic beverages has an appearance of evil (Proverbs 20:1).

Christians should not drink alcoholic beverages.

_____

_____

_____

_____

_____

_____

_____

3. Take a teaching you believe to be implied in the Bible, state it as a syllogism, and support it with Scripture. (Do not use those mentioned in the book or in this study guide.) _____

_____

_____

_____

_____

_____

_____

CASE STUDIES

1. A person says to you, "I have done a topical study on the Holy Spirit from Acts. Now I plan on preaching a series of messages on it." What principles of interpretation would you counsel him or her to remember? Write out your answer on a separate sheet of paper.

2. Bill is a conscientious objector on the basis of the sixth commandment, "Thou shalt not kill" (Exodus 20:13). Apart from your own personal bias on the subject, how would you counsel Bill, using the twenty-four rules of interpretation? Include in your comments the rules you would use.

3. On the basis of Matthew 19:21–23 and Luke 14:33, you are told by someone that to be a follower of Christ you must rid yourself of all possessions. Biblically, how would you answer this person and which of the rules of interpretation would you use?

4. A Jehovah's Witness argues that Jesus denied being divine in John 10:33–36. Using the rules of interpretation just studied, interpret this passage and answer the Jehovah's Witness' assertion. List the rules used as you do this.

SECTION

V The
Principles
of Application

19 Foundational Principles of Application

CERTAIN FOUNDATIONAL TRUTHS MUST BE EMBRACED TO BEGIN THE PROCESS OF OBEDIENCE.

In all endeavors, foundational truths must be understood before the effort is begun. In business, the customer is always right. This credo has been the guideline for many corporations over the last hundred years, and it is foundational to all efforts and decisions made within such companies.

Scriptural application is based on foundational truths as well. The following rules are foundational principles for any consideration of Scriptural application:

1. Application must be focused on pleasing God rather than pleasing others.

2. Every problem a person has is related to his or her concept of God.

3. Attitude is as important as action in obeying God's commands.

4. Surrender is the cornerstone of all application. Refusal to surrender blurs our ability to discover and do God's will.

5. Application is a process, not a single event.

An understanding of these principles is essential in beginning the process of obedience.

RULE ONE

Application must be focused on pleasing God rather than pleasing others.

The author of Hebrews reminds us that the descendants of Aaron were well suited to be priests. The priest's ability to identify with people is one of the subjects of Hebrews 5: "He is able to deal gently with those who are ignorant and are going astray, since he himself is subject to weakness" (Hebrews 5:2).

Empathy with the people was possible for these Old Testament priests simply because they were plagued with the same problem—sin. For that reason, they couldn't help the people. A sinner cannot impart righteousness to another sinner.

The solution to man's sin problem had to be found in "one who has been tempted in every way, just as we are—yet was without sin" (Hebrews 4:15). That is, He had to be a man who could understand our problem, but not have the problem.

In our quest for godliness we must seek to emulate the "Perfect High Priest" rather than a priest "from among men." This is for two reasons. First, people inevitably establish extra-biblical standards for us and judge our spirituality on the basis of our conformity to their standards. Second, when we do meet their expectations, they will cease nudging us towards Christlikeness.

The Scribes and Pharisees of Jesus' day established rules and regulations not found in the Bible. These became normative not only for the religious leaders but also for all who would be godly. Jesus felt no obligation to keep these extra-biblical standards. He did obey the laws of the Scriptures, as He Himself testified: "Do not think that I have come to abolish the Law or the Prophets; I have not come to abolish them but to fulfill them" (Matthew 5:17).

But keeping the Old Testament statutes was not enough for these custodians of right and wrong. They expected Jesus to follow their rules as well. The Savior's refusal was a major reason the Sanhedrin wanted Him dead. If the focus of Jesus' application had been toward pleasing men rather than God, He would have become a Pharisee.

Mores and taboos change from generation to generation. In the nineteenth century, for instance, most of the evangelical churches in the United States taught that drinking tea and coffee was wrong. Often these man-made rules not only add to, but clash with God's laws. On this subject, Jesus said to the Pharisees: "You have a fine way of setting aside the commands of God in order to observe your own traditions! For Moses said, 'Honor your father and mother,' and, 'Anyone who curses his father or mother must be put to death.' But you say that if a man says to his father or mother: 'Whatever help you might otherwise have received from me is Corban' (that is, a gift devoted to God), then you no longer let him do anything for his father or mother. Thus you nullify the word of God by your tradition that you have handed down. And you do many things like that" (Mark 7:9–13).

When we meet the expectations of people, they cease to nudge us toward Christlikeness. Converted out of a life of debauchery, Jean becomes part of the believing fellowship. Her past lifestyle is unacceptable to any moral individual—much less to the church. So, pressure is exerted on Jean to "clean up her act." Within a couple of years she fits very nicely into her new-found environment. Her lifestyle matches that of the congregation.

Now the pressure is off. Jean is a member in good standing, and her fellow Christians' expectations are met. No longer do they exhort her to godliness; she is as godly as they are.

Does this mean that the Holy Spirit is satisfied and that the sanctification process has come to an end? Not at all. As long as Jean compares herself with her fellow believers, her spiritual ears will be dulled; for instance, she may lie and be reluctant to confess it. If her application focus is on meeting God's expectations, she will jump the hurdle of her reluctance, obey the Holy Spirit's nudging, and rectify her wrong. But if the focus of her application is people, she will justify her wrong, suppress the convicting voice of the Holy Spirit, and walk away from application.

The focus of our application must be toward pleasing God rather than pleasing others.

RULE TWO

Every problem a person has is related to his or her concept of God.

Not only is God sovereign and in control, He also has believers' best interests at heart as He monitors the flow of circumstances through their lives. As Joseph's life unfolds in the book of Genesis, we see God manipulating history to accomplish His own goals.

In Genesis 37:28 Joseph's brothers sell him to a Midianite caravan on its way to Egypt. In 39:1, the captain of Pharaoh's guard buys Joseph. By verse 20 Joseph is in prison because of the wiles of Potiphar's wife. Genesis 40 records that Pharaoh's butler and baker are cast into the same prison. Because Joseph has maintained a good attitude, he is trusted, and the butler and baker come under Joseph's care. When the butler and the baker have mysterious dreams, Joseph interprets them, predicting the restoration of the butler and the demise of the baker. The butler is restored.

Now Pharaoh has a dream (Genesis 41). No one can interpret it, and the butler suggests that Joseph might be able to help. Joseph interprets the dream for Pharaoh and ends up becoming Egypt's prime minister. In the morning Joseph is in prison; that afternoon he is in the palace—a clear illustration of God ordering events to accomplish His own purpose.

At the end of Joseph's life his testimony to his brothers is: "You intended to harm me, but God intended it for good to accomplish what is now being done, the saving of many lives" (Genesis 50:20).

Joseph's story is an illustration of the biblical teaching that God is in control and has our best interests at heart. Other people cannot hurt us except by divine permission. This principle does not absolve others of their responsibility, but it does mean that when I have a problem, my problem is with God, not with others.

David's response in the Psalms also illustrates this truth. In Psalm 18:16–19, he testifies:

He reached down from on high and took hold of me;
  he drew me out of deep waters.
He rescued me from my powerful enemy,
  from my foes, who were too strong for me.
They confronted me in the day of my disaster,
  but the LORD was my support.
He brought me out into a spacious place;
  he rescued me because he delighted in me.

When things are going poorly for David and when his enemies seem to be gaining on him, he takes his case before God. He does not, however, simply abandon the issue; a recognition of God's control is never an excuse for inactivity.

Frequently the Bible calls on us to respond to circumstances differently than we would naturally want to respond. When we bless our enemies or turn the other cheek or go to war, the application of the Scriptures requires risk taking—first because we do not know how the situation will turn out; second, because application runs counter to how we naturally feel. As Job goes through the trauma of defending himself from his friends as they challenge his integrity, he cries out for an opportunity to take his case directly to God. Time and again he expresses a longing to confront God with some difficult questions. When he finally meets God and is given the opportunity to address the issue, he declines. He merely says, "My ears had heard of you but now my eyes have seen you. Therefore I despise myself and repent in dust and ashes" (Job 42:5–6). When Job met God, his problems appeared superfluous.

Every problem in life requires an application of the Scriptures, either in attitude or in conduct. How we respond will be determined by our concept of God.

RULE THREE

Attitude is as important as action in obeying God's commands.

Twice during Saul's brief reign in Israel the prophet Samuel came with a reprimand from God. The first, in 1 Samuel 13, occurs before the battle with the Philistines. Israel's army, arrayed for battle, waited for Samuel to come and offer a sacrifice on their behalf.

He waited seven days, the time set by Samuel; but Samuel did not come to Gilgal, and Saul's men began to scatter. So he said, "Bring me the burnt offering and the fellowship offerings." And Saul offered up the burnt offering. Just as he finished making the offering, Samuel arrived, and Saul went out to greet him.

"What have you done?" asked Samuel.

Saul replied, "When I saw that the men were scattering, and that you did not come at the set time, and that the Philistines were assembling at Micmash, I thought, 'Now the Philistines will come down against me at Gilgal, and I have not sought the LORD's favor. So I felt compelled to offer the burnt offering."

"You acted foolishly," Samuel said. "You have not kept the command the LORD your God gave you; if you had, he would have established your kingdom over Israel for all time. But now your kingdom will not endure; the LORD has sought out a man after his own heart and appointed him leader of his people, because you have not kept the LORD's command." (1 Samuel 13:8–14)

This was not the first time a non-Levite intruded into the priest's office, nor would it be the last. Gideon, Jephthah, and Elijah all offered sacrifices with impunity, and Scripture gives no indication that they were related to Levi.

Samuel's second rebuke followed Saul's return from fighting the Amalekites. God had sent Saul to avenge the way Amalek had treated Israel during the exodus. God commanded Saul to destroy the Amalekites. "When Samuel reached him, Saul said, 'The LORD bless you; I have carried out the LORD's instructions'" (1 Samuel 15:13). Saul claims to have kept God's commandment, and in a sense he did. He merely saved some of the spoil for a future sacrifice.

In both encounters, no moral issue was at stake, as there was in the case of King David when he committed adultery with Bathsheba and murdered her husband, Uriah (2 Samuel 11). Saul had not broken one of the Ten Commandments. Yet Saul was alienated from God the rest of his life while God calls David "a man after my own heart" (Acts 13:22).

The issue is deeper than the actions of these two men; the difference relates to their attitudes toward God.

Samuel reproves Saul for his disobedience: "Does the LORD delight in burnt offerings and sacrifices as much as in obeying the voice of the LORD? To obey is better than sacrifice, and to heed is better than the fat of rams. For rebellion is like the sin of divination, and arrogance like the evil of idolatry. Because you have rejected the word of the LORD, he has rejected you as king" (1 Samuel 15:22–23).

Rebellion lies at the heart of Samuel's charge. Rebellion and sinful acts are not synonymous; a person can be rebellious and not *do* anything wrong. Conversely, a person can do wrong and not be in rebellion. Rebellion is primarily, though not exclusively, an act of the heart.

In 1 Samuel 15:13 Saul protests to Samuel that obedience was his intent. But he wanted to take God's command and filter it through his own conviction of what was reasonable. Instead of abandoning himself and carrying out God's request, he evaluated it in light of his own value system—and that is rebellion.

Many centuries later, as Jesus and His disciples walked through the grain fields, the Pharisees challenged them for gleaning and eating grain on the Sabbath: "Jesus answered them, 'Have you never read what David did when he and his companions were hungry? He entered the house of God, and taking the consecrated bread, he ate what is lawful only for priests to eat. And he also gave some to his companions.' Then Jesus said to them, 'The Son of Man is Lord of the Sabbath' " (Luke 6:3–5).

To justify the disciples' actions, Jesus referred to the time when David, fleeing from Saul, ate the bread in the tabernacle (see Leviticus 24:5–9 and 1 Samuel 21:1–6). David broke the law, and not only was he not reprimanded for it, but Jesus also excuses it.

Does this mean we can break God's law as long as we have a good attitude? Not at all!

Isaiah addresses this issue in the opening paragraphs of his prophecy:

> "The multitude of your sacrifices—
>   what are they to me?" says the LORD.
> I have more than enough of burnt offerings,
>   of rams and the fat of fattened animals;
> I have no pleasure

in the blood of bulls and lambs and goats.
When you come to meet with me,
    who has asked this of you,
    this trampling of my courts?
Stop bringing meaningless offerings!
    Your incense is detestable to me.
New Moons, Sabbaths and convocations—
    I cannot bear your evil assemblies.
Your New Moon festivals and your appointed feasts
    my soul hates.
They have become a burden to me;
    I am weary of bearing them.
When you spread out your hands in prayer,
    I will hide my eyes from you;
even if you offer many prayers,
    I will not listen.
Your hands are full of blood;
    wash and make yourselves clean.
Take your evil deeds
    out of my sight!
Stop doing wrong,
    learn to do right!
Seek justice,
    encourage the oppressed.
Defend the cause of the fatherless,
    plead the case of the widow.

"Come now, let us reason together,"
    says the LORD.
"Though your sins are like scarlet,
    they shall be as white as snow;
though they are red as crimson,
    they shall be like wool.
If you are willing and obedient,
    you will eat the best from the land;
but if you resist and rebel,
    you will be devoured by the sword."

For the mouth of the Lord has spoken.
                                        (Isaiah 1:11–20)

Israel, in a perfunctory fashion, kept the ceremonial and sacrificial aspects of the law. The people's hearts, however, were not in their obedience, because they failed to keep the law's "weightier matters." Isaiah told them to abandon their ritualistic practices, but he did not suggest that they stop keeping the moral law.

God summarizes his complaint against Israel in Isaiah: "These people come near to me with their mouth and honor me with their lips, but their hearts are far from me. Their worship of me is made up only of rules taught by men" (Isaiah 29:13). Nowhere does the prophet imply that, since God does not have His people's hearts, they can stop keeping His commandments.

Proper action is important to God, but that action should be based on a spirit of dependence and submission. As long as I vote on a command's reasonableness and modify it based on how I evaluate it, I am in rebellion. My heart's attitude is as important as my action in obeying God's commands.

RULE FOUR

Surrender is the cornerstone of all application. Refusal to surrender blurs our ability to discover and do God's will.

We can easily see the connection between surrender to God and applying His commandments. We obey what He says because we are submissive to Him, and we are in submission to Him because of who He is.

Many of the New Testament epistles are written from this perspective; Ephesians is a case in point. The first three chapters remind us who Jesus Christ is and what He did for us. Beginning with chapter four, we are told of our responsibility. Because He is Lord, we are to submit to His expectations. The last three chapters enumerate the various applications expected.

Although the connection between surrender to God and knowing His will is not readily apparent, it is nonetheless compelling. To help the believer discover and do God's will, God provides counsel through proven people and leads through the Scriptures and the Holy Spirit. These indicators become blurred, however, if the believer does not seek God's will with a submissive attitude.

Hebrews 3 discusses Israel's sojourn to Canaan after years of slavery in Egypt. Quoting from Psalm 95, the author says: "Do not harden your hearts as you did in the rebellion, during the time of testing in the desert, where your fathers tested and tried me and for forty years saw what I did" (Hebrews 3:8–9).

In verse 8, God tested them; in verse 9, Israel tested God. The controversy was the giants in Canaan—God wanted Israel to face the giants, but Israel did not want to. Both God and Israel had Israel's best uppermost in their minds. Conflict resulted from disagreeing on what that best interest looked like. The Bible is filled with assurances that God loves His children and designs all circumstances so that they contribute to the children's good. Paul assures the Romans: "And we know that in all things God works for the good of those who love him, who have been called according to his purpose" (Romans 8:28).

We question God's commitment to us either when events we don't like invade our lives or when we suspect God is asking us to do something we don't want to do. Circumstances we don't like frequently interrupt our lives with varying degrees of magnitude. On a recent trip to Fort Campbell, a soldier sought counsel from me on how to handle a tragedy. He had just returned from overseas, and his wife and two daughters were driving to meet him. A drunk lost control of his vehicle, crossed the lane, hit the car, and the young soldier's family burned to death in the accident. "If God truly loves us and is in control, why did He allow this to happen?" the distraught soldier asked.

God is not obliged to tell His children why such things happen. He rarely takes us into His confidence with what we consider is an adequate explanation. He does assure us, however, that He is in control, that there is purpose behind such events, that He loves us and has our best interests at heart. Believing this without understanding why is faith. Our confidence is in God's character rather than our ability to understand why He does what He does. If our submission to Him is based on our ability to understand His ways, we will wander in the wilderness of confusion just as Israel did when they refused to fight the giants.

All of us have chuckled at the *Peanuts* sequence in which Lucy holds the football for Charlie Brown, only to pull it away at the last minute. Wary of a repeat performance, he extracts from her assurances that she won't pull the ball away next time. Having been placated with soothing words, he tries again. Each time she jerks the ball away, and each time Charlie Brown slams to the ground.

When circumstances go awry, the tendency is to question God's commitment. We feel we have entered into a Charlie Brown–Lucy relationship with God in which we are never sure if God is going to pull away the football as we try to kick it. The next step, withholding our submission to God, is a short one.

Surrender is the cornerstone of all application, and it is based on our concept of God. If He is sovereign and has our best interests at heart, then we can submit to Him assured that, although we may not know why He does what He does, his loving purpose rules. The only tragedy in life we need fear is the tragedy of self-will.

In addition to questioning God's commitment to us when circumstances are difficult, we also may question His goodness when we fear He may ask us to do something we don't want to do. A graduating high-school student was accepted at several different colleges. He prayed about the one he should accept and sought counsel from people who knew and loved him. Weeks turned into months, and still he didn't know where to go. What was God's will?

The roadblock was his lack of neutrality. He couldn't look his Lord in the face and say, "Thy will be done," because he didn't want to attend one of the colleges and feared that, if he surrendered, God would ask him to go there. Normally a confident, decisive person, he found himself in the valley of indecision, desperately trying to climb out—on his own terms. His refusal to surrender blurred his ability to discover and do God's will.

RULE FIVE

Application is a process, not a single event.

This principle is the heart of understanding biblical application. We have seen it illustrated in the lives of such people as Rebekah, Rahab, Joseph, Saul, Daniel, and Jesus; it is further illustrated by Abraham.

Abraham is one of the recognized "greats" in the Bible; he is referred to no less than seventy-five times in the New Testament. In Genesis, however, we find that he led a rather uneventful life. He wrote no books; he built no cities; he made no great discoveries; he did not become a ruler. He simply lived.

In the morning Abraham got up, sat in front of his tent, probably gave some instruction to his herdsmen, and went to bed at night. Periodically he moved from Shechem to Peniel, from Peniel to Hebron, from Hebron back to Shechem. He did have an adventurous moment when he saved Lot from his enemies (Genesis 14). But most of the time he simply believed God's promises and waited for God to fulfill them.

Abraham is not great in the economy of God because of what he did; he didn't do much! He is great because: "Abram believed the LORD, and he credited it to him as righteousness" (Genesis 15:6).

Many of God's greats were significant leaders. In God's Hall of Fame in Hebrews 11, many great leaders are mentioned. Joseph, for example, became prime minister of Egypt, but Hebrews says he was great because: "By faith Joseph, when his end was near, spoke about the exodus of the Israelites from Egypt and gave instructions about his bones" (Hebrews 11:22).

Moses, obviously a great man, led the children of Israel out of captivity and was God's vehicle for communicating the law. But God considered him great because of his faith: "By faith Moses, when he had grown up, refused to be known as the son of Pharaoh's daughter. He chose to be mistreated along with the people of God rather than to enjoy the pleasures of sin for a short time. He regarded disgrace for the sake of Christ as of greater value than the treasures of Egypt, because he was looking ahead to his reward. By faith he left Egypt, not fearing the king's anger; he persevered because he saw him who is invisible. By faith he kept the Passover and the sprinkling of blood, so that the destroyer of the firstborn would not touch the firstborn of Israel" (Hebrews 11:24–28).

Nowhere in Hebrews 11 are people considered great because of worldly accomplishments. All these men and women were great because they understood God's program and were willing participants. In short, they were process-oriented rather than product-oriented.

Abraham and those who followed him as God's "greats" did not view application as a single event. They did not try to evaluate their holiness on the basis of faithful acts. They understood that walking with God was a day-by-day, moment-by-moment process, and that process included responding properly to what God asked them to do.

For Abraham that process began when God called him: "The LORD had said to Abram, 'Leave your country, your people and

your father's household and go to the land I will show you'"
(Genesis 12:1).

As an act of faith, Abraham cooperated with God in the
process: "By faith Abraham, when called to go to a place he
would later receive as his inheritance, obeyed and went, even
though he did not know where he was going" (Hebrews 11:8).

On entering the promised land, Abraham had not "arrived" in
his relationship with God. When famine hit Canaan, he and
Sarah went to Egypt. Abraham suggested to Sarah: "Say you are
my sister, so that I will be treated well for your sake and my life
will be spared because of you" (Genesis 12:13).

The famine ended, and Abraham returned to Canaan. They
still had not arrived in the process of trusting God. In Gerar, he
takes the same action with Sarah: "And there Abraham said of
his wife Sarah, 'She is my sister.' Then Abimelech king of Gerar
sent for Sarah and took her" (Genesis 20:2).

If Abraham, the man of faith, had arrived in the process, there
would have been no need for God to test him with Isaac: "Some
time later God tested Abraham. He said to him, 'Abraham!'

"'Here I am,' he replied.

"Then God said, 'Take your son, your only son, Isaac, whom
you love, and go to the region of Moriah. Sacrifice him there as a
burnt offering on one of the mountains I will tell you about'"
(Genesis 22:1-2).

Each step of faith, each testing, prepared Abraham for his next
step with God. Because application is not a single event, at no
time in Abraham's life had he arrived. The same is true for every
believer. Application must be viewed not as a single event, but
as a lifelong process of responding properly to God.

20 Principles on Personal Responsibility

CERTAIN COMMITMENTS TO PERSONAL RESPONSIBILITY ARE REQUIRED TO PROCEED IN THE APPLICATION OF SCRIPTURES.

God holds the believer responsible for certain commitments to proceed in personal application. These commitments, coupled with the foundational truths, begin the application process. As with the foundational truths, these commitments must be accepted, understood, and acted on. If we are to accept responsibility for our actions, we must understand what actions are required.

In training children we often deal with the fundamentals, teaching them their basic responsibilities so that they can begin to create habits for good living. This practice holds true in

275

scriptural growth. God has given us specific responsibilities in the application process. Rules 6–10 profile five areas of personal responsibility to which we must commit ourselves:

6. In those areas of life not directly addressed by the Scriptures, we must develop personal convictions to govern our behavior.

7. When applying the Scriptures, we must make a distinction between the positive and negative commandments.

8. Each person is individually responsible for applying the Scriptures to his or her own life.

9. In all things we must be teachable. We must be willing to admit that we are wrong, change direction and appear inconsistent.

10. The acknowledgment of wrong must be followed by restitution when it is within our power.

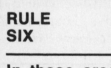

RULE SIX

In those areas of life not addressed by the Scriptures, we must develop personal convictions to govern our behavior.

The Scriptures specify few prohibitions. If we were to list them, they would scarcely fill more than a page. This is in contrast to most societies, which have volumes of laws. Believers are free to do whatever the Bible does not prohibit. Christians have considerable freedom.

The Word includes no commandments that prohibit gambling, frequenting night clubs, having more than one spouse, or drinking alcoholic beverages. It does not suggest that we *ought* to do these things, of course, but rather, the Bible does not *demand* that we abstain. If the state has no laws governing such behavior, the believer is free to do them.

But to exercise one's freedom in Christ and indulge in all behavior not expressly prohibited by God can cause irreparable harm, as Paul implied when he said, " 'Everything is permissible'—but not everything is beneficial. 'Everything is permissible'—but not everything is constructive" (1 Corinthians 10:23). Because there are so few negative commands in the Bible, and most of them are self-evident, nonbelievers can and often do abide by them as successfully as believers. If we don't establish limits in areas other than those mentioned in the Bible, we run the risk of becoming emotionally yoked with the world.

While in Midian, Moses encountered God at the burning bush. God commissioned Moses to free Israel from Egyptian slavery. The Lord said: "The elders of Israel will listen to you. Then you and the elders are to go to the king of Egypt and say to him, 'The LORD, the God of the Hebrews, has met with us. Let us take a three-day journey into the desert to offer sacrifices to the LORD our God' " (Exodus 3:18).

Moses went before Pharaoh and repeated God's command: "This is what the LORD , the God of Israel, says: 'Let my people go, so that they may hold a festival to me in the desert' " (Exodus 5:1).

As the plagues increased in intensity, Pharaoh began to compromise with Moses. Israel can sacrifice to the Lord, he said, but not leave Egypt. "Then the Pharaoh summoned Moses and Aaron and said, 'Go, sacrifice to your God here in the land' " (Exodus 8:25).

During the negotiations, Pharaoh sought accommodation, and Moses *increased* the demand: "Then Pharaoh summoned Moses and said, 'Go, worship the LORD. Even your women and children may go with you; only leave your flocks and herds behind.'

"But Moses said, 'You must allow us to have sacrifices and burnt offerings to present to the LORD our God. Our livestock too must go with us; not a hoof is to be left behind. We have to use some of them in worshiping the LORD our God, and until we get

there we will not know what we are to use to worship the LORD' "
(Exodus 10:24–26).

The Lord did not say that the flocks and herds had to go. This
was Moses' idea—his conviction. He went beyond what God
required, and God backed him.

The same principle can be seen in Daniel's life. Darius had
decreed that for thirty days people could worship only the king.
"Now when Daniel learned that the decree had been published,
he went home to his upstairs room where the windows opened
toward Jerusalem. Three times a day he got down on his knees
and prayed, giving thanks to his God, just as he had done
before" (Daniel 6:10).

Nothing in Scripture requires a person to have devotions three
times a day. Daniel could have said, "I'll get up early and have
my quiet time before the rest of the city rises." Or he could have
shut the windows. Scripture even suggests that the windows be
closed: "When you pray, do not be like the hypocrites, for they
love to pray standing in the synagogues and on the street corners
to be seen by men. I tell you the truth, they have received their
reward in full. But when you pray, go into your room, close the
door and pray to your Father, who is unseen. Then your Father,
who sees what is done in secret, will reward you" (Matthew
6:5–6).

To pray three times a day with the windows open was *Daniel's*
idea. Evidently it pleased God. When Daniel was caught and
sentenced to the lion's den, the Lord closed the lions' mouths.

As we seek to obey the Lord, we are to be sensitive to the
Holy Spirit's leading. Part of that leading relates to prohibitions
not mentioned in the Bible.

We have some good friends who feel they should not join the
country club. They can afford it, but they feel they shouldn't
belong. Others that we know, equally godly, belong to country
clubs.

The Holy Spirit may prohibit one Christian from doing

something while allowing another to do it. I must resist the temptation to judge others as less spiritual because they do what the Lord has forbidden me to do.

At times, evangelical Christians have tended to make biblical absolutes out of such issues as gambling, drinking alcohol, and dancing. Failure to comply brought condemnation, and the system resulted in Pharisaism. We should formulate our own convictions, but we should not make them normative for others.

Our generation is freer; the environment is healthier. But now we err in allowing our freedom to become license. Those who have a heart for application must develop God-given convictions in those areas of life not addressed by the Scriptures.

RULE SEVEN

When applying the Scriptures, we must make a distinction between the positive and negative commandments.

By and large, negative commandments deal with what we are to do away with. Positive commands state what we are to add in our lives. Negative commandments tend to be clear, crisp, and easy to evaluate. In contrast, positive commandments tend to be nebulous and difficult to evaluate.

Paul, in his letter to the Colossians notes the difference between positive commandments and negative commandments:

Put to death, therefore, whatever belongs to your earthly nature: sexual immorality, impurity, lust, evil desires and greed, which is idolatry. Because of these, the wrath of God is coming. You used to walk in these ways, in the life you once lived. But now you must rid yourself of all such things as these: anger, rage, malice, slander, and filthy language from your lips. Do not lie to each other, since you have taken off your old self with its practices and have put on the new self, which is being renewed in knowledge in the image of its Creator. Here there is no Greek or Jew, circumcised or uncircumcised, barbarian, Scythian, slave or free, but Christ is all, and is in all.

> Therefore, as God's chosen people, holy and dearly loved, clothe yourselves with compassion, kindness, humility, gentleness and patience. Bear with each other and forgive whatever grievances you may have against one another. Forgive as the Lord forgave you. And over all these virtues put on love, which binds them all together in perfect unity.
>
> Let the peace of Christ rule in your hearts, since as members of one body you were called to peace. And be thankful. Let the word of Christ dwell in you richly as you teach and admonish one another in all wisdom, and as you sing psalms, hymns and spiritual songs with gratitude in your hearts to God. And whatever you do, whether in word or deed, do it all in the name of the Lord Jesus, giving thanks to God the Father through him. (Colossians 3:5–17)

In verse 5, Paul says that we are not to commit fornication. We all know immediately whether or not we have broken this negative commandment. Again, in verse 9, he says: "Do not lie to each other." When evaluating ourselves in light of all the negative commandments, we know immediately where we stand because they tend to deal with conduct.

Not so with the positive commandments. In Colossians 3:12, Paul says we are to be compassionate, kind, humble, patient. If we ask ourselves, "Am I humble?" in all probability we would have a difficult time answering. We would hesitate and say that we try to be but are more humble at some times than at others, and maybe not as humble as we should be or possibly more humble than we used to be. The positive commandments deal with heart attitudes, making evaluation difficult, if not impossible. A person can obey the command "thou shalt not kill" but have a bad attitude in the process.

Sometimes we can use the negative commandments in evaluating the positive commandments. The Bible says, for example, that I am to love my wife—a positive commandment. The Bible also says that I am not to divorce my wife—a negative commandment. If I love my wife, I will not divorce her. The negative commandment serves as a guide in helping me to evaluate the positive one. But this approach has obvious limitations because it is a one-way street. If I love my wife, I will not divorce her. Yet just because I have not divorced my wife does not mean that I love her.

Both positive and negative commandments require personal application. Whenever we apply the Scriptures we look for some way to evaluate how we are doing. The negative commandments make that task easy through objective evaluation. With the positive commandments, objective evaluation is impossible; all evaluation of the positive commandments is subjective. We must be careful in evaluating our success in keeping the positive commandments. If we seek to apply objective standards of measurement to them, we will either become guilt-ridden or rigid and pharisaical. So when we apply the Scriptures, we must make a distinction between the positive and negative commandments to know how to respond to them.

RULE EIGHT

Each person is individually responsible for applying the Scriptures to his or her own life.

Beginning with conversion, Christians are taught to function in the community of believers. Within this community, we are responsible for helping to monitor the behavior of our fellow Christians. The author of Hebrews says, for example: "Encourage one another daily, as long as it is called Today, so that none of you may be hardened by sin's deceitfulness" (Hebrews 3:13).

Paul says essentially the same thing to Timothy: "Preach the Word; be prepared in season and out of season; correct, rebuke and encourage—with great patience and careful instruction" (2 Timothy 4:2).

If the recalcitrant believer does not heed exhortation or rebuke, then the Christian community is to follow the method of discipline prescribed by Jesus in Matthew 18:15–19:

"If your brother sins against you, go and show him his fault, just between the two of you. If he listens to you, you have won your brother over. But if he will not listen, take one or two others along, so that 'every matter may be established by the testimony of two or three witnesses.' If he refuses to listen to them, tell it to the church; and if he refuses to listen even to the church, treat him as you would a pagan or a tax collector.

"I tell you the truth, whatever you bind on earth will be bound in heaven, and whatever you loose on earth will be loosed in heaven.

"Again, I tell you that if two of you on earth agree about anything you ask for, it will be done for you by my Father in heaven."

Community responsibility does not, however, absolve the individual of his or her own personal responsibility to apply the Scriptures. Most of the commands and admonitions in the Bible are given to the community, but their application is an individual responsibility. Sin may appear to be corporate when many people are transgressing God's commandments, but in the final analysis, it is always an individual problem in God's eyes.

Because no one likes to assume responsibility, society will always have those who shift responsibility for failure to someone else: Either the individual was improperly raised; society did not give him or her the "breaks" that were needed; or circumstances were such that the person *had* to behave wrongly.

Although this approach is attractive, because it absolves an individual of responsibility, it is unacceptable in the light of biblical teaching. Each person is responsible for applying the Scriptures to his or her own life. Failing to make application is a personal matter.

Paul, in writing to the Corinthians, warns: "For we must all appear before the judgment seat of Christ, that each one may receive what is due him for the things done while in the body, whether good or bad" (2 Corinthians 5:10).

Judgment is individual, not corporate. Each of us is responsible for applying the Scriptures to our lives, and each of us must give an account before God of how we have done.

RULE NINE

In all things, we must be teachable. We must be willing to admit that we are wrong, change direction, and appear inconsistent.

Nothing sticks in the throat of the proud believer like the need to admit that he or she is wrong: "It was the way I was raised," "I didn't really mean what I appeared to have said," "I've always believed this way, it's just that I didn't know how to say it."

We are ingenious in our ability to waltz around accountability. One of the most humorous illustrations of this is found in Exodus when Aaron made the golden calf: "'Do not be angry, my Lord,' Aaron answered. 'You know how prone these people are to evil. They said to me, "Make us gods who will go before us. As for this fellow Moses who brought us up out of Egypt, we don't know what has happened to him." So I told them, "Whoever has any gold jewelry, take it off." Then they gave me the gold, and I threw it into the fire, and out came this calf!' " (Exodus 32:22–24).

The need to backtrack is not surprising and should not be embarrassing. All of us "see but a poor reflection," to use Paul's phrasing in 1 Corinthians 13:12. Only Jesus the Messiah was able to see clearly. John testifies in his gospel: "Jesus would not entrust himself to them, for he knew all men. He did not need man's testimony about man, for he knew what was in a man" (John 2:24–25).

Acts 9:1–9 is the record of Paul's conversion. Years later he reflects on it before King Agrippa. Here he discusses the implications of his encounter with Christ and says, "So then, King Agrippa, I was not disobedient to the vision from heaven. First to those in Damascus, then to those in Jerusalem and in all Judea, and to the Gentiles also, I preached that they should repent and turn to God and prove their repentance by their deeds" (Acts 26:19–20).

One day Paul is preaching that Christianity is a heresy, and he seeks with all he has to expunge it, and a week later he is preaching that Jesus is the Messiah, and Paul is expending his energies propagating the Gospel. Paul expresses his dramatic reversal beautifully: "They only heard the report: 'The man who formerly persecuted us is now preaching the faith he once tried to destroy' " (Galatians 1:23).

Ron, a close friend of ours, is sharp, articulate, a man of conviction. What he believes to be true he preaches unashamedly. But often he has found himself wrong. With no self-justification, no defense, he simply reverses himself and begins to preach what he now understands to be true. It is easy to see why people like this are a source of consternation to others.

Ghandi, the great spiritual and political leader of India, was not a Christian, but he had this characteristic. Often people saw him take one position only to find later that he had reversed himself. When challenged with inconsistency, he would simply reply, "I have more facts now than I did then."

Such people are a bewilderment to the insecure. Only those who understand who they are can display this kind of flexibility, yet it is foundational for the life committed to applying God's Word. We must be willing to admit we are wrong, change direction, and appear inconsistent.

RULE TEN

The acknowledgment of wrong must be followed by restitution when it is within our power.

Restitution is a key application principle. Confession is not sufficient when it is within our power to make right the wrong. Sadly, we are a generation of people who feel they can walk away from the consequences of wrong with scarcely a nod of acknowledgment. Society has nourished the idea of such "easy-outs" as bankruptcy laws and divorce. Not only is commitment to covenants and obligations lacking, but so also is the acknowledgment of sin followed by restitution.

Psychology deals with guilt by placing the emphasis on the symptom rather than the disease. But guilt can never be abolished by dealing with guilt; it can only satisfactorily be handled by dealing with the root problem—sin. People *feel* guilty because they *are* guilty.

One of Jesus' claims that shook the religious community of His day was the assertion that He could forgive sin. At the heart of the Christian message is the assurance that forgiveness comes through Christ's finished work. This forgiveness, however, should be followed by restitution whenever possible. Jesus told Zacchaeus, the dishonest tax collector in Luke 19: "Today salvation has come to this house, because this man, too, is a son of Abraham." What evoked such a response was not only Zacchaeus' willingness to believe but also his willingness to follow that belief with restitution: "Zacchaeus stood up and said to the Lord, 'Look, Lord! Here and now I give half of my possessions to the poor, and if I have cheated anybody out of anything, I will pay back four times the amount' " (Luke 19:8).

This willingness to right wrongs is in keeping with John the Baptist's ministry. He cried out to the people of his generation, "Produce fruit in keeping with repentance" (Matthew 3:8).

At times restitution is impossible. Years ago I cheated a man out of forty dollars. After I became a Christian, I sought in vain to find him. Since I was unable to make it right with him, I gave the forty dollars to the Lord's work.

Many times, however, restitution is possible. A good friend of ours from Oklahoma City was forced into bankruptcy, leaving behind a trail of debts. Although the law had absolved him of any responsibility for repayment, he vowed before God to make it right. After many years, every creditor was repaid, and his story has become a testimony to other conscientious Christians who understand their obligation to make restitution.

21 Principles on Our Perception of God's Word

OUR PERCEPTION OF GOD'S WORD IS VITAL FOR SUSTAINED AND MEANINGFUL GROWTH IN SCRIPTURAL APPLICATION.

All the great men and women of the Bible were committed to the purity and holiness of the Word of God and to obedience to it. In his later years Daniel still studied the works of Jeremiah (Daniel 9), and he governed and controlled his life by what the Word of God instructed him to do. Christ was also committed to the holiness of the Bible: "Do not think that I have come to abolish the Law or the Prophets; I have not come to abolish them but to fulfill them. I tell you the truth, until heaven and earth disappear, not the smallest letter, not the least stroke of a pen, will by any means disappear from the Law until everything is accomplished.

287

Anyone who breaks one of the least of these commandments and teaches others to do the same will be called least in the kingdom of heaven, but whoever practices and teaches these commands will be called great in the kingdom of heaven" (Matthew 5:17–19).

The author of the book of Hebrews says that God's Word is alive and active, cutting more keenly than any double-edged sword (Hebrews 4:12). Such an attitude toward the Bible must be true of us also.

Principles 11–13 address key perceptions concerning the Word of God, concepts essential to the maturing process:

11. We must consider God's command rather than His chastisement as the motive for application.

12. Knowledge carries with it both privilege and responsibility.

13. There is no such thing as a nonessential command.

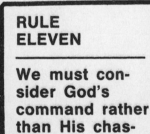

**RULE
ELEVEN**

We must consider God's command rather than His chastisement as the motive for application.

About seventy guests had gathered at Jim's home for a discussion. Most were uncommitted and had come to this friendly, open environment to ask questions about God. As the discussion moved to whether a literal heaven and hell exist, Bob said, "I wish I could know for sure whether there is a hell. If there isn't, I wouldn't spend so much time trying to be good."

Like many, Bob works hard at "being good" out of fear that if he is bad, he will be the object of God's wrath. He is motivated by fear.

Love is a higher and more noble motive for application than fear. Such a motive causes a person to think, "I know that God is absolute purity and holiness. There is nothing false or evil about Him. Simply because He said it, His word is worthy of obedience. To do His will is best for all concerned.''

Although most people agree that this is how we should respond, none of us can consistently execute these intentions. Not only do we frequently fail to meet God's expectations, but when we do meet them, it is often out of fear of His rod.

If, however, our gaze is fixed on what will happen to us if we fail to conform to His will, we will receive mixed signals. God's rebuke varies in intensity, and not just according to the size of the transgression. For reasons known only to Him, the severity of the chastisement and the seriousness of the infraction do not always seem to match.

In Exodus, Aaron, the high priest designate, makes an idol in the likeness of a golden calf. Although God is angry, Aaron apparently receives no punishment. Later, however, when Nadab and Abihu, the sons of Aaron, offer "unauthorized fire" before the Lord, they are destroyed. Aaron is told that if he weeps over their deaths, he too will be destroyed (Leviticus 10:1–7). Aaron makes an idol and nothing happens to him. But if he mourns his sons' deaths, God will kill him.

Exodus 2:11–12 narrates an incident in Moses' life: "One day, after Moses had grown up, he went out to where his own people were and watched them at their hard labor. He saw an Egyptian beating a Hebrew, one of his own people. Glancing this way and that and seeing no one, he killed the Egyptian and hid him in the sand." Another incident in the life of Moses demonstrates the seeming inconsistency of God's rebuke:

> The LORD said to Moses, "Take the staff, and you and your brother Aaron gather the assembly together. Speak to that rock before their eyes and it will pour out its water. You will bring water out of the rock for the community so they and their livestock can drink."
> So Moses took the staff from the LORD's presence, just as he commanded him. He and Aaron gathered the assembly together in

front of the rock and Moses said to them, "Listen, you rebels, must
we bring you water out of this rock?" Then Moses raised his arm and
struck the rock twice with his staff. Water gushed out, and the
community and their livestock drank.

But the LORD said to Moses and Aaron, "Because you did not trust
in me enough to honor me as holy in the sight of the Israelites, you
will not bring this community into the land I give them" (Numbers
20:7–12).

Moses strikes a man dead, but God never calls him to account.
He strikes a rock out of frustration over Israel's unbelief, and
God says he can never enter into the promised land.

A man gathers sticks for a fire on the Sabbath, and the
punishment is death (Numbers 5:32), while seemingly far greater
infractions of God's law are recorded without severe consequences. If we look at retribution as a means of motivating us to
obedience, we will be confused. Accountability to God is
certain, but it cannot always be seen clearly. Our analysis of an
act of disobedience is frequently different than God's. He warns:
" 'For my thoughts are not your thoughts, neither are your ways
my ways,' declares the LORD. 'As the heavens are higher than
the earth, so are my ways higher than your ways and my
thoughts than your thoughts' " (Isaiah 55:8–9).

God's accountability system appears to change but His
commandments never change. We must consider the commands
and that the Sovereign of the universe has asked us to keep them
as the source of our motivation rather than fear of His
retribution.

RULE TWELVE

Knowledge carries with it both privilege and responsibility.

Acquiring knowledge is both liberat-
ing and enjoyable. To understand
truth, to come to grips with things as
they are, to have one's mind broad-
ened and expanded—these are some
of the most pleasurable experiences
that life affords. Conversely, to be

ignorant is to live in bondage. Ignorant people are often guided by their superstitions and are open to exploitation by both man and the devil. People who have no desire or no opportunity to learn are bound in darkness.

The psalmist exalted: "Your word is a lamp to my feet and a light for my path" (Psalm 119:105). The Bible likens knowledge of God's Word to a light that reveals where a person is going; it "lights the path."

Another delightful aspect of knowledge involves the love two people have for one another. When I love others, I want to get to know them. I want to understand how they think, feel, and perceive reality. Such love lies at the very heart of the devotional life for the Christian. When an individual falls in love with Jesus Christ, he develops an insatiable appetite for knowing Him. Knowing all about a person is the natural by-product of loving that person.

An awesome responsibility, however, accompanies knowledge. Again and again, the Scriptures remind us that knowledge demands application. James pointed out that to hear or know the Word and to fail to apply it is to live in self-deception (James 1:22).

Nothing dismays God more than when we know and do not apply. Conversely, nothing delights God more than to see us apply what we know.

Matthew 13 records a series of parables that Jesus gave in His public ministry, all dealing with the kingdom of heaven. After the first one, the Parable of the Sower, the disciples asked:

"Why do you speak to the people in parables?"
He replied, "The knowledge of the secrets of the kingdom of heaven has been given to you, but not to them. Whoever has will be given more, and he will have an abundance. Whoever does not have, even what he has will be taken from him. This is why I speak to them in parables: 'Though seeing, they do not see; though hearing, they do

not hear or understand.' In them is fulfilled the prophecy of Isaiah: 'You will be ever hearing but never understanding; you will be ever seeing but never perceiving. For this people's heart has become calloused; they hardly hear with their ears, and they have closed their eyes. Otherwise they might see with their eyes, hear with their ears, understand with their hearts and turn, and I would heal them.' But blessed are your eyes because they see, and your ears because they hear. For I tell you the truth, many prophets and righteous men longed to see what you see but did not see it, and to hear what you hear but did not hear it.

"Listen then to what the parable of the sower means." (Matthew 13:10–18)

Jesus' answer is extraordinary. He says that He speaks in parables so that the people can hear but not understand.

The people to whom Jesus ministered had absorbed vast quantities of knowledge but were short on application. Jesus spoke in parables so that these people would fail to understand, simply because their mindset demonstrated a refusal to apply God's Word.

In formal education, knowledge and application are considered synonymous; testing is often intended to determine how much knowledge the students have retained. But no effort is made to discover how much of it the student is applying. Perhaps the nature of education eliminates any endeavor to evaluate application. Not so with the Scriptures; God insists that knowledge be followed by application. Knowledge is a wonderful and delightful privilege, but it is also a responsibility.

RULE THIRTEEN

There is no such thing as a nonessential command.

By definition, a command is essential; commandments are given to be obeyed. When we skirt them with fancy logic, such as "cultural context" or "unreasonableness," we do injustice to Scripture. The Pharisees ignored the commands and thereby provoked the ire of Jesus. The probing question of our Lord relates to us as well: "Why do you break the command of God for the sake of your tradition?" (Matthew 15:3).

If nonessential commands do exist, what is the standard or criteria for deciding which ones are essential and which are not? Even an objective evaluation would tend to make the decision on the basis of culture. Culture is an insidious impediment to application. Whenever we dismiss scriptural commands or teachings because of culture, it is the culture of our day rather than the culture of the Scriptures that causes us to come to such a conclusion. Increasingly the moral standards of the church are being eroded by the misconception that some commands are cultural and, therefore, nonessential. In some congregations "alternate lifestyles" are encouraged, including premarital sex and homosexuality. Some even argue for the ordination of homosexuals.

The problem is not culture. In the United States we find a generation of people who feel that the voice of authority is negotiable. In an editorial, *Time* magazine pointed out that disregard for the law is becoming epidemic. People feel free to transgress the vehicle codes, running red lights and stop signs, and disregarding rights of way. Flagrant abuse of drugs abounds, along with an utter disregard for the law. Young men feel that they can disregard with impunity the law that says they must register for the draft. Teachers feel that they have to function as policemen in the classroom rather than educators.

Writing to the Ephesians, Paul deals with the various roles of authority and our need to comply: "Children, obey your parents in the Lord, for this is right. 'Honor your father and mother'— which is the first commandment with a promise—'that it may go well with you and that you may enjoy long life on the earth'" (Ephesians 6:1–3).

The command is not for parents to make their children obey, but rather for children to obey and honor their parents. The responsibility is with the child, not the parent. If a child does not learn to respect the voice of authority, that disobedience has far-reaching ramifications. A child who does not learn to obey his parents will have a difficult time obeying teachers, the law of the land, and any voice of authority, including the Bible.

Imposed discipline builds self-discipline. If our children do not learn to obey and honor their parents, they grow up seeing no need for self-discipline. The good of the individual as that individual perceives it, rather than the good of the society, becomes paramount. The laws of God and the state are not to be obeyed; they are to be taken under advisement, evaluated in light of the person's own perception of his or her needs, and handled accordingly.

One young couple recently went through a divorce. She reasoned: "I know that the Bible says that I am not to divorce, but I also know that God loves me and has my best interests at heart. He wants me to be happy. We are not under law but under grace. Because God loves me and is gracious toward me, my happiness is more important than the law 'do not divorce.' I have tried to make the marriage work; I cannot. I am unhappy, and God would rather have me break the law and be happy than keep the law and be perpetually unhappy. Therefore, I feel that God would rather have me divorce than remain unhappily married."

As well-reasoned as this appears, it is predicated on the assumption that God's commandments and one's happiness are mutually exclusive. The insidiousness of such reasoning stems from concluding that all authority, irrespective of its origin, is negotiable. Such reasoning destroys the individual, the society, and the person's relationship with God. God views this as rebellion. Nothing provokes His ire more quickly. A person cannot have a heart for application and conclude that God's commandments are negotiable. There simply is no such thing as a nonessential command.

**RULE
FOURTEEN**

We must not insist that we will obey only after a seeming contradiction in commandments is resolved.

Some commandments in the Bible seem to contradict one another. In Luke 14:26, for example, Jesus says we must hate our family and our own lives if we are to be disciples. But then Paul states in 1 Timothy 5:8 that if we do not provide for our families we have denied the faith and are worse than unbelievers.

One could easily conclude that these two statements are mutually exclusive concepts, for how can an individual do both? The temptation is to say, "Since Jesus' words are more authoritative that Paul's, I will obey Jesus rather than Paul." Or we may conclude that we will obey neither command until their apparent contradictions are resolved.

We cannot, however, allow seeming contradictions to paralyze us into inactivity. We must seek, rather, to obey the commands with equal zeal. I am my brother's keeper. My brothers, sisters, father, mother, wife, and children are my responsibility. If I do not provide for them, I am, as the apostle Paul says, "worse than an infidel."

On the other hand, my commitment to Christ is singularly unique above all other commitments that I have in life. Every relationship I have on earth pales in comparision to the significance of my relationship with Jesus Christ. In that sense, as a Christian, my loyalty and allegiance is first and foremost to Christ. Obedience to other authorities, including those in the family unit, must defer to Christ's authority.

In applying Scripture we must be careful not to insist on seeming contradictions to be resolved as a prerequiste for obedience.

22 Principles on the Product of Disobedience

NO MATTER WHAT THE RATIONALE FOR DISOBEDIENCE, DISOBEDIENCE ALWAYS LEADS TO BEING AT ODDS WITH GOD AND CONTRIBUTES TO OUR DEMISE.

The first three groups of principles in this book discuss preparing to apply God's Word and developing right attitudes to apply His word. Each principle affirms our positive responses to God. But to keep the picture in perspective, we must also understand the price to be paid for disobedience.

As the difficulty of becoming Christlike increases, we can easily rationalize adjusting God's commands. We begin to compromise morality an inch at a time. But we must always uphold God's law as the standard, not our opinion of the moment. If we are to err, we must err toward the Word, not toward our personal rationalizations and insights. Proverbs 3:5–6 exhorts: "Trust in the LORD with all your heart and lean not on your own understanding; in all your ways acknowledge him, and he will make your paths straight."

Disobedience only produces confusion and breaks down our relationship with God. Major principles regarding disobedience include:

15. Although there is no distinction between sins, there is a difference in consequences.

16. Disobedience adds to confusion when adverse circumstances come.

17. God's permissive will is entered only through a failure to apply the Scriptures.

18. We must refuse to yield to what we know is wrong. Satisfying the drive will only momentarily alleviate the hunger and will stimulate a desire for more.

19. "Culture" cannot serve as an excuse for not obeying God's commands.

20. The difference between a trial and a temptation lies in the response.

RULE FIFTEEN

Although there is no distinction between sins, there is a difference in consequences.

In His teaching, Jesus presents sin as sin. There is no such thing as little sins and big sins. The distinction between venial and mortal sins is a human, not a biblical, distinction, for sin alienates a person from God, regardless of what type of sin it is.

For example, in Jesus' Sermon on the Mount, He said:

You have heard that it was said to the people long ago, "Do not murder, and anyone who murders will be subject to judgment." But I tell you that anyone who is angry with his brother will be subject to judgment. Again, anyone who says to his brother, "Raca," is answerable to the Sanhedrin. But anyone who says, "You fool!" will be in danger of the fire of hell. . . .

You have heard that it was said, "Do not commit adultery." But I tell you that anyone who looks at a woman lustfully has already committed adultery with her in his heart. . . .

You have heard that it was said, "Eye for eye, and tooth for tooth." But I tell you, Do not resist an evil person. If someone strikes you on the right cheek, turn to him the other also. (Matthew 5:21–22; 27–28; 38–39)

Jesus seems to suggest that the thought behind an act or the intent of an act are as bad as the act itself. He makes no distinctions between big and little sins.

Suppose I play golf. I stand on the first tee, hit the ball, and put a hook on it so that it leaves the golf course and goes through a huge window in a department store across the street. The manager comes out and says, "Who broke the window?" I respond, "Sir, I broke your window." He says, "That will cost you six thousand dollars." I counter, "Sir, I do not have six thousand dollars." He answers, "You broke the window, you pay." "How big was the golf ball?" I ask, and he answers by lifting his hand to show me the size. Pleased with where my argument is about to carry me, I suggest, "I put the ball through the window one time. I will buy you one piece of glass that big, and then we are even." His predictable response is, "No, you broke the window, you buy the whole window." We argue about it and go to court. Any objective jury would award the case to the manager.

God's law is like that plate-glass window. Some people put only a few holes in it, others put many holes in it. Some periodically put a hole here or there. Others destroy it with a howitzer. Still others seem to delight in jumping up and down on the pieces of broken glass until they grind them into sand. But one hole is all it takes; the window is broken, and the one who broke it is responsible for the purchase of the whole window.

In our relationship with God, as James said, "whoever keeps the whole law and yet stumbles at just one point is guilty of breaking all of it" (James 2:10). Sin is sin, and only one sin is necessary to require Jesus Christ's death on the cross in payment.

Although there is no distinction between sins, there is a difference in consequences. Jesus' words in Matthew 5:21–22 indicate that the consequences here on earth of my being angry at my brother are far different than the consequences if I kill him. In my mind, I can covet the money that is in the bank, and that is sin. If, however, I go the next step and rob the bank, the consequences of that act will be far more severe than coveting the money.

In all of life, a clear distinction must be maintained between how God views sin and the repercussions of that sin as they are expressed here on earth.

RULE SIXTEEN

Disobedience adds to confusion when adverse circumstances come.

Calamity is traumatic. When difficulties enter our lives, serious ones, such as death, disease, losing a job, or having a home destroyed by fire, the natural question to direct to God is "Why?" Why did the Lord allow these circumstances to happen?

The Bible reminds us that trials and tribulations come to all people— Christian and non-Christian alike. As a matter of fact, the Scriptures seem to suggest that Christians receive additional trials simply because we are identified with Christ and His sufferings. Peter writes: "Dear friends, do not be surprised at the painful trial you are suffering, as though something strange were happening to you. But rejoice that you participate in the sufferings of Christ, so that you may be overjoyed when his glory is revealed'' (1 Peter 4:12–13).

There is another aspect of adverse circumstances, however, as the author of Hebrews reminds us:

> You have forgotten that word of encouragement that addresses you as sons: "My son, do not make light of the Lord's discipline, and do not lose heart when he rebukes you, because the Lord disciplines those he loves, and he punishes everyone he accepts as a son.''
>
> Endure hardship as discipline; God is treating you as sons. For what son is not disciplined by his father? If you are not disciplined (and everyone undergoes discipline), then you are illegitimate children and not true sons. Moreover, we have all had human fathers who disciplined us and we respected them for it. How much more should we submit to the Father of our spirits and live! Our fathers disciplined us for a little while as they thought best; but God disciplines us for our good, that we may share in his holiness. No discipline seems pleasant at the time, but painful. Later on, however, it produces a harvest of righteousness and peace for those who have been trained by it. (Hebrews 12:5–11).

Here we are told that because the Lord loves us, He disciplines us. As His children, we can count on His chastening. He does not say that He punishes us; He merely corrects us. Punishment is given to achieve justice; chastisement is given to correct behavior. Our punishment has been borne by Christ on the cross. But when we err, we are chastened by the Lord.

"The law of the harvest" is different from chastisement; it is the natural reaping of what a person sows. Reaping may occur immediately after the transgression, or it may be postponed until the day of judgment, but the promise of the Scriptures is that all people will reap what they sow (Galatians 6:7).

When we live in willful disobedience to the Lord, and then calamity strikes, our spirit gives us unclear signals as to how we ought to evaluate the situation. We know that we all must go through trials and tribulations, but still we might be reaping God's chastisement, or we might be reaping what we have sown. Tragedy torments the guilty conscience when the believer has been living in disobedience to the Lord.

Such was the experience of Joseph's brothers. They sold Joseph into slavery. Years passed, and through a series of circumstances, Joseph became Egypt's prime minister. When famine hit Canaan, his brothers journeyed to Egypt to buy grain from the prime minister, not knowing that he was their brother. Before revealing himself to his brothers, Joseph tested them to see if they were still willing to betray one of their brothers. When the crisis developed, note what the brothers said to one another: "Surely we are being punished because of our brother. We saw how distressed he was when he pleaded with us for his life, but we would not listen; that's why this distress has come upon us" (Genesis 42:21).

The brothers had sinned, and they knew it. As a result, when adverse circumstances entered their lives, they were confused and could not understand what was taking place. Traumatic experiences will always be difficult, but they are further complicated when the believer lives in willful disobedience to the Lord.

RULE SEVENTEEN

God's permissive will is entered only through a failure to apply the Scriptures.

Nothing should terrify the believer so much as the thought of abiding in God's permissive will.

Israel's exodus from Egypt is filled with illustrations of what it means to live in His permissive will. The psalmist picks up this theme in Psalm 106: "They soon forgot his works; they waited not for his counsel: But lusted exceedingly in the wilderness, and tempted God in the desert. And he gave them their request; but sent leanness into their souls" (Psalm 106:13–15 KJV).

Similarly, the prophet Balaam did not consider God's Word to be final. As Israel journeyed between Egypt and Canaan, they made contact with the country of Moab. Balak, the Moabite king, feared the Israelites and sought to have Balaam curse them.

Balak's ambassadors made a proposition to Balaam, who talked it over with God. "God said to Balaam, 'Do not go with them; you must not put a curse on those people, because they are blessed' " (Numbers 22:12).

The answer was clear enough, and Balaam reported the outcome to Balak's emissary: "The next morning Balaam got up and said to Balak's princes, 'Go back to your own country, for the LORD has refused to let me go with you' " (Numbers 22:13).

Refusing to take no for an answer, Balak returned to Balaam who again asked the Lord. The Lord answered: " 'Since these men have come to summon you, go with them, but do only what I tell you.'

By the time we get to Numbers 24, we plainly see Balak's stubbornness. He would have been wiser if he had asked Balaam to *bless* Moab rather than *curse* Israel. But cursing Israel was all he could think about.

Balaam obeyed the letter of God's law. He did not curse Israel. But he did violate God's perfect will in refusing to view Israel as special in God's sight. He suggested to Balak that if he would cause the Moabites to sin sexually with the people of Israel, God would curse the Hebrews. Moses writes: "They were the ones who followed Balaam's advice and were the means of turning the Israelites away from the LORD in what happened at Peor, so that a plague struck the LORD's people" (Numbers 31:16).

When God spoke to him, Balaam did not consider His Word final. Balaam negotiated with God to get what he wanted. When that failed, he sought by devious means to get his way. Three

times in the New Testament he is referred to as an evil man
(2 Peter 2:15; Jude 11; Revelation 2:14).

Many people fear that they have entered into God's permissive
will or received God's second best because of some decision
they have made. Yet nothing in Scripture indicates that anybody
enters into God's permissive will except through a flagrant
violation of His known will.

Paul reminded Timothy: "God did not give us a spirit of
timidity, but a spirit of power, of love and of self-discipline"
(2 Timothy 1:7). Those who have a heart for application need
not fear God's permissive will. The emphasis of our lives should
not be on wondering whether we are in God's permissive will,
but on living in obedience to what we understand to be His
perfect will. Obedience is always the issue.

When God speaks, we must not argue. If we do, we may get
what we want, but He will "send leanness" to our soul. God's
permissive will is not an attractive place.

**RULE
EIGHTEEN**

**We must refuse
to yield to what
we know is
wrong. Satisfy-
ing the drive
will only mo-
mentarily allevi-
ate the hunger
and will stimu-
late a desire for
more.**

The Bible speaks a great deal about
making no provision for the flesh.
Paul, writing to the churches of Galatia, reminded them that "those who
belong to Christ Jesus have crucified
the sinful nature with its passions and
desires" (Galatians 5:24). To the
Romans he wrote: "So then, the law
is holy, and the commandment is
holy, righteous and good.

"Did that which is good, then,
become death to me? By no means!
But in order that sin might be recognized as sin, it produced death in me
through what was good, so that
through the commandment sin might
become utterly sinful" (Romans 7:12–13).

Later he said: "And do not think about how to gratify the desires of the sinful nature" (Romans 13:14).

Appetites and drives are God-given and are, therefore, good. But God does establish boundaries. When we exceed those boundaries under the pretext that it is "natural," not only are His commandments broken, but one's own life is also put in jeopardy.

Sex is a perfect example. Yielding to the drive does not lessen its urge; it only offers momentary relief. Satisfaction merely feeds the urge, and the desire for continued fulfillment increases. Like a boiler building a head of steam, each act increases the passion.

Marriage is the biblical norm for sexual fulfillment. When sex is practiced outside of marriage, guilt is incurred; the desire for continued fulfillment increases; and the willingness to yield grows with each transgression.

Commitment to the fulfillment of our appetites produces a vicious cycle. One experience, no matter how exotic, can never satisfy us. We always crave more, both qualitatively and quantitatively. In the quest for fulfillment, we search for larger and greener pastures.

A friend of ours changes jobs every two or three years. Once he has mastered a job, it loses its attractiveness; he becomes bored. His restless spirit looks elsewhere for a richer experience. This is the result of a life committed to fulfillment. Commitment must be to God's perfect will, never to self-gratification. We must be committed to a conviction rather than to a fulfilling experience.

If marriage is based on the meeting of my personal needs rather than commitment to my God-given partner, before long the marriage will show signs of stress. Marriage can, of course, be a perpetually fulfilling, even exotic, experience where my needs are met. But fulfillment is a by-product of commitment.

To concentrate on our needs is to concentrate on the

insatiable. A well-known casanova of our day is currently undergoing treatment for impotence. His condition may appear ludicrous, but it illustrates the sad plight of those who live for their own fulfillment.

An unused limb of the body will atrophy; use makes it strong. Similarly, human drives that are unbiblical or impossible to fulfill in a scriptural manner can best be controlled by starvation. Feeding them does not alleviate the hunger but only stimulates a desire for more. Abstinence causes the drive to atrophy.

RULE NINETEEN

Culture cannot serve as an excuse for not obeying God's commands.

When we consider the difference between American culture and Oriental society, we see certain principles in action. It is possible, for example, for one person to consider "good food" what another considers inedible. Convictions in these matters, are greatly influenced by the experiences that make up a person's culture. Truth is not relative, but our ability to see truth is hindered by a world view that is a product of our culture.

Every generation needs to sort through its convictions to determine which are biblically based and which are based on culture. This must be done in two areas: First, and most easily discerned, are the prohibitions not biblically based, such as gambling and the use of alcohol. Although the believer is free to do those things not prohibited in the Bible, we are wise to think through why we believe what we believe.

Second, and possibly more subtle, are the biblical commands that we ignore because of the pressure of our culture. In Paul's letter to the Corinthians he said:

If any of you has a dispute with another, dare he take it before the ungodly for judgment instead of before the saints? Do you not know that the saints will judge the world? And if you are to judge the world, are you not competent to judge trivial cases? Do you not know that we will judge angels? How much more the things of this life! Therefore, if you have disputes about such matters, appoint as judges even men of little account in the church! I say this to shame you. Is it possible that there is nobody among you wise enough to judge a dispute between believers? But instead, one brother goes to law against another—and this in front of unbelievers!

The very fact that you have lawsuits among you means you have been completely defeated already. Why not rather be wronged? Why not rather be cheated? Instead, you yourselves cheat and do wrong, and you do this to your brothers" (1 Corinthians 6:1–8).

The passage denies a believer the right to take a fellow Christian to court. Yet the command is virtually ignored because our culture expects such matters to be settled in the courts rather than in the church. The excuse for such disobedience is a common one: In our culture the church is fragmented. Because we don't present a unified front, a believer can walk away from the authority of his church when displeased and go elsewhere.

In Sweden a large segment of the church condones premarital sex. It is an "accepted" practice. Is it possible that in a few years the church in the United States will follow Sweden's lead regarding premarital sex?

Society exerts great pressure on people to conform to its norms; yet not all that culture teaches is wrong. Culture is a mixture of iron and clay; much of what it teaches is good, but certainly not all. On one hand, God has used culture from the time of creation; on the other hand, we are urged not to allow it to "squeeze us into its mold" (Romans 12:2 PHILLIPS).

Whenever we are told that a biblical command need not be obeyed because it was cultural in its original context, and our culture is different from theirs, we should suspect that *our* culture, not the culture of Bible days, is the issue. It is not the cultural context of the Scriptures, but the cultural context of the believer that pressures him into not applying biblical teachings.

The Scriptures, along with their commands, transcend time and culture. Therefore, we must not allow culture to serve as an excuse for not obeying God's commands.

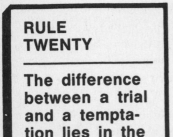

RULE TWENTY

The difference between a trial and a temptation lies in the response.

In the New Testament there are two words that are used for our English words "tried," "tempted," "temptation," "tested," and "trial." The first, *peira,* is used in passages such as Matthew 4:1; Mark 1:12–13; 1 Corinthians 10:13; James 1:12–14; and Hebrews 11:17, 36.

Hebrews 11:17 says: "By faith Abraham, when God tested him, offered Isaac as a sacrifice. He who had received the promises was about to sacrifice his one and only son." This verse refers to Genesis 22 where God called on Abraham to offer his son Isaac on Mount Moriah. Hebrews 11:17 tells us that God tried or tested Abraham to see if his faith was strong enough to obey.

James, however, makes an interesting observation: "Blessed is the man who perseveres under trial, because when he has stood the test, he will receive the crown of life that God has promised to those who love him.

"When tempted, no one should say, 'God is tempting me.' For God cannot be tempted by evil, nor does he tempt anyone; but each one is tempted when, by his own evil desire, he is dragged away and enticed" (James 1:12–14).

The word for "temptation" in James is the same word used for "tried" in Hebrews 11:17—*peira.* Yet James 1:13 says: "God cannot be tempted by evil, nor does he tempt anyone." At first this seems to be a contradiction, but James implies that although God *tests* the believer, He does not *tempt* him in the sense that He seeks his downfall. God's motive is never the believer's demise but the strengthening of faith and character.

When a trial or temptation comes into the believer's life, if it is handled properly, it can serve to his or her advantage. If the believer yields to temptation or succumbs to unbelief, then it works to his or her disadvantage.

In Job's life, we see an apparent contradiction. Job 2:3 says: "Then the LORD said to Satan, 'Have you considered my servant Job? There is no one on earth like him; he is blameless and upright, a man who fears God and shuns evil. And he still maintains his integrity, though you incited me against him to ruin him without any reason.'" Later, Job 2:7 says: "So Satan went out from the presence of the LORD and afflicted Job with painful sores from the soles of his feet to the top of his head."

Verse 3 says that God afflicted Job; verse 7 says Satan did the afflicting. Because God is sovereign and in control, and in His providence does not allow anything to touch the believer without His divine permission, no real distinction exists between the two. As Paul says: "No temptation has seized you except what is common to man. And God is faithful; he will not let you be tempted beyond what you can bear. But when you are tempted, he will also provide a way out so that you can stand up under it" (1 Corinthians 10:13).

God does not allow testing and temptation to come into a believer's life that exceeds his or her ability to overcome them; every trial and temptation includes the power to overcome. In the overcoming process the believer is strengthened.

Jesus is an illustration of this truth: "Then Jesus was led by the Spirit into the desert to be tempted by the devil" (Matthew 4:1). The Holy Spirit leads Jesus into the wilderness to be tempted by the devil, for through testing one discovers one's convictions.

The second word used in the New Testament for "tried," "trial," "temptation," and "tempted" is *dokime*. It is used in James 1:12 and in 1 Peter 1:7 and 4:12. It means "an object that is tested to prove its genuine value; certified; tested and proved worthy." 1 Peter 1:7 says that our faith is of greater worth than gold, the most valuable commodity on earth. In almost every generation gold has stood as the standard of value. The more uncertainty there is in the currency of a country, the more the people tend to invest in gold which does not lose its value.

God never brings trials and testings into our lives to cause us to fall into sin. According to Peter, the "trying of our faith" actually works to our advantage; the sufferings and difficulties encountered in the world establish that our faith is real, valuable, and certified as pure. Regardless of its source, the difference between a trial and a temptation lies in our response to it.

23 Principles on The Life of Application

PART 1:
WE CANNOT MEASURE PROGRESS IN
APPLICATION.

Measurement is an important concept in our society; it is the foundation of worth and accomplishment. Through measurement, we make long-range projections and establish goals; without it we do not know how far we have gone, and we have a difficult time planning for the future.

Without it, control is impossible. If a company cannot measure the quantity and quality of its product, it cannot control its future. Not to measure is to be out of control, and to be out of control is to be insecure.

Every individual has a built-in desire to control. We want to control our environment, our destiny—in short, the world in which we live. Many people refuse to become Christians out of a fear that they will lose control of their lives.

A superficial analysis, however, reveals our lack of control. None of us determines such things as our sex, appearance, nationality, era of history, color of skin, size, gifts and abilities, longevity, or circumstances. What we do control is our response to those things over which we have no control.

When we are out of control, we are dependent. When we are in control, we are independent. Control is at the very heart of our relationship to God. He wants us to be dependent, walking by faith. Because measurement is essential for control, it can be a problem in striving for dependence and faith.

We can measure the quantitative aspects of the Christian life—the number of days a person has private devotions, the frequency of church attendance, the number of people to whom one witnesses. But the qualitative dimension of the Christian life is, for the most part, unmeasurable. The time a person spends in prayer is measurable; the quality of that prayer is not.

The characteristics of Christlikeness defy measurement, such as the fruit of the Spirit: "love, joy, peace, patience, kindness, goodness, faithfulness, gentleness and self-control" (Galatians 5:22). Lordship is qualitative; so are patience, humility, and a host of other virtues. God has designed the Christian life so that the qualities that are important in God's economy can only be attained by maintaining a posture of dependence and faith.

Measurement should not be confused with evaluation. We evaluate all that comes into our lives. But measurement implies a standard; a person reaches the standard or does not quite measure up. Evaluation has no standard; it is comparative.

Janice is a Christian disciple. We cannot measure her walk with God—unless by the standard of perfection (Matthew 5:48), in which case she, like everyone else, falls short. On the other hand, we can evaluate Janice by comparing where she is today with where she was a year ago.

We must resist the temptation to measure. We cannot look to people and circumstances for feedback in our growth, nor must we measure the growth of others.

21. Circumstances do not indicate God's approval or disapproval.

22. The validity of personal application is not dependent on another's acceptance or approval.

23. We must resist the temptation to judge others as less spiritual when they do what the Lord has forbidden us to do.

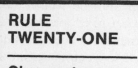

RULE TWENTY-ONE

Circumstances do not indicate God's approval or disapproval.

God in His providence allows circumstances to enter our lives. They may heighten our awareness of the need for application, but they are poor indicators of God's approval or disapproval. We view most of our circumstances as either negative or positive, but our perception of them is not always the same as God's.

We tend to be experience-oriented, or feeling-oriented; circumstances are construed to be either good or bad depending on how we feel. If the circumstance is positive, making me feel good, I conclude that God loves me. On the other hand, if the circumstance is negative, making me unhappy, I conclude that God is either angry with me or does not care.

Using circumstances as a barometer of God's pleasure or displeasure is not new. The psalmist wrestled with the same problem; in Psalm 73 he expresses dismay over the triumph of wicked men. The psalmist, in contrast, seems to have kept God's law in vain. He struggles with the contradiction, finding himself envying the prosperity of the wicked until God reveals to him the ultimate outcome: "When I tried to understand all this, it was oppressive to me till I entered the sanctuary of God; then I understood their final destiny" (Psalm 73:16–17).

The writer undergoes a transformation in his thinking, but not through anything he saw or experienced. His conclusion was derived through faith. His hope was based on God's promises.

Experience tells us that the righteous do not always prosper. Frequently the wicked prosper and oppress the righteous. Clearly, we cannot depend on circumstances to indicate God's approval or disapproval.

As Job's three friends sought to evaluate his predicament, they reasoned that because God blesses the righteous and punishes the wicked, Job's adverse circumstances were an indication of God's displeasure. If Job would but repent, God would bless him. Yet in Job 2:3 God says that he had destroyed Job "without any reason," which means the calamity that befell Job was not a product of Job's sin or unrighteousness. His circumstances, like ours, could not be interpreted as an indicator of God's approval or disapproval.

RULE TWENTY-TWO

The validity of personal application is not dependent on another's acceptance or approval.

People often view applying God's Word as a risk because the Scriptures appear illogical—the Bible calls on us to do things that the world considers foolish. For example, Jesus said: "If anyone would come after me, he must deny himself and take up his cross daily and follow me. For whoever wants to save his life will lose it, but whoever loses his life for me will save it" (Luke 9:23–24).

In Mark 10:31 Jesus said that those who wish to be first must be last; in Luke 6:38, He suggested that the secret to getting is giving.

If we evaluate such truths from the world's perspective, they appear to be nonsense. When we try to put them into practice in our lives, we can count on a certain amount of disapproval.

Little of what Abraham did in obedience to God would have gained approval from the people of his—or any—generation: "By faith Abraham, when called to go to a place he would later receive as his inheritance, obeyed and went, even though he did not know where he was going" (Hebrews 11:8).

If he were alive today, Abraham would arrive at the office some Monday morning and announce his plans to quit. When asked why, he would answer that he was leaving town. As people asked where he was going, his answer according to this verse would be, "I don't know." We can imagine the approval we would gain for such a plan—quitting our jobs, selling our homes, leaving town without any idea where we were going.

Years later when Abraham is in the Promised Land of Canaan, God comes to him again: "Take your son, your only son, Isaac, whom you love, and go to the region of Moriah. Sacrifice him there as a burnt offering on one of the mountains I will tell you about" (Genesis 22:2). If God were to ask me to take my only child and offer him as a sacrifice, how many people would I find who would approve or accept? No doubt if Abraham had sought counsel on this command from God, the vote would have been unanimously in favor of not offering Isaac.

Those who love us most are often the strongest in their objections to our obeying "illogical" commands. They do not want us to disobey God, but they also do not want us to suffer or do foolish things. When the Bible says that we are to be crucified with Christ (Galatians 2:20), we cannot expect universal acceptance or approval when we seek to obey. A command's validity, or the application of any Scripture, for that matter, is not determined by another person's acceptance or approval.

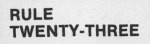

RULE TWENTY-THREE

We must resist the temptation to judge others as less spiritual when they do what the Lord has forbidden us to do.

Because it is so easy to forget, we must constantly remind ourselves that application is simply responding properly to what God says. The process of sanctification is different in each person's life. The common core of application that we all share is the standard expressed in the absolute commandments of the Bible. Our culture, however, prohibits certain activities that the Bible does not say are wrong, such as smoking, drinking, and gambling.

Among the extra-biblical prohibitions found in the Mormon Church, for instance, is the drinking of beverages containing caffeine. The Mormons borrowed this, along with a host of other extra-biblical prohibitions, from evangelical Christianity a century or so ago. Most evangelical Christians have dropped the prohibition; the Mormons have not.

Because we are each in a different place in the application process, we cannot judge those whose convictions differ from our own. J. Gresham Machen, the founding president of Westminster Seminary, once said, "When the church forbids what God allows; it soon allows what God forbids."

Paul gives us a proper perspective on judging in his first epistle to the Corinthians and in his letter to the Colossians. First Corinthians 4:3–5 says: "I care very little if I am judged by you or by any human court; indeed, I do not even judge myself. My conscience is clear, but that does not make me innocent. It is the Lord who judges me. Therefore judge nothing before the appointed time; wait till the Lord comes. He will bring to light what is hidden in darkness and will expose the motives of men's hearts. At that time each will receive his praise from God."

Paul reminds the Corinthians that he does not even know his

own motives, much less those of another. We cannot, therefore, judge one another's motives. First Corinthians 5:1–5 contrasts this principle with another kind of judging: "It is actually reported that there is sexual immorality among you, and of a kind that does not occur even among pagans: A man has his father's wife. And you are proud! Shouldn't you rather have been filled with grief and have put out of your fellowship the man who did this? Even though I am not physically present, I am with you in spirit. And I have already passed judgment on the one who did this, just as if I was present. When you are assembled in the name of our Lord Jesus and I am with you in spirit, and the power of our Lord Jesus is present, hand this man over to Satan, so that the sinful nature may be destroyed and his spirit saved on the day of the Lord."

Paul is talking about the transgression of a negative command-ment: one of the Corinthians is having an incestuous relationship with his father's wife. This kind of behavior must be judged by the Christian community.

In Colossians 2:16–17 Paul talks about a third kind of judging: "Therefore do not let anyone judge you by what you eat or drink, or with regard to a religious festival, a New Moon celebration or a Sabbath day. These are a shadow of the things that were to come; the reality, however, is found in Christ."

In this passage Paul refers to activities that are not prohibited in the Scriptures but may be avoided by certain Christians out of personal conviction. He says, in essence, that we cannot judge those who do what our personal convictions forbid us to do. We must resist the temptation to judge others as less spiritual than us when they do the things the Lord has forbidden us to do.

PART 2:
THE OBJECTIVES OF APPLYING GOD'S WORD TO OUR LIVES ARE TO PLEASE GOD, TO STRIVE FOR MORAL EXCELLENCE, AND TO LEAVE A GODLY LEGACY.

God speaks of these three major products of obedience. They are discussed in rules 1, 24, and 25. Rather than attempting to measure the results of application, we must learn to wait and view the product of our commitment to the Word of God and its application from God's perspective. God's promised results are exciting but not quantitative. His feedback comes to us in ways that bring joy but exclude measurement. If we commit our tasks to Him, we receive His pleasure, moral excellence, and a positive impact on posterity.

1. Application must be focused on pleasing God rather than pleasing others.

24. The path to intellectual excellence is curiosity, investigation, and experimentation, but the path to moral excellence is obedience.

25. Our conduct, good or bad, will affect the generations to follow.

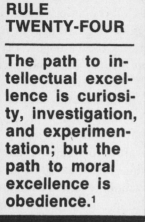

RULE TWENTY-FOUR

The path to intellectual excellence is curiosity, investigation, and experimentation; but the path to moral excellence is obedience.[1]

Risk taking, or faith, is at the heart of the believer's life, but the risk is always toward being moral, never toward being immoral. Nowhere in the Scriptures do we find believers admonished to indulge in acts of immorality to gain knowledge. As a matter of fact, we find just the opposite: "Everyone had heard about your obedience so I am full of joy over you; but I want you to be wise about what is good, and innocent about what is evil" (Romans 16:19).

The word "innocent" connotes being half-witted regarding evil; that is, there is no need for the believer to know all there is to know about unrighteous matters.

Paul reiterates the same idea in 1 Corinthians 14:20: "Brothers, stop thinking like children. In regard to evil be infants, but in your thinking be adults."

In understanding life, the apostle encourages us to understand as adults, with one exception—in evil matters. In this area we are to be as children, naïve and innocent.

Our permissive age teaches us to experiment in moral matters as one would experiment in scientific matters: "Try it! You don't know what it's like until you do it." We are encouraged to experiment with sex, drugs, and trial marriages. Even if such experimentation leads an individual to Christ, such a conversion comes at the cost of moral bankruptcy. Experimentation can never lead a person to moral excellence.

From a biblical perspective, the path to moral excellence is always obedience. Paul says in Colossians 3:5–10: "Put to death, therefore, whatever belongs to your earthly nature: sexual

---

[1] Chambers, Oswald, *Shade of His Hand.*

immorality, impurity, lust, evil desires and greed, which is idolatry. Because of these, the wrath of God is coming. You used to walk in these ways, in the life you once lived. But now you must rid yourselves of all such things as these: anger, rage, malice, slander, and filthy language from your lips. Do not lie to each other, since you have taken off your old self with its practices and have put on the new self, which is being renewed in knowledge in the image of its Creator."

The scientific method is appropriate in amoral matters where scriptural commands are not at stake. But to treat the moral realm as one would treat the scientific realm is to lead to degradation and depravity. When psychology and psychiatry encourage using the scientific method in moral areas, such application can lead to nothing but personal ruin.

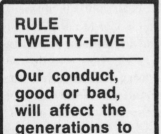

RULE TWENTY-FIVE

Our conduct, good or bad, will affect the generations to follow.

This theme is repeated throughout the Scriptures. When we do well, our children reap the benefits. When we do evil, our children suffer the consequences. This truth can be seen by observation as well as learned through Scripture.

As the children of Israel were making their exodus from Egypt, en route to Mount Sinai, they were hindered by the Amalekites who fought them at Rephidim: "The LORD said to Moses, 'Write this on a scroll as something to be remembered and make sure that Joshua hears it, because I will completely blot out the memory of Amalek from under heaven.'

"Moses built an altar and called it The LORD is my Banner. He said, 'For hands were lifted up to the throne of the LORD. The LORD will be at war against the Amalekites from generation to generation'" (Exodus 17:14–16).

Hundreds of years later God instructed the prophet Samuel to have King Saul fulfill this vow: "Samuel said to Saul, 'I am the one the LORD sent to anoint you king over his people Israel; so listen now to the message from the LORD. This is what the LORD Almighty says: "I will punish the Amalekites for what they did to Israel when they waylaid them as they came up from Egypt. Now go, attack the Amalekites and totally destroy everything that belongs to them. Do not spare them; put to death men and women, children and infants, cattle and sheep, camels and donkeys"'" (1 Samuel 15:1–3).

The Amalekites were destroyed even though the generation that died did no wrong to Israel. Their forefathers, hundreds of years before, provoked God's wrath.

God reminded the prophet Ezekiel: "The soul who sins is the one who will die. The son will not share the guilt of the father, nor will the father share the guilt of the son. The righteousness of the righteous man will be credited to him and the wickedness of the wicked will be charged against him" (Ezekiel 18:20).

Each person is responsible for his or her own sin; the father does not bear responsibility for the son's sin, nor does the son bear responsibility for the father's sin. Nevertheless, the consequences of one's sin linger and are inherited by future generations, just as the blessings of one person or family linger and are inherited by future generations.

Isaac is an illustration of a person who is blessed because of his father's faithfulness. The Lord reaffirmed His covenant with Isaac, appearing to him with the words: "I am the God of your father Abraham. Do not be afraid, for I am with you; I will bless you and will increase the number of your descendants for the sake of my servant Abraham" (Genesis 26:24). Isaac was promised blessing because of Abraham's relationship with God.

A man's sin also affects his progeny. A man of God comes to Eli, the high priest of Israel, rebuking him for his failure to raise his sons properly: "Therefore the LORD, the God of Israel, declares: 'I promised that your house and your father's house would minister before me forever.' But now the LORD declares: 'Far be it from me! Those who honor me I will honor, but those who despise me will be disdained. The time is coming when I will cut short your strength and the strength of your father's house, so that there will not be an old man in your family line and you will see distress in my dwelling. Although good will be done to Israel, in your family line there will never be an old man. Every one of you that I do not cut off from my altar will be spared only to blind your eyes with tears and grieve your heart, and all your descendants will die in the prime of life" (1 Samuel 2:30–33). Because of Eli's failure, he is told twice, "There will not be an old man in your family line."

In contrast, an evil man, because of his forefathers' righteousness, does not receive fully what he deserves. Concerning Abijah, son of Rehoboam, it is written: "He committed all the sins his father had done before him; his heart was not fully devoted to the LORD his God, as the heart of David his forefather had been. Nevertheless, for David's sake the LORD his God gave him a lamp in Jerusalem by raising up a son to succeed him and by making Jerusalem strong. For David had done what was right in the eyes of the LORD and had not failed to keep any of the LORD's commands all the days of his life—except in the case of Uriah the Hittite" (1 Kings 15:3–5).

Abijah committed all the sins his father Rehoboam did. Yet God said that for David's sake He would not utterly destroy his lineage. David's faithfulness affected the generations that followed.

In 1 Kings 14:6–14, the infant son of Jeroboam was ill, and Jeroboam sent his wife to inquire from the prophet, Ahijah, what would happen:

> So when Ahijah heard the sound of her footsteps at the door, he said, "Come in, wife of Jeroboam. Why this pretense? I have been sent to you with bad news. Go, tell Jeroboam that this is what the LORD, the God of Israel, says: 'I raised you up from among the people

and made you a leader over my people Israel. I tore the kingdom away from the house of David and gave it to you, but you have not been like my servant David, who kept my commands and followed me with all his heart, doing only what was right in my eyes. You have done more evil than all who lived before you. You have made for yourself other gods, idols made of metals; you have provoked me to anger and thrust me behind your back.

" 'Because of this I am going to bring disaster on the house of Jeroboam. I will cut off from Jeroboam every last male in Israel— slave or free. I will burn up the house of Jeroboam as one burns dung, until it is all gone. Dogs will eat those belonging to Jeroboam who die in the city, and the birds of the air will feed on those who die in the country. The LORD has spoken!' "

"As for you, go back home. When you set foot in your city, the boy will die. All Israel will mourn for him and bury him. He is the only one belonging to Jeroboam who will be buried, because he is the only one in the house of Jeroboam in whom the LORD, the God of Israel, has found anything good.

"The LORD will raise up for himself a king over Israel who will cut off the family of Jeroboam." (1 Kings 14:6–14)

Three principles emerge from this passage: (1) What a person does appreciably affects his progeny (v. 10). (2) Children generally repeat their fathers' sins. The one who does not still dies early, yet remains in the grace of God (v. 13). (3) Many events in life are worse than death. From a biblical perspective, death is not a disaster, as verse 13 indicates. Life, therefore, must not be focused toward living but rather toward being the Lord's obedient servant.

This truth can be observed in everyday life. Scientists tell us that if we abuse our bodies with drugs, alcohol, tobacco, and other harmful substances, we affect the physical well-being of our children. Conversely, if parents work hard, discipline themselves, live moral, exemplary lives, gain fine reputations in the community, and excel in what they do, their children profit.

This principle began with Adam's and Eve's sin in the Garden of Eden. The suffering of humanity for thousands of years is the direct consequence of their sin. Plus people in every age have emulated Adam and Eve by living disobediently.

In every age people argue that there is no cause-and-effect relationship between what a person does today and what happens years later. God's word to Moses should sober us: "You shall not bow down to them or worship them; for I, the LORD your God, am a jealous God, punishing the children for the sins of the fathers to the third and the fourth generation of those who hate me" (Exodus 20:5).

Moses, prayed in Psalm 90:12: "Teach us to number our days aright, that we may gain a heart of wisdom." He understood the responsibility of continuity. Wise people have an appreciation for the process that brought them to where they are and sense their responsibility to the future.

24 Principles on People in the Process of Application

GOD USES PEOPLE TO HELP US GROW.

Community is an important part of the Christian life. Christ designed His Body in such a way that "maverick" existence is impossible. In 1 Corinthians 12–14, for example, we learn that the distribution of spiritual gifts insures that everyone has some gift and no one has all. The gifts that I have that the rest of the Body does not have make me important; the gifts that the Body has that I do not have make me dependent.

The importance of community is highlighted in Hebrews 10:24–25: "Let us consider how we may spur one another on toward love and good deeds. Let us not give up meeting together, as some are in the habit of doing, but let us encourage one another—and all the more as you see the Day approaching."

People have a powerful influence on each other's lives, either for better or for worse. The apostle John warns of the need to avoid negative influence: "If any one comes to you and does not bring this teaching, do not take him into your house or welcome him" (2 John 10).

By and large, however, fellowship with like-minded believers has a positive impact. We become like the people with whom we associate; if we want to be godly, we need to associate with godly people. Our fellow Christians influence us in specific ways.

26. We must maintain an accountability relationship with a group of people who will exhort us to faith and good works.

27. Godly counsel is helpful in the quest for obedience, but it should never be used to avoid personal responsibility.

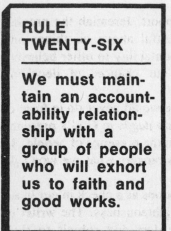

RULE TWENTY-SIX

We must maintain an accountability relationship with a group of people who will exhort us to faith and good works.

The focus of application must be to please God rather than others (Rule 1). As important as this truth is, the balancing truth must also be remembered—we need people who love us enough to tell us when we are wrong and call us to account.

The Scriptures are full of admonitions and illustrations of accountability. Hebrews 3:13 admonishes us to "encourage one another daily, as long as it is called Today, so that none of you may be hardened by sin's deceitfulness."

Jesus laid down the procedure we are to follow when a brother falls into sin: "If your brother sins against you, go and show him his fault, just between the two of you. If he listens to you, you have won your brother over. But if he will not listen, take one or two others along, so that 'every matter may be established by the testimony of two or three witnesses.' If he refuses to listen to them, tell it to the church; and if he refuses to listen even to the church, treat him as you would a pagan or a tax collector" (Matthew 18:15–17).

In 2 Samuel 12 Nathan the prophet rebuked David. David with an amazing spirit of submission, responded to Nathan's charge: "I have sinned against the LORD" (2 Samuel 12:13). We should have such an attitude as we stand accountable to our brothers and sisters in the faith.

Not all accountability, of course, comes as rebuke. Often it is counsel: "The purposes of a man's heart are deep waters, but a man of understanding draws them out" (Proverbs 20:5). Other times it is encouragement: "Saul's son Jonathan went to David at Horesh and helped him find strength in God" (1 Samuel 23:16).

All believers need this kind of support. Jeremiah the prophet reminds us that "the heart is deceitful above all things and beyond cure" (Jeremiah 17:9). Accountability to other believers gives us objectivity and reduces our chances of deceiving ourselves.

We will do in front of God what we would never do in front of people. We will think thoughts and do deeds in God's presence that we would be ashamed of doing in the presence of people. So also, we will do in the presence of strangers what we won't do before friends.

The support group, therefore, functions as a check in our lives. Its very presence prods us toward righteousness. The writer of Hebrews exhorted: "Obey your leaders and submit to their authority. They keep watch over you as men who must give an account. Obey them so that their work will be a joy, not a burden, for that would be of no advantage to you" (Hebrews 13:17).

Many will find this support in their local congregation. Other churches are so large that support must be found in the Sunday-school class or some small informal group. Whatever the source, the component parts are counsel, support, rebuke when necessary, and a willingness to uphold one another in prayer. Such accountability is rooted in a loving, caring concern for one another.

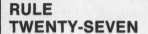

RULE TWENTY-SEVEN

Godly counsel is helpful in the quest for obedience, but it should never be used to avoid personal responsibility.

In Jesus' ministry, he repeatedly emphasized to His disciples their need to walk by faith.

Faith plays a strategic role in the application process. Because application involves doing what we "know" God wants us to do, and because we cannot "know" in the scientific sense, we therefore must walk by faith as we apply the Scriptures.

In trying to minimize the risk, if not entirely eliminate it, we use godly counsel. But counsel can never be used to answer the question, "What should I do?" None of us can avoid the personal responsibility of trusting God in the application process.

What is the purpose of godly counsel? It can accomplish two things for the person who has an obedient heart. First, it can help us check the validity of our thinking. Some of us do not always think straight as we try to sort out how to respond to what we feel God wants us to do. Counsel can help us in that sorting process. Second, counsel can help us gain additional or new insights. As we wrestle with a decision, we may easily overlook certain truths that can be identified by people who take a fresh and objective view of our situation.

Judges 7 records God's deliverance of the children of Israel from the hand of the Midianites. As Gideon sought to obey God, he recognized the risk involved in facing the Midianite hoards.

He used a fleece to help affirm in his own heart that God was really leading him:

> Gideon said to God, "If you will save Israel by my hand as you have promised—look, I will place a wool fleece on the threshing floor. If there is dew only on the fleece and all the ground is dry, then I will know that you will save Israel by my hand, as you said." And that is what happened. Gideon rose early next day; he squeezed the fleece and wrung out the dew—a bowlful of water.
> Then Gideon said to God, "Do not be angry with me. Let me make just one more request. Allow me one more test with the fleece. This time make the fleece dry and the ground covered with dew." That night God did so. Only the fleece was dry; all the ground was covered with dew. (Judges 6:36–40)

The Bible does not prohibit a person from using a "fleece" to decide what he or she ought to do. The fleece, however, does not eliminate the need to walk by faith, it simply shifts the risk taking to a more objective form.

Counsel differs from authority in that all of us are under authority, and authority is to be obeyed. In seeking counsel the issue is obtaining help in clarifying one's thinking. At times, an individual may use godly counsel to help determine what is to be done. There is nothing unbiblical in this approach, as long as we recognize that: (1) in using this approach we do not shift the burden of responsibility from ourselves to the counselor—the individual is always accountable for his or her own decision; (2) using godly counsel as a fleece does not eliminate risk taking or the need to walk by faith.

25 An Example of Application, from the Life of David

Bill, a man in his twenties, is a partner with his father. Together they run a large, successful insurance agency.

Bill's dad is a "self-made man." He started the company from scratch and is proud of his accomplishments. He is also proud of Bill and delighted that they are working together. Dad wants Bill to run the business, but he can't resist the temptation to step in and make unilateral decisions. When this happens, the employees become confused, and Bill becomes frustrated.

Since Bill is a Christian, he has wrestled before the Lord over how he should respond. In studying David's life, he found his answer. His application came from his study of 1 Samuel 24 and 26. It is both an illustration of what biblical application is all about and how to draw an application from an Old Testament example.

WAIT UPON THE LORD—1 SAMUEL 24 AND 26
A STUDY OF MY RELATIONSHIP WITH DAD
AND THE BUSINESS

1. David would not take matters into his own hands. He knew he was going to be king—but he also knew Saul was the Lord's anointed. It was up to God to remove him.

   Application: Dad is president by God's choice. I should do nothing directly to change that. I can make my feelings known, but I should not demand or push.

2. David was at peace knowing that his time to be king would come; sooner or later Saul would be removed by the Lord (1 Samuel 26:10).

331

Application: In God's time, I will have the leadership role in the company—or in some other area that God chooses.

3. David recognized that the Lord repays each man for his righteousness and his faithfulness (1 Samuel 26:23; Psalm 18:20). Therefore he knew that by refusing to kill Saul, he would be *positively* repaid by the Lord.

   Application: Not taking matters into my own hands (obedience and faithfulness) will be rewarded by the Lord.

4. David did not want to talk negatively about Saul or undermine him in any way. He even regretted cutting off the corner of Saul's robe (1 Samuel 24:4–6).

   Application: I should do nothing to undermine Dad's authority or influence. I should not put him down in any way. I have indirectly talked against him by letting employees know that I wanted to get certain things done before he returned.

5. David knew it would be a *sin* to take matters into his own hands prematurely (1 Samuel 26:9). He would be heavy with guilt.

   Application: It would be a sin for me to act prematurely— ahead of God.

6. It was because of his devotion to God, not because of his devotion to Saul, that David spared Saul (1 Samuel 24:6: "Far be it from me *because of the Lord* that I should do this thing").

   Application: Far be it from me to try to change Dad or take matters into my own hands, not just because he is my Dad but because of my devotion to God.

7. David's decision to spare Saul was not because of good behavior on Saul's part or because Saul deserved to be spared (1 Samuel 24:11, 27; 1 Samuel 26:21).

Application: My reactions are not to be a response to Dad's behavior or what I think he deserves.

8. David let Saul know the limits of his options—that he would not try to unseat or move Saul aside but instead would wait upon God (1 Samuel 24:11; 26:11).

Application: I need to let Dad know that he is *secure* in our company as president until he or God changes that.

9. Saul was convicted of his offense against David but then returned to his old ways of chasing David (1 Samuel 24:17; 26:2; I Samuel 26:21).

Application: Don't expect Dad's behavior to change. He will probably still struggle with his ego and need to control at times. Also, he may be unwilling to have less ownership interest and will desire to keep money in the business.

10. David did not listen to the worldly advice of those around him (1 Samuel 24:4; 26:8).

Application: The counselor who told me not to take responsibility for Dad's ego but to push forward, gave me wrong advice.

11. David had a young man killed who had killed Saul (or said he killed Saul at Saul's request), because he stretched out his hand to kill the Lord's anointed (2 Samuel 1:14–16).

Application: I cannot allow others to undermine Dad's position.

12. David truly loved Saul and built him up even after his death (1 Samuel 1:19–27). He wrote a song about Saul and Jonathan.

    Application: My entire relationship should be one of love for Dad, and I should build him up.

13. After Saul's death, David first asked the Lord how to proceed (2 Samuel 2:1). He was then satisfied to be king only over Judah for seven and a half years (2 Samuel 5:5). He was thirty when he became King of Judah.

    Application: Don't rush ahead, even if you see a green light. Move slowly as God leads.

WHY COULD DAVID HAVE THIS ATTITUDE?

1. He recognized that the battle was the Lord's. He could rest in this assurance because of his experiences of God's faithfulness and a proper understanding of his limitations and God's position. 1 Samuel 17:47 says: "It is not by sword or spear that the Lord saves; for the battle is the Lord's, and he will give all of you into our hands."

2. He believed that God would deliver him, no matter what the circumstances (1 Samuel 17:37).

3. He received strength when he needed it from the Lord. 1 Samuel 30:6: "But David found strength himself in the Lord his God."

4. He had a pure heart. 1 Samuel 16:7: "The Lord looks at the heart."

5. The Holy Spirit's power worked through his life. 1 Samuel 16:13: "From that day on the Spirit of the Lord came upon David in power."

6. He remembered past times of deliverance by the Lord. 1 Samuel 17:37: "The Lord who delivered me from the paw of the lion and the paw of the bear will deliver me from the hand of this Philistine."

7. He was vocal that all battles were in God's name (strength), not his own. 1 Samuel 17:45: "I come against you in the name of the LORD Almighty, the God of the armies of Israel, whom you have defied."

8. He sought godly counsel. He spent time with Samuel and sought his counsel on how to handle the situation (1 Samuel 19:18).

9. He had the support of others—Jonathan and all Israel and Judah (1 Samuel 18:16; 20:4).

10. David truly loved Saul and Jonathan in spite of his treatment by Saul (1 Samuel 20:41, 42).

Conclusion

Biblical application is a lifelong process. If any of us were able to completely assimilate and put the Scripture into practice, we would "arrive." Then application would cease to be a process and become a product. "Doing" is the outcome of "being." To the degree that we assimilate the ingredients that make up the process of Biblical application, we will "do" what is right. Meanwhile, we continue to wrestle with the issues God raises in our lives. That, after all, is the process.

We want to hear from you. Please send your comments about this book to us in care of the address below. Thank you.

ZONDERVAN™

GRAND RAPIDS, MICHIGAN 49530

WWW.ZONDERVAN.COM